Maxims And Opinions
of
His Grace The Duke of Wellington,

by

Arthur Wellesley, Duke of Wellington

The Echo Library 2006

Published by

The Echo Library

**Echo Library
131 High St.
Teddington
Middlesex TW11 8HH**

www.echo-library.com

Please report serious faults in the text to complaints@echo-library.com

ISBN 1-40680-606-4

MAXIMS AND OPINIONS OF FIELD-MARSHAL HIS GRACE THE DUKE OF WELLINGTON, SELECTED FROM HIS WRITINGS AND SPEECHES DURING A PUBLIC LIFE OF MORE THAN HALF A CENTURY.

With a Biographical Memoir,
BY
GEORGE HENRY FRANCIS, ESQ.

"Cujus gloriae neque profuit quisquam laudando, nec vituperando quisquam nocuit."

ADVERTISEMENT

So many works have already appeared of which the Duke of Wellington has been the subject, that an explanation is due to the public on the occasion of adding one more to the number.

That explanation consists in the fact, that those works have been almost exclusively occupied with the military exploits of the Duke, which rendered him so illustrious during the first twenty years of his public life; while his political career, which may be said to have constituted a second life, distinct and different from the other, has been comparatively neglected.

To meet the want thus left unsatisfied, the Editor of the following pages has endeavoured to supply materials, by which a just estimate may be formed of the Duke of Wellington's claims as a minister and as a statesman.

The volume will be found to contain the Duke's deliberate opinions as a member of the House of Peers, and, during many years, as a minister, upon the great questions which have agitated the public mind since the commencement of the present century.

If there are those who hold the Duke of Wellington in light estimation as a politician, they will not continue to entertain that opinion, the Editor believes, after having dispassionately read the extracts of which this work is composed.

Interspersed with the Duke's more elaborate OPINIONS, will be found his MAXIMS on public policy, which, though few and unpretending, may be said to have sunk into the national mind.

The Editor has added a few remarkable sentences and passages from the dispatches of the Duke; with a cursory memoir of his life, which becomes more elaborate from the commencement of his political career; and has also attempted to portray some of his characteristics, as a soldier and as a civilian.

LONDON, *February*, 1845.

MEMOIR

OF

HIS GRACE THE DUKE OF WELLINGTON.

Arthur Wellesley, Duke of Wellington, is the fourth son of Garret, second Earl of Mornington, by Anne, the eldest daughter of Arthur Hill, Viscount Dungannon. He was borne at Dangan Castle, in the county of Meath, Ireland, on the 1st of May, 1769.

As in the case of many of the chief nobility and landholders in Ireland, the ancestors of the Duke were scions of an English house—the Colleys (afterwards Cowley), two of whom, named Walter and Robert Colley, proceeded to Ireland in the reign of Henry VIII., and located themselves in the County of Kilkenny. The two brothers were lawyers by profession, and in the year 1531, were invested with the office of Clerk of the Crown in Chancery, which they were to hold jointly during their lives. Six years afterwards, we find the elder brother Master of the Rolls in Ireland, and the other Solicitor-General. In 1549, Walter was made Surveyor-General of Ireland. It was from this Walter that the immediate ancestors of the Duke of Wellington were, by the mother's side, descended.

His eldest son, Henry, acquired some distinction as a soldier in the reign of Elizabeth. He was also a member of the Irish Parliament for the borough of Thomastown. He was, moreover, a Privy Councillor, and was knighted.

Sir Henry Sydney, who was, perhaps, the wisest and most able of all the Lords Deputy whom Elizabeth sent over to Ireland, appears to have entertained a very high opinion of Sir Henry Colley's abilities; for, in recommending him to his successor in the Government, he describes him as "valiant, fortunate, and a good servant;" and speaks of him as his "sound and fast friend." But he more especially praises the "order," in which he kept his county.

Thus early did a member of this family earn praise for good service to the State; and if we compare the measure of that praise with what we know of the temper of the times, we might almost suppose that some portion of the spirit of the "sound and fast friend," the "valiant, fortunate, and good servant," had been inherited by his illustrious descendant.

The immediate descendants of Sir Henry Colley were more or less distinguished. His great-great grand-daughter, Elizabeth, married into the family of the Westleys (afterwards Wellesleys) of Dangan, in the county of Meath. This family also was of English extraction, having originally come from Sussex. Richard Colley, the nephew of the Elizabeth abovementioned, was adopted by Garret Wellesley, whose name and estates he took in the year 1728, by patent from the Herald's office. He was auditor and registrar of the Royal Hospital of Kilmainham, and a Chamberlain of the Court of Exchequer. He sat in parliament several years for Carysford, and was, in 1747 raised to the peerage by George II., being created Baron Mornington. His son, Garret, was, in 1760, created Viscount Wellesley and Earl of Mornington. He married, on the 6th February, 1759, Anne, eldest daughter of the Right Honourable Arthur Hill, Viscount Dungannon, by whom he had issue, Richard the late Marquis Wellesley, Arthur Gerald, who died in infancy, William Wellesley Pole, Baron Maryborough, Arthur Duke of Wellington, Gerald Valerian, D.D., Sir Henry, G.C.B., Francis Seymour, Anne, and Mary Elizabeth.

The Earl of Mornington, who was chiefly remarkable for his strong passion for music, in which science he acquired no slight celebrity as a composer, died in 1781, leaving his property very much encumbered. Its management was entrusted to Lady Mornington, who appears, by universal assent, to have been one of those remarkable women to whose care the world is indebted, so much more than it conceives or will admit, for its great men. Although it may have been upon severer models, and by the lessons of more pretending teachers, that the Marquis Wellesley was formed into the vigorous ruler, and the wise, far-seeing statesman; or if his scarcely more illustrious brother must, from other sources, have imbibed that stern unswerving spirit which, in his after career, insured truth to his views and certainty to his enterprises, yet one can scarcely allow a doubt that it is to the direction given by their admirable mother to the minds of these two great men, while still in the pliant season of youth, that we owe that high appreciation of truth and honour, and that sense of the identity of virtue and duty, which, while their wisdom and prowess were spreading our military fame, and extending the sphere of our civilising influence, enabled them also, by the exaltation of our national character, to secure for their country the respect of all the world.

One of the first fruits of early lessons or of later reflection upon the mind of the young Earl of Mornington was, that he took upon himself the payment of his father's debts, an act entirely voluntary on his part.

Of Lord Mornington, afterwards the celebrated Marquis Wellesley, it is unnecessary to say more in this place than that he was in the year 1797 appointed to the Governor-Generalship of India, in which high office he was enabled to develop, without the suspicion of undue preference, the peculiar talents of his younger brother—talents which his discriminating mind would probably have discovered even without the assistance of such close proximity.

To return to the immediate subject of these Memoirs:—His education commenced at Eton, from whence he went to the military academy at Angers, in the department of the Maine and Loire, there being at that period no institution of the kind in this country.

On his return from the Continent, young Wellesley received (on the 7th of March, 1787), an ensigncy in the 41st regiment, he being then in his eighteenth year. He became lieutenant on the 25th of December in the same year; captain, on the 30th of June, 1791; major, on the 30th of April, 1798; and lieut.-colonel on the 30th of September following. These promotions were chiefly by purchase, and the lieut.-colonelcy (of the 33rd) was bought for him by his brother. He was returned to the Irish parliament at the general election of 1790, for Trim, a borough belonging to his brother.

Brilliant as was the reputation which, within a very few years, he acquired as a soldier and a politician in the East, it will not excite surprise to hear that his parliamentary displays did not in his early life excite much attention. A friend of the writer of this memoir, a gentleman who was in the habit of being present, almost daily, in the Irish House of Commons, and who took critical notice of the remarkable men of his time, states that the Duke never made any striking impression as a speaker; indeed; there was nothing whatever to distinguish him from the herd of young parliamentary nominees, except a certain simple, straightforward, firm, though unassuming statement of his opinions; and even this took place but seldom. The recollection of this gentleman confirms the account of Sir Jonah Barrington, that—"His address was unpolished; he spoke occasionally, and never with success; and evinced no promise of that unparalleled celebrity which he reached afterwards."

The following anecdote is not inconsistent with that reputation for inflexible honour which, in successive eras of his life, procured for the Duke of Wellington the confidence of the Indian government, of the British army, and ultimately of the whole English nation. It is taken from the excellent detailed account of the Duke's military career, recently published by Mr. Maxwell:—

"The appointment of Captain Wellesley to the staff of the Earl of Westmorland, had placed him in the household of the viceroy, and as aid-de-camp required his constant attendance at the castle. The Irish court at that period was celebrated alike for its hospitality, its magnificence, and its dissipation. The princely display of the lords lieutenant of those days entailed a heavy expenditure upon the numerous attachés of the court, and too frequently plunged young men of high family and limited fortunes into very distressing embarrassments. Captain Wellesley's patrimony was small, his staff appointment more fashionable than lucrative, and it is not surprising that soon after he had come of age he found himself involved in pecuniary difficulties. At the time he lodged in the house of an opulent bootmaker, who resided on Lower Ormand Quay. The worthy tradesman discovered, accidently, that his young inmate was suffering annoyance from his inability to discharge a pressing demand. He waited on Lieutenant Wellesley, told him that he was apprised of his embarrassments, mentioned that he had money unemployed, and offered a loan, which was accepted. The obligation was soon afterwards duly repaid; and the young aid-de-camp was enabled in a few years to present his humble friend to an honourable and lucrative situation. Nor did death cancel the obligation; the Duke's patronage, after his parent's death, was extended to the son of his early friend, for whom he obtained a valuable appointment."

To enter into any detailed account of the military career of the Duke of Wellington, would be wholly beyond the scope of a work devoted more especially to his Grace's character and services as a civilian; but were it not so, it would be unnecessary, after the many able biographies which have appeared since the publication of the dispatches by Lieut.-Colonel Gurwood. The following is, therefore only a short summary of the Duke's proceedings from

1794, when he first entered on active service, to 1815, when his functions as a military commander in the field finally ceased.

It was in June, 1794, that Lieut.-Colonel Wellesley embarked at Cork, in command of the 33rd regiment, to join the Duke of York's army in the Netherlands. In the subsequent retreat from Holland he commanded, as senior officer, three battalions, and conducted himself in a manner that already drew on him the attention of military men.

In October, 1795, he again embarked, in the command of the 33rd, for the West Indies, on board the fleet commanded by Admiral Christian. This fleet was, however, repeatedly driven back by the strong equinoctial gales, and in the January following it returned to port. Before it could again sail, the 33rd regiment was ordered to India, and Colonel Wellesley arrived at Bengal in February, 1797. When we consider the fate of a large portion of his fellow soldiers who went to the West Indies, and at the same time look forward to the peculiar facilities which the service in India afforded for developing the great qualities of mind which lay hid under the rigid exterior of the young soldier, it may truly be said, that the moment at which the destination of the 33rd regiment was countermanded, was the point at which the fate of the Duke of Wellington turned. Nay more, if it be admitted that you rarely find in one man a combination of those peculiar qualities, which enabled the Duke to withstand, and ultimately to destroy, the military and political system established by the contrary tendencies which ruled the mind of Napoleon; if, too, it be conceded that the British government, even while the Duke was winning battles in Spain, were accustomed to resort to his counsel with regard to their more extended operations against the common enemy; if, in fact, it is owing to the sagacity, steadfastness, and perseverance of the Duke of Wellington, that we owe the peace of Europe; then must it be admitted, that upon the accident of tempests which obstructed Admiral Christian's fleet, and upon the accident of military disposition, which altered the destination of the regiment, depended not merely the fortunes of the Duke of Wellington, but also the fate of nations, and the peace of the world.

By this time, the Earl of Mornington had been appointed Governor-general of India, and the inveterate hatred of Tippoo Sultaun against the English name was arming the natives to resistance. The first achievement of Colonel Wellesley, that drew attention to his name, was the storming of Seringapatam, in which he commanded the reserve in the trenches. On the capture of Seringapatam Colonel Wellesley was appointed governor, and at the same time named as one of the commission appointed to dispose of the territory conquered. But an office more honourable to his character, was his selection to superintend the removal of the family of Tippoo Sultaun. Lord Mornington in his instructions says:—"The details of this painful but indispensable measure cannot be entrusted to any person more likely to combine every office of humanity with the prudential precautions required by the occasion than Colonel Wellesley; and I therefore commit to his discretion, activity, and humanity, the whole arrangement."

In July, 1799, Colonel Wellesley was appointed to the sole command of Seringapatam and Mysore; and here his capacity for civil government, as well as in military affairs, was fully developed. He had by this time begun to feel his own strength, and to make it felt by others. The reader of his dispatches will perceive that, from the moment when he was placed in a position of independent command, his mind appears to have taken a higher stand: he recognised higher responsibilities: and one may almost detect, in the confirmed self-reliance of his judgment even in this comparatively limited sphere, a prescience of future greatness.

The year 1803 was signalised by Major-General Wellesley's conquests in the Mahratta territory, and the battle of Assaye. Passing over the details of these campaigns, in which the rising commander displayed military genius of the highest order, we come to the more pleasing task of enumerating the honours he received. A monument was erected in Calcutta to commemorate the last-named battle: the inhabitants of that city presented him with a sword of the value of £1000: the officers of his division presented him with a golden vase, afterwards changed for a service of plate, on which the word "Assaye" was engraved: the British parliament voted him public thanks, he was made a Knight Companion of the Bath: and addresses of the warmest praise were voted to him by the inhabitants of Seringapatam, and other places, which had benefitted by his skill and prowess in the field, and his wisdom on the seat of government.

In February, 1805, having resolved on returning to England, he resigned the political and military powers that had been entrusted to him in the Deccan. On the 5th of March, a grand entertainment was given him at the Pantheon at Madras, by the officers of the Presidency, civil and military. On the 10th of September following, he arrived in the Downs; and, in the following month, he was appointed to the Staff, for the Kent District.

In the November following, Sir Arthur Wellesley, as he had now become, commanded the brigade in the expedition to Hanover under Lord Cathcart, which was withdrawn immediately after the battle of Austerlitz. In January, 1800, on the death of the Marquis Cornwallis, he was appointed colonel of the 33rd regiment; and on the 12th of April, in the same year, he was returned to the House of Commons as member for Newport, Isle of Wight.

In this year, Sir Arthur Wellesley married the Honourable Catherine Pakenham, third daughter of the second Earl of Longford.

On the 8th of April, 1807, he was made a privy councillor; and on the 19th of the same month, appointed chief secretary for Ireland, under the lord lieutenancy of the Duke of Richmond. On the 22nd, he was presented by the corporation of the city of Dublin with the freedom of that city. The address in which it was conveyed was most complimentary, and shows the high estimation in which he was already held on account of his brilliant military and civil services in India. In June of the same year, he accompanied Lord Cathcart in the expedition against Copenhagen; and in the only important action which took place at the affair at Kioge—he commanded, and obtained distinction. The result of the action was a capitulation, which Sir Arthur Wellesley was appointed to arrange. On his return home, he received the thanks of parliament for his services. Alluding to Sir Arthur Wellesley, the speaker said:—"But I should indeed be wanting in the full expression of those sentiments which animate this house and the whole country, if I forebore to notice, that we are on this day crowning with our thanks one gallant officer, long since known to the gratitude of this house, who has long trodden the paths of glory,—whose genius and valour have already extended our fame and empire,—whose sword has been the terror of our distant enemies, and will not now be drawn in vain to defend the seat of empire itself, and the throne of his sovereign."

A new and wider field of operations was now preparing for the rising hero. Napoleon, the unquestioned despot of the rest of continental Europe, had also grasped at the Peninsula. Both Spain and Portugal were in his possession, as far as military occupation and nominal sovereignty could ensure them to him. The hostile efforts of England were suspended as far as regarded Europe; but an expedition had been fitted out at Cork against part of Spanish America, and Sir Arthur Wellesley was appointed to the command. Again a marvellous interposition of accidents prevented this his second projected service in America. Before the troops could set sail, the insurrection at Madrid on the 2nd of May, 1808, against the French under Murat, drew the attention of England to the Peninsula, where some hope of successful resistance to Napoleon began to dawn. Once more the destination of the future conqueror was averted from the West, and he was ordered in command to the South.

Sir Arthur Wellesley landed at the mouth of the river Mondego in Portugal on the 3rd of August. Here he received intimation that re-inforcements under Sir John Moore were about to be sent. Moore was his superior officer, and there was also Sir Hew Dalrymple and Sir Harry Burrard on their way, the former of whom would take the chief, and the latter, the second command of the army. There was but little time for Sir Arthur to strike the decisive blow, and although he was not the man to force a battle for the sake of fame, he could not but feel anxious for distinction in this new sphere before all opportunity should be cut off, by the arrival of his superiors in command. Fortune in this was on his side; and he had not been many days in Portugal before he was enabled to defeat the French at the pass of Roliça, and, on the 21st of August, to gain the battle of Vimeiro.

While this battle was at its height, Sir Harry Burrard arrived, but would not interfere with Sir Arthur's dispositions. The French were soon after beaten on the left, and Sir Arthur then urged on Sir Harry the advance of our right wing upon Torres Vedras, while our left would pursue the enemy: his object being to cut off Junot's retreat on Lisbon. No man now doubts that this was counsel wise as well as bold; but Sir Harry Burrard declined to take it, and the golden opportunity was lost. Sir Arthur, who carried military obedience almost to the extent of a chivalrous sentiment, submitted to the orders, though he did not acquiesce in the judgment of his superior officer; but he could not help saying to one of his officers who stood by, "well, then, we have nothing to do but to go and shoot red-legged partridges!" the common game of that part of Portugal.

Sir Arthur Wellesley's subsequent conduct to Sir Harry Burrard was highly honourable. He declared voluntarily before the Court of Inquiry that, though he still differed in opinion with Sir Harry as to the not advancing after the battle of Vimeiro, his opinion was, that Sir H. Burrard "had decided upon fair military grounds, in the manner which appeared to him to be the most conducive to the interests of the country;" and his belief, "that Sir Harry had no motive for his decision which could be supposed personal to him, or which as an officer he could not avow."

The untoward convention of Cintra, which followed the victory of Vimeiro, was received in England with one universal cry of indignation. Sir Arthur Wellesley was no farther implicated in it than that he signed it as one of the generals, although disapproving of it from the first. Pending the inquiry, instituted in England on the convention, he returned thither, and his evidence was satisfactory alike to the court and to the public.

On the 27th January, 1809, Sir Arthur received the thanks of parliament for the battle of Vimeiro. The speaker, in delivering the thanks of the House of Commons, said:—

"Amidst the contending opinions which have prevailed
upon other questions, the public voice has been
loud and general in admiration of your splendid
achievements. It is your praise to have inspired
your troops with unshaken confidence and unbounded
ardour—to have commanded, not the obedience alone,
but the hearts and affections of your companions in
arms; and having planned your operations with the skill
and promptitude which have so eminently characterised all
your former exertions, you have again led the armies of
your country to battle, with the same deliberate valour,
and triumphant success which have long since rendered your
name illustrious in the remotest parts of this empire.
Military glory has ever been dear to this nation; and great
military exploits, in the field or upon the ocean, have
their sure reward in royal favour, and the gratitude of parliament."

Sir Arthur, in his reply, observed:--
"No man can value more highly than I do the
honourable distinction which has been conferred upon
me—a distinction which it is in the power of the
representatives of a free people alone to bestow, and
which it is the peculiar advantage of the officers and
soldiers in the service of his majesty to have held out
to them as the object of their ambition, and to receive
as the reward of their services."

The opening allusion of the speaker to "contending opinions on other matters," was intended to mark the sense of the house that Sir Arthur Wellesley, at least, was free from blame as regarded recent transactions in the Peninsula. That the government thought so also, and had at last learned to appreciate the value of an officer whom they had so recently trammelled, was evidenced by the appointment of Sir Arthur, on the 2nd of April, to the command of the army in Portugal.

Towards the close of the previous year, complaint had been made, in the House of Commons, of Sir Arthur holding the office of secretary for Ireland while in the Peninsula. On the 14th of April, he resigned that office, and on the 22nd, he arrived at Lisbon and assumed the command of an army, disproportioned, indeed, to the service expected of it, and still more to that which they afterwards achieved, but strong in its confidence in a general who had never made a false step, or suffered a defeat.

On the 12th of May, he carried Oporto by a *coup de main*. So complete was the surprise, that Sir Arthur and his staff sat down to the dinner which had been prepared for the French commander.

On the 28th July following, the battle of Talavera was fought, after which (on the 26th August), Sir Arthur was raised to the peerage by the titles of Baron Douro of Wellesley and Viscount Wellington of Talavera. In the February following, he received the thanks of parliament for Talavera, and a pension of £2000 per annum was voted to him and his two next heirs male.

So inferior was the numerical force of his army to that of the enemy that Lord Wellington found his operations must for some time be confined to the defence of Portugal; and he, therefore, gave orders for the fortification of the lines of Torres Vedras, by which the capital of the country was covered. They extended from the sea to the Tagus, at a point where the width of that river is such as to afford an adequate protection.

It was characteristic of the mind of the man of whom we are writing, that these works were planned and executed with a secrecy that baffled the penetration of the enemy, and equally the suicidal curiosity of the English newspapers.

Massena was now the general of the French army. Wellington, before retiring within the lines, fought the action of Busaco (ten months after the battle of Talavera), in which the French lost 5000 men, killed or wounded, and as many more disabled. After this victory, the English withdrew within the lines, to cover Lisbon. Massena took up a position at Santaren, from whence he gradually retreated towards the frontiers, several affairs occurring between his troops and the English, by whom he was closely followed. At length, he crossed the frontier, and Wellington's object was, thus far, attained. On the 26th of the same month, he received the thanks of both houses of parliament for the liberation of Portugal.

In the meanwhile, the army of Massena had been re-organized and reinforced, and on the 3rd of May he again attacked the allied British and Portuguese forces, for the purpose of relieving the fortress of Almeida, which was under blockade. The action was fought at Fuentes D'Onoro, and resulted in the defeat of the French. Massena was then superseded, and Marmont appointed in his place.

The next object of the British commander was to take Badajoz and Ciudad Rodrigo. The latter was stormed on the 19th January, and the former on the 9th of April. For both, the thanks of parliament were voted; and Lord Wellington, after having been created Conde de Vimeiro in Portugal, and Duke of Ciudad Rodrigo in Spain, was raised to an earldom (of Wellington) at home, with another vote of 2000 l. per annum to maintain the title.

On the 22nd of July, Marmont's army, which had been strongly reinforced, attacked the allies near Salamanca. The two armies had been watching each other for a considerable time, waiting for the favourable moment to attack. At length Marmont began, and having superior numbers, extended his left for the purpose of turning the British right. Wellington, when informed of this by one of his staff, was seated on the ground eating some cold beef; suddenly starting up, he exclaimed, "Marmont's good genius has forsaken him." He immediately attacked the French where they had weakened their line, and overthrew them from left to right. The loss of the enemy was severe, and Marmont himself lost an arm in the battle.

On the 12th of August following, Lord Wellington entered Madrid, and was appointed generalissimo of the Spanish armies—a troublesome honour which there was some difficulty in inducing him to accept. He was created a marquis at home, thanks were voted to him for the battle of Salamanca, and he received a grant of 100,000 l. to purchase land. He was also in December of the same year made Duque da Vittoria in Portugal.

In the meantime, the enormous force which had been brought together by the French, the refusal of the Spanish generals to co-operate, the failure of an attempt to capture the fortress of Burgos, and other causes, compelled the allies to retreat to Ciudad Rodrigo, with the determination of returning to Spain at a more fitting time. This retreat was conducted in the most admirable manner, and closed the campaign of 1812.

The foregoing is necessarily a most meagre outline of events, on which volumes have been written. Those who may be anxious to read the Duke of Wellington's own account of the military operations, will find in the public despatches his annual summaries: for 1809, in despatch No. 343; for 1810, No. 504; and for 1811, No. 615. For 1812 there is no such summary.

It would be a mistake, however, to suppose that the difficulties with which the Duke of Wellington had to contend during these the three first years of his service in Spain, were confined to the making of military dispositions and the winning of battles. Other causes there were, operating as a drawback at every forward step, and obstacles sufficient to have wearied a less stout heart or a less determined spirit. To oppose to a skillful and veteran enemy he had but an inadequate force, most scantily supplied with provisions, and even with money. The French generals, restrained by no principle of honour or even of policy, were accustomed to plunder mercilessly for the subsistence of their troops: the

English commander would take nothing from the people but what was paid for on the spot in money or in bills on the English government. Yet, such was the apathy (or worse) of the Portuguese authorities, that even on these terms provisions were not forthcoming; and important operations were constantly delayed or frustrated by the want of the necessary subsistence for the troops.

The reader of the Duke's despatches will glean much of his character from the letters written from time to time to these persons; and, scattered through the extracts which form a part of this volume, will be found characters of both Spaniards and Portuguese, (that is to say in the civil service) that are not very flattering to the national vanity. Well may he say, in a letter to Mr. Villiers on the 25th of May 1811, "No man can appreciate better than yourself the difficulties with which I have had to contend; but I believe you are not aware of all of them. I persevered in the system which I thought best, notwithstanding that it was the opinion of every British officer in the country that I ought to embark the army; while, on the other hand, the Portuguese civil authorities contended that the war ought to be maintained on the frontier, for which they wanted not only physical force, but the means of providing for the force which they could produce in the field. I believe that nothing but *something worse than firmness could have carried me through* the nine months' discussion with these contending opinions. To this add that people in England were changing their opinions almost with the wind, and you will see that I had not much to look to, excepting myself."

Nothing could be more ignoble than the conduct of the people of Lisbon as to the billeting of the very soldiers who had saved them from the enemy. On one occasion the Duke writes to order his wine, &c. to be removed from the house of a Signor Bandeira, and to have a house taken for him, "in order," he says, "to mortify the people of Lisbon a little as to their conduct about billets. I am slaving like a negro for them: I have saved the people, in Lisbon particularly, from the enemy, and I take nothing from them, while they continually torment me with their frivolous complaints on subjects on which they ought to have no feeling. * * I shall not be sorry if the government and principal people of Lisbon know the reason why I take this house; viz., that I will not lay myself under obligation to any of them." Strong language this, from a man of the Duke's impassible temperament. But unfortunately there was too much reason for this, and indeed, for much more animadversion on more serious subjects, as regards many of the chief men of the Peninsula.

Nor were these the only annoyances he had to submit to. In the early part of his service in the Peninsula, before he had by his brilliant deeds utterly silenced for the present and the future the cavillings of the envious, he was subjected to repeated attacks in Parliament, to predictions of failure—to everything in short that was calculated to dispirit him and his army. The government, too, seemed hardly to have "backed him up" as they might have done, either with respect to the force at his command, or their approval of his plans.

Nor were these attacks confined to parliament. On the 2nd January, 1810, writing to Mr. Villiers, he says: "You see the dash the Common Council have made at me![1] I act with a sword hanging over me, which will fall upon me, whatever may be the result of affairs here; but they may do what they please,—I shall not give up the game here as long as it can be played." Again, two months after, he refers to what has passed in parliament about him, and observes, "that it does not give him one moment's concern."

[Footnote 1: They had voted an address for an inquiry into his conduct.]

Throughout the dispatches and letters will be found very interesting passages referring to all these difficulties in his path.

In May, 1819, the British again advanced into Spain, and on the 21st of June completely defeated the French at Vittoria, for which the thanks of parliament were voted on the 8th of July. What was felt in another quarter will be seen by the following letter written by the Prince Regent.

To Field Marshal the Marquis of Wellington, K.G.
Carlton House, 3rd July, 1818
My dear Lord.—Your glorious conduct is beyond all human praise, and far above my reward. I know no language the world affords worthy to express it. I feel I have nothing left to say, but most devoutly to offer up my prayer of gratitude to Providence, that it has, in its Omnipotent bounty, blessed my country and myself with such a general. You have sent me, amongst the trophies of your unrivalled fame, the staff of a French marshal, and I send you in return that of England.
The British army will hail it with rapturous enthusiasm, while the whole universe will acknowledge those valorous exploits which have so imperiously rallied for it. That uninterrupted health and still increasing laurels may continue to crown you through a glorious and long career of life, are the never ceasing and most ardent wishes of, my dear lord, your very sincere and faithful friend.
G.P.R.

On the 22nd, the Regency of Spain gave the Marquis of Wellington the estate of the Soto de Roma, in Granada, "in the name of the Spanish nation, in testimony of its sincere gratitude."

On the 28th of July, the French, under Marshal Soult, having re-entered Spain, the battle of Sovauren was fought; and on the 8th of September, St. Sebastian fell. On the 7th of October, the passage of the Bidassoa was effected; and on the 10th of November, the whole of the army descended into France. Other battles ensued; and on the 10th of April, 1814, was fought the final battle of Toulouse, which ended the war.

On the 3rd of May, the illustrious commander was advanced in the peerage by the titles of Marquis of Douro and Duke of Wellington; and, soon after, a grant of £400,000 was voted him by parliament. He arrived in England on the 23rd of June, and on the next day proceeded to Portsmouth to the Prince Regent, who was there with the allied monarchs.

A few days afterwards, a scene took place in the House of Lords—when for the first time the Duke took his seat there—enough to make a nation's heart beat with gratitude, pride, and exultation. It is thus described:

"On the 28th of June, shortly after 3 o'clock, the Lord Chancellor having taken his seat, the Duke of Wellington was introduced, supported by the Dukes of Richmond and Beaufort, in military uniform, and in their ducal robes. Being arrived in the body of the House, the Duke made the usual obeisance to the Lord Chancellor, and shewed his patent and right of summons: these noblemen then approached the table, where his Grace's various patents, as baron and viscount, earl, marquis, and lastly as duke, were each read by the clerks. The oaths were then administered, and the Test Rolls were signed by him. He then, accompanied by his noble supporters, took his seat on the dukes' bench, and saluted the house in the usual manner, by rising, taking off his hat, and bowing respectfully. The Lord Chancellor then rose, and, pursuant to their lordships' orders, addressed his Grace:—

"My Lord Duke of Wellington,—I have received the commands of this house, which I am persuaded has witnessed with infinite satisfaction your Grace's personal introduction to this august assembly, to return your grace the thanks and acknowledgments of this house, for your great and eminent services to your king and country."

"In the execution of these commands, I cannot forbear to call the especial attention of all who hear me to a fact in your Grace's life, singular, I believe, in the history of the country, and infinitely honourable to your Grace, that you have manifested, upon your first entrance into this house, your right, under various grants, to all the dignities in the peerage of this realm which the crown can confer. These dignities have been conferred at various periods, but in the short compass of little more than four years, for great public services, occurring in rapid succession, claiming the favour of the crown, influenced by its sense of justice to your grace and the country; and on no one occasion in which the crown has thus rewarded your merits have the Houses of Parliament been inattentive to your demands upon the gratitude of the country. Upon all such occasions, they have offered to your Grace their acknowledgments and thanks, the highest honours they could bestow."

"I decline all attempts to state your Grace's eminent merits in your military character; to represent those brilliant actions, those illustrious achievements, which have attached immortality to the name of Wellington, and which have given to this country a degree of glory unexampled in the annals of this kingdom. In thus acting, I believe I best consult the feelings which evince your Grace's title to the character of a truly great and illustrious man."

"My duty to this house cannot but make me most anxious not to fall short of the expectation which the house may have formed as to the execution of what may have been committed to me on this great occasion; but the most anxious consideration which I have given to the nature of that duty has convinced me that I cannot more effectually do justice to the judgment of the house, than by referring your Grace to the terms and language in which the house has so repeatedly expressed its own sense of the distinguished and consummate wisdom and judgment, the skill and ability, the prompt energy, the indefatigable exertion, perseverance, the fortitude and the valour, by which the victories of Vimeiro, Talavera, Salamanca and Vittoria were achieved; by which the sieges of Ciudad Rodrigo and Badajoz were gloriously terminated; by which the deliverance of Portugal was effectuated; by which the ever memorable establishment of the allied armies on the frontiers of France was accomplished; armies pushing forward, in the glory of victory at Orthes, to the occupation of Bordeaux. These achievements, in their immediate consequence infinitely beneficial to the common cause, have, in their final results, secured the peace, prosperity, and glory of this country; whilst your Grace's example has animated to great exertions the other nations of Europe, exertions rescuing them from tyranny, and restoring them to independence, by which there has been ultimately established among the nations of Europe that balance of power which, giving sufficient strength to every nation, provides that no nation shall be too strong. I presume not to trespass upon the house by representing the personal satisfaction which I have derived from being the honoured instrument of conveying to your Grace the acknowledgments and thanks of this house upon every occasion upon which they have been offered to your Grace, or by endeavouring to represent the infinite gratification which I enjoy in thus offering, on behalf of the house, on this day, to your Grace in person, those acknowledgments and those thanks. Your Grace is now called to aid hereafter, by your wisdom and judgment, the great council of that nation, to the peace, prosperity, and glory of which your Grace has already so essentially contributed; and to tender your Grace, now taking your seat in this house, in obedience to its commands, the thanks of the house in the words of its resolution—That the thanks of this house be given to Field-marshal the Duke of Wellington, on his return from his command abroad, for his eminent and unremitting services to his majesty and the public."

The Duke answered the address to the following effect:--
"My lords, I have to perform a duty to which I feel myself very inadequate, to return your lordships my thanks for the fresh mark of your approbation of my conduct and of your favour."
"I assure your lordships that I am entirely overcome by the honours which have been conferred upon me; and by the favour with which I have been received in this country by the Prince Regent, by your lordships, and by the public."
"In truth, my lords, when I reflect upon the advantages which I enjoyed in the confidence reposed in me, and the support afforded by the government, and by his royal highness the commander-in-chief, in the cordial assistance which I invariably received upon all occasions from my gallant friends, the general officers of the army, who are an honour to their country, the gallantry and discipline of the troops, and in the manner in which I was encouraged and excited to exertion by the protection and gracious favour of the prince, I cannot but consider that, however great the difficulties with which I had to contend, the means to contend with them were equal to overcome them; and I am apprehensive that I shall not be found so deserving of your favour as I wish."

"If, however, my merit is not great, my gratitude is unbounded; and I can only assure your lordships, that you will always find me ready to serve his majesty to the utmost of my ability in any capacity in which my services can be at all useful to this great country."

His Grace then retired to unrobe; he wore a field-marshal's uniform, with his insignia of the garter. On his return into the House he sat for a few minutes on the extremity of one of the benches, and then retired for the evening.

In addition to the pecuniary remuneration voted by Parliament to the Duke of Wellington for his distinguished services, the House of Commons resolved to pay him the highest tribute of respect and applause that it was possible to bestow on a subject, that of its thanks, accompanied with a deputation of its members to congratulate him on his return to this country Lord Castlereagh rose in the house, on the 27th June, to make a motion for this purpose, which was unanimously agreed to; and a committee was appointed to wait on his Grace, to know what time he would name for receiving the congratulations of the house. Lord Castlereagh having reported from the committee that it was the Duke's desire to express to the house his answer in person, the following day, July 1, was appointed for the solemnity.

At about a quarter before five, the speaker being dressed in his official robes, and the house being crowded with members, some of them in military and naval uniforms, and many of them in the court dresses in which they had been attending the speaker with an address to the Prince Regent on the peace, the house was acquainted that the Duke of Wellington was in waiting. His admission being resolved on, and a chair being set for him on the left hand of the bar towards the middle of the house, his Grace entered, making his obeisances, while all the members rose from their seats. The speaker then informing him that a chair was placed for his repose, he sat down in it for some time, covered, the serjeant standing on his right hand with the mace grounded, and the members resumed their seats. He then rose, and spoke, uncovered, to the following effect:—

"Mr. Speaker,—I was anxious to be permitted to attend this house, in order to return my thanks in person for the honour they have done me in deputing a committee of their members to congratulate me on my return to this country; and this, after the house had animated my exertions by their applause upon every occasion which appeared to merit their approbation, and after they had filled up the measure of their favours by conferring upon me, upon the recommendation of the Prince Regent, the noblest gift that any subject had ever received."

"I hope it will not be deemed presumptuous in me to take this opportunity of expressing my admiration of the great efforts made by this house and the country at a moment of unexampled pressure and difficulty, in order to support the great scale of operations by which the contest was brought to so fortunate a termination. By the wise policy of parliament, the government was enabled to give the necessary support to the operations which were carried on under my direction; and I was encouraged by the confidence reposed in me by his majesty's ministers, and by the commander-in-chief, by the gracious favour of his royal highness the Prince Regent, and by the reliance which I had on the support of my gallant friends the general officers of the army, and on the bravery of the officers and troops, to carry on the operations in such a manner as to acquire for me those marks of the approbation of this house, for which I have now the honor to make my humble acknowledgments."

"Sir, it is impossible for me to express the gratitude which I feel; I can only assure the house that I shall always be ready to serve his majesty in any capacity in which my services can be deemed useful, with the same zeal for my country which has already acquired for me the approbation of this house."

This speech was received with loud cheers, at the end of which the speaker, who had sat covered during its delivery, rose, and thus addressed his Grace:—

"My Lord,—Since last I had the honour of addressing you from this place, a series of eventful years has elapsed; but none without some mark and note of your rising glory."

"The military triumphs which your valour has achieved upon the banks of the Douro and the Tagus, of the Ebro and the Garonne, have called forth the spontaneous shouts of admiring nations. Those triumphs it is needless on this day to recount. Their names have been written by your conquering sword in the annals of Europe, and we hand them down with exultation to our children's children."

"It is not, however, the grandeur of military success which has alone fixed our admiration, or commanded our applause; it has been that generous and lofty spirit which inspired your troops with unbounded confidence, and taught them to know that the day of battle was always a day of victory; that moral courage and enduring fortitude, which, in perilous times, when gloom and doubt had beset ordinary minds, stood nevertheless unshaken; and that ascendancy of character, which, uniting the energies of jealous and rival nations, enabled you to wield at will the fate of mighty empires."

"For the repeated thanks and grants bestowed upon you by this house, in gratitude for your many and eminent services, you have thought fit this day to offer us your acknowledgments: but this nation well knows that it is still largely your debtor. It owes to you the proud satisfaction, that, amidst the constellation of great and illustrious warriors who have recently visited our country, we could present to them a leader of our own, to whom all, by common acclamation, conceded the pre-eminence; and when the will of heaven, and the common destinies of our nature, shall have swept away the present generation, you will have left your great name and example as an imperishable monument, exciting others to like deeds of glory, and serving at once to adorn, defend, and perpetuate the existence of this country amongst the ruling nations of the earth."

"It now remains only that we congratulate your Grace upon the high and important mission on which you are about to proceed, and we doubt not that the same splendid talents, so conspicuous in war, will maintain, with equal authority, firmness, and temper, our national honour and interests in peace."

His Grace then withdrew, making the same obeisance as when he entered; and all the members rising again, he was reconducted by the serjeant to the door of the house.

On the 7th July, when the Prince Regent went in state to St. Paul's, to return public thanksgiving for the restoration of peace, the Duke of Wellington was seated on the right hand of his royal highness, with the sword of state before him.

On the 9th, the Duke was entertained by the corporation of London in the Guildhall, and previously to the banquet he was presented with a sword of exquisite workmanship, which had been voted him by the common council. Four years and a half before, as will be remembered, the Duke was publicly attacked by this same common council, and he then says, "I act with a sword hanging over me." During the interval, the common council had learned to apply their sword to a better purpose. In fact, all ranks, from the highest to the lowest, now combined to do honour to the Duke of Wellington.

When Buonaparte landed from Elba, the Duke was at Vienna, the representative of this country at the congress of the allied sovereigns. From that point he wrote to Lord Castlereagh, stating the interview he had had with the sovereigns on the subject of Buonaparte's movements, and adding that he had no doubt whatever of their support, and their determination not to lay down their arms until Buonaparte was put down. A numerous force was assembled, and of the whole, whether British or foreign, in Belgium (already seen to be the point on which the fate of Napoleon would be decided), the Duke of Wellington assumed the command. The campaign was closed by the decisive victory of Waterloo, on the 18th June, followed by the abdication of Napoleon, and the convention of Paris.

During the subsequent proceedings, the Duke of Wellington was instrumental in stopping the savage revenge of Blucher and the Prussians, who were on the point of destroying the beautiful bridge on the Seine, called the bridge of Jena, because it had been named in honour of Napoleon's victory over the Prussians at that place.

The Duke, however, did not interpose to prevent another act, which was one of real justice, the restoration to the several nations of the various works of art of which they had been plundered by the French. It was in answer to complaints of his conduct in this respect that the Duke wrote his letter to Castlereagh, in which he said—"It is to be wished, as well for the happiness of France as of the world, that if the French people are not already convinced that Europe is too strong for them, they may be made to feel that, however extensive for a time their temporary and partial advantages over one or more of the powers of Europe may be, the day of retribution must at length come. According to my feelings, then, it would not only be unjust in the sovereigns to gratify the French people, but the sacrifice they would make would be impolitic, as it would deprive them of the opportunity of giving the French nation a *great moral lesson.*"

The thanks of both houses were voted to the Duke for the battle of Waterloo, and an additional grant of 200,000 l.

From the year 1815 until 1823 the Duke of Wellington's name rarely appears in connexion with any public transactions, with the exception that in December, 1818, he was appointed Master-General of the Ordnance, an office which he continued to fill for some years.

In 1819 he made one speech in parliament in which his declared his belief that Roman Catholic Emancipation was impossible, unless there could be a proper security for the Protestant religion, which he doubted.

In the year 1823, on the appointment of Mr. Canning to be Secretary for Foreign Affairs, Duke of Wellington was named as the Plenipotentiary of the King of Great Britain at the Congress of Verona. It was supposed that the subject matter of the discussions of the sovereigns at that congress would be the relations of Russia and Turkey. On the Duke's arrival at Paris, however, he found that Spain would form the main subject. He wrote back for fresh instructions, and Mr. Canning's answer distinctly stated that should France attempt to interfere in Spain either by force or by menace, he was to instruct the Duke "frankly and peremptorily to declare, that to any such interference, come what may, his majesty will not be a party."

The words "frankly and peremptorily" could not have been better chosen, or more agreeable to the character of the Duke. He stuck simply and stedfastly to his text throughout the negotiations, and when at last, in consequence of the state of affairs in Spain, the three great powers agreed to withdraw their ministers from Madrid, the Duke told them he should not withdraw ours but leave him there in the hope of allaying the irritation which the measures of the others were calculated to produce.

The Duke returned to Parts in December, and found the French not indisposed to some arrangement. When it subsequently became necessary to send a special communication to the Spanish government, a mark of respect was paid by Mr. Canning to the Duke of Wellington, more gratifying perhaps to him than his titles or honours. The desire of the British Government was to attach a special character of friendliness to this communication, and for that purpose the Duke of Wellington was requested to make it. This course was taken because it was believed that the private opinions of a man who had conferred such distinguished benefits on Spain, and who had been on terms of personal intercourse and friendship with many of the leading men, would be listened to with more deference than even an official communication. It is unnecessary to pursue this subject farther, as the Duke of Wellington's connexion with it ceased; except that he gave, in the House of Lords, on the 24th of April, a full explanation of his share in the proceedings.

In 1826, the Duke having been appointed ambassador to St. Petersburgh, on the anniversary of the entrance of the allied army into Paris under his command, the Emperor Nicholas addressed a letter to him, in which he told him that in order to testify to him his particular esteem for his great qualities and for the distinguished services he had rendered to the whole of Europe, he had given orders that the Smolensko regiment of infantry, formed by Peter the Great, and one of the most distinguished of his army, which was formerly under the Duke's command in France, should thenceforward be called the Duke of Wellington's regiment.

In 1827, on the death of the Duke of York, the public mind pointed to the Duke of Wellington as the fit successor of his royal highness in the important post of Commander-in-Chief, and he was immediately appointed. The Duke held this office until the appointment of Mr. Canning to be Prime Minister, when he resigned it, and also the Master-Generalship of the Ordnance.

The circumstances attending this resignation must of course hold a prominent place in any memoir of the Duke. But there were personal matters mixed up in the affair, which make it necessary to enter into it at some length, for the better understanding of his Grace's character.

On the death of the Earl of Liverpool, in the beginning of the year 1827, the king called on Mr. Canning to form an administration. As Mr. Canning had all along advocated Roman Catholic Emancipation, and as the cabinet of Lord Liverpool had firmly opposed that measure, it became a question how far the premiership of Mr. Canning would compromise the position of those who had hitherto acted with him in the cabinet of Lord Liverpool. The question very soon received a practical solution, by the simultaneous (though not concerted) resignation of six of the most influential members of the government, including the Duke of Wellington.

The political friends of Mr. Canning, and those of his opponents with whom he was agreed on the Roman Catholic question, concurred in representing this act of the seceding ministers as a cabal against Mr. Canning; and the Duke of Wellington, more especially, was made the subject of most unsparing abuse. The ground of this was that he had not contented himself with resigning the office he held directly under the government, but had also resigned the command of the army, an office unconnected with politics. This was supposed to indicate some special determination to crush Mr. Canning.

Now with regard to the motives of the Duke on this occasion all men will form their own opinion, not so much with reference to facts, as to their political feelings. It may however be fairly laid down as a principle that where admitted facts sufficiently supply an explanation of a man's conduct, all reference to motives are unnecessary; and the more so because in all cases, however strong suspicion or presumptive evidence may be, the truth with regard to a man's motives must ever remain locked in his own breast. The open, manly and fearless character of the Duke would however, except in the heated imagination of partisans, almost preclude suspicion in the first instance.

But let us turn to the facts, as stated in the house of lords on the 2nd of May, when the peers met after the Easter recess. On the 10th of April Mr. Canning wrote to the Duke of Wellington the following letter:—

To his Grace the Duke of Wellington.
Foreign Office, April 10, 6 P.M., 1827.

My dear Duke of Wellington,—The king has, at
an audience from which I have just returned, been
graciously pleased to signify to me his majesty's commands,
to lay before his majesty, with as little loss as
time as possible, a plan of arrangements for the re-construction of
the administration. In executing these commands it will be as much my
own wish, as it is my duty to his majesty, to adhere to the principles
upon which Lord Liverpool's government has so long acted together. I
need not add how essentially the accomplishment must depend upon your
Grace's continuing a member of the cabinet.

Ever, my dear Duke of Wellington, your Grace's sincere and faithful servant,

GEORGE CANNING.
To this the Duke of Wellington replied in a characteristic way:--
To the Right Hon. George Canning.
London, April 10, 1827.

My dear Mr. Canning,—I have received your letter of
this evening, informing me that the king had desired
you to lay before his majesty a plan for the re-construction
of the administration; and that, in executing
these commands, it was your wish to adhere to the
principles on which Lord Liverpool's government had
so long acted together. I anxiously desire to be able
to serve his majesty, as I have done hitherto in his
cabinet, with the same colleagues. But before I can
give an answer to your obliging proposition, I should
wish to know who the person is you intend to propose
to his majesty as the head of the government?

Ever, my dear Mr. Canning, yours most sincerely,
WELLINGTON.
On the next day came the following from Mr. Canning:--

To his Grace the Duke of Wellington.
Foreign Office, April 11, 1897.
My dear Duke of Wellington,—I believed it to be
so generally understood, that the king usually intrusts
the formation of an administration to the individual
whom it is his majesty's gracious intention to place at
the head of it; that it did not occur to me, when I

communicated to your Grace yesterday the commands
which I had just received from his majesty, to add, that,
in the present instance, his majesty does not intend to
depart from the usual course of proceeding on such
occasions. I am sorry to have delayed some hours this
answer to your Grace's letter; but from the nature of
the subject, I did not like to forward it without having
previously submitted it (together with your Grace's
letter) to his Majesty.

Ever, my dear Duke of Wellington, your Grace's
sincere and faithful servant,
  GEORGE CANNING.

And finally, on the evening of the same day, the Duke wrote thus to Mr. Canning.—

London, April 11, 1837.

My dear Mr. Canning,—I have received your letter
of this day, and I did not understand the one of yesterday
evening as you explained it to me. I understood
from yourself that you had in contemplation another
arrangement, and I do not believe that the practice to
which you refer has been so invariable as to enable me to affix a
meaning to your letter which its words did not, in my opinion, convey. I
trust that you will have experienced no inconvenience from the delay of
this answer, which I assure you has been occasioned by my desire to
discover a mode by which I could continue united with my recent
colleagues.—I sincerely wish that I could bring my mind to the
conclusion that, with the best intentions on your part, your government
could be conducted practically on the principles of that of Lord
Liverpool; that it would be generally so considered; or that it would be
adequate to meet our difficulties, in a manner satisfactory to the king,
or conducive to the interests of the country. As, however, I am
convinced that these principles must be abandoned eventually, that all
our measures would be viewed with suspicion by the usual supporters of
the government; that I could do no good in the cabinet; and that at last
I should be obliged to separate myself from it, at the moment at which
such separation would be more inconvenient to the king's service than it
can be at present, I must beg you to request his majesty to excuse me
from belonging to his councils. Ever, my dear Mr. Canning, yours most
sincerely,

WELLINGTON.

This closed the correspondence; and it is needless to add that the Duke continued to hold aloof from the new administration.

The Duke's explanation in the House of Lords related to two branches of charge. The first was a charge of want of personal courtesy to Mr. Canning, as exhibited in the foregoing correspondence; the second was a general charge of hostility to the new premier, founded on personal jealousy, and on every other ground, probable or improbable, which the malice of party could suggest. The Duke began by observing, that the House of Lords was scarcely the proper place to enter on such subjects, but that his only excuse was the necessity of vindicating his character against what had been said in another place, to say nothing of the manner in which he had been treated by a corrupt press, which if not in the pay, was under the control of the government. He then proceeded to meet the first charge, that of personal discourtesy. It was said, that his asking in reply to Mr. Canning's first letter, "who was to be at the head of the new government?" was intended as an insult to Mr. Canning. This he denied. The letter of Mr. Canning, he said gave no information who were to form the new cabinet, or what members of the old one had resigned, or were expected to resign. Nor was he invited, as he found the other ministers had been, to receive personal explanations on the subject. Under those circumstances the inquiry was made. But that was not the first communication that had passed between them on the subject. Early in the month of April, continued the Duke, he had had a conversation with Mr. Canning, in which, anticipating the possibility of his being called upon to reconstruct the government, one of his plans was to recommend that Mr. Robinson (now the Earl of Ripon) should be raised to the peerage and be made premier. Of this plan the Duke at the time approved, and it was with this in his mind that he wrote the first answer, which gave Mr. Canning so much offence. Precedent, also, he contended, was against Mr. Canning; for it appeared that in 1812, when Lord Liverpool, by command of the Prince Regent, waited on Mr. Canning, to know whether he would form part of the proposed administration, the first question Mr. Canning asked of the noble earl (then in the same position Mr. Canning was in now) was, "who was to be at the head of the new administration?" The Duke's letter was written on the 10th, and Mr. Canning only kissed hands as minister on the 12th; so that, even in that point of view, the Duke's question was, he contended, necessary.

It may be said that there is enough on the face of this communication to show that the Duke of Wellington took a narrow, and, so to speak, technical, view of the relative positions of himself and Mr. Canning; that the latter expected a more conventional and generous construction of his position and proposal from one with whom he was on terms of intimate friendship.

In answer to this, it may be as well to remind the reader that, where the slightest movements of public men may be construed into a compromise of public principles, a rigid attention to etiquette becomes a matter of duty. Many acts of the Duke of Wellington, not merely as a civilian, but even as a military commander, have been misjudged, because this obvious principle has been overlooked.

In answer to the second charge—that of hostility to the new administration on personal grounds—the Duke referred to the known opinions of Mr. Canning on the Catholic question. How could he be in office under a minister whom he must oppose on, at least, one vital question of domestic policy? How could he give the right honourable gentleman that fair support which one member of a cabinet had a right to expect from another? The principles of the new government could not be those of that of the Earl of Liverpool. The principle of the latter was to maintain the existing laws; of the former, to change them in a fundamental particular. The absurd calumny that he had threatened the king to resign, unless he were prepared to make him prime minister, hardly deserved an answer; and then came his celebrated *nolo episcopari* speech, which created against him in a year after, so much ridicule and rancour. He said—"Was it likely that he would resign the office of commander-in-chief," a situation so consonant to his feelings and his habits, "for the mere empty ambition of being placed at the head of the government. I know," continued the Duke, "I am disqualified for any such office; and I, therefore, say, that, feeling as I do with respect to the situation which I recently filled at the head of the army; liking it as I did from the opportunity it gave me to improve the condition of my old comrades in arms; knowing my own capacity for filling that office, and my incapacity for filling the post of first minister, I should have been mad, and worse than mad, if I had ever entertained the insane project which certain individuals, for their own base purposes, have imputed to me."

His reason for retiring from the command of the army was founded on the peculiar circumstances of his dispute with Mr. Canning. "No political opinions would have prevented him," he said, "under ordinary circumstances, from continuing either at the Horse Guards or at the head of the army in the field; but, from the tone and tenor of the communication he had received from his majesty; from the nature of the invitation to join the administration, contained in Mr. Canning's post letter, and from the contents of the last letter he received from Mr. Canning, by his majesty's commands, he saw it would be impossible to continue his relations with that gentlemen, either with service to the country or credit to himself. His resolution had been adopted after the most mature deliberation."

The foregoing is the substance of the Duke of Wellington's explanation of his own share in the general resignation of the chief members of Lord Liverpool's cabinet.

Another circumstance occurred a few days afterwards, which still further increased the public belief that there was a serious quarrel between the Duke and the new premier. The former moved an amendment in committee on the corn bill, which had the effect of defeating the new government on that measure. This was regarded as an act of hostility on the part of the Duke, and, shortly after, a correspondence was made public between him and Mr. Huskisson, then President of the Board of Trade, in which it appeared clear that the Duke had moved the amendment in the belief that the government had agreed to it through Mr. Huskisson, and equally clear that the Duke had been mistaken. There were not wanting those who asserted roundly that the Duke had taken advantage of an ambiguity in Mr. Huskisson's letters, in order to have a pretext for inflicting this injury on the government. And, unhappily, Mr. Canning himself, carried out of parliamentary decorum by an irritability of temper, springing from the difficulties of his position and from his advancing illness, went so far as publicly to declare that the Duke of Wellington, great man as he was, had been but in instrument in the hands of others. History, he said, afforded parallel the actions of other great men.

The Duke maintained a dignified silence with respect to this attack; but, in the following year, long after Mr. Canning's death, and when he had himself become prime minister, he took an opportunity of disclaiming, in strong language, the existance of any personal hostility on his part to the deceased statesman.

On the formation of the new administration, under Lord Goderich, the Duke of Wellington resumed the command of the army. This was on August the 27th.

Early in January, 1828, this administration fell to pieces, and the Duke of Wellington was called on by the king to form another. He was at first reluctant to do so, but ultimately gave way. He rallied round him Mr. Peel, and most of those who had seceded on the accession of Mr. Canning; so that his administration was nearly identical with that of the Earl of Liverpool, except that Mr. Huskisson and some two or three of the coalitionary whigs, were retained.

In the following May, these were got rid of. Mr. Huskisson gave a vote on the East Retford Bill, adverse to those of his colleagues; and on leaving the house, sat down (at two in the morning), and wrote a letter to the Duke, which was construed into a positive resignation of office. An amusing correspondence took place between the two statesmen, Mr. Huskisson declaring he never meant to resign, and the Duke as positively adhering to his original construction of the first letter. Mr. Huskisson's place was filled up, and he resented that proceeding by declaring in the House of Commons his belief that he had been sacrificed as a peace-offering to gain the support of some of the old tories.

The whole of the Duke's share in this correspondence is highly characteristic; and it was in the course of negotiations for the return of Mr. Huskisson that the Duke uttered the sentence so often quoted of him: "It is no mistake; it can be no mistake; and it shall be no mistake!" Strange to say, although the Duke's mode of proceeding to Mr. Huskisson was somewhat arbitrary, it gained him a sort of popularity, on account of the firmness with which he stuck to his point. The laugh was fairly on his side; and many of the vessels in the Thames hoisted flags, and exhibited other signs of rejoicing at Mr. Huskisson's dismissal.

On his appointment to be Prime Minister, the Duke again resigned the command of the army (Feb. 14th).

The first important measure, during the Duke's administration, was the repeal of the Test and Corporation Acts. In giving his support to that bill, the Duke met an argument, that it was a step towards Roman Catholic emancipation, by a declaration that, though he voted for the measure, no man could be a more determined opponent of those claims than he; and he added, "Until I see a great change in that question, I shall certainly oppose it." In the June following, however, the commons having in the meanwhile passed a resolution indicating favour to emancipation, the Duke declared that he looked on the question as one of expediency; and concluded his speech by recommending that the public mind should be allowed to rest. In the end, it might be possible to do something; for he was most desirous of seeing the subject brought to an amicable conclusion.

Causes altogether independent of parliamentary majorities or discussions had in the mean time been at work, and had proposed this change in the tone of ministers. Mr. O'Connell, although a Catholic, had been returned to parliament as member for the county of Clare; and during the summer and autumn, the whole of the Catholic population had become so organized, under the Catholic Association, as seriously to threaten the continuance of the existing system in Ireland. These events produced their effects upon English statesmen on either side of the question; and the more moderate of the Conservative party began to think that some concession to the Catholics would be inevitable.

Still, however, the government gave no sign of yielding. On the contrary, a circumstance occurred, in the month of December, which led to an opposite inference. Dr. Curtis, a Roman Catholic prelate, who had been on terms of personal acquaintance with the Duke of Wellington at Salamanca, wrote a letter to him on the position of the Catholic question, to which the Duke wrote an answer, which seemed to deny all hope of a speedy settlement. It was immediately made public by Dr. Curtis through the Catholic Association. The effect of the letter was to make that body redouble their efforts.

In a few days after, the Marquis of Anglesea, the lord lieutenant, who had always been the avowed supporter of the Catholics, also addressed a letter in reply to one he received from Dr. Curtis, in which he gave the Catholics advice as to the best mode of proceeding in order to attain emancipation. This conduct on the part of the viceroy, together with the open countenance he gave to the leading catholics in Dublin, gave the strongest offence to the king, and amounted to such a breach of duty that the Duke of Wellington was compelled to recall the marquis from Ireland.

The public mind was now in the greatest perplexity. On the one hand, the state of Ireland seemed to render some measure of concession inevitable, while on the other there was the letter to Dr. Curtis, and the dismissal of the lord lieutenant—facts which seemed to discountenance all hope.

The year 1829 was the most eventful in the civil career of the Duke of Wellington. He had been throughout his life the opponent of Roman Catholic emancipation: he was now to come before the public in the new character of a prime minister prepared to grant, as a measure of free grace, that which he had hitherto denounced as inconsistent with the safety of the Protestant constitution.

Up to within a few days of the opening of parliament, however, the design of the government was wholly concealed, but in the speech from the throne parliament was recommended to entertain the question. In the debate on the address the Duke of Wellington announced it as the intention of the government to introduce a measure for the emancipation of the Catholics. And now arose a political storm almost unparalleled in the history of party, from the effects of which we are scarcely yet recovered.

The Duke and Mr. Peel were immediately made the objects of the most unrelenting hostility by the opponents of emancipation. Seeing the favour in which the two statesmen are now held by their party, it would be almost impossible to believe that such abusive language as was then poured forth could have been used towards them, were it not on record.

The Duke especially was charged with a treble treachery; to Mr. Canning, on account of the transactions previously referred to; towards the Protestant party, of whom he had been the chosen leader, and whom he was about to betray; and lastly a personal treachery in the concealment of his design until the moment of execution, by which he prevented others from coming forward and taking the station he had abandoned, as leader of the opponents of emancipation.

The Duke's replies to all these charges will be found at length in the following pages. But the charge of personal treachery was afterwards put in a shape which compelled the Duke of Wellington to take a very different notice of it. The Earl of Winchelsea wrote a letter to the secretary of King's College, in which, after adverting to the support which the Duke had given on Protestant principles to that institution, he stated that he now believed that the Duke's conduct had been only a blind to the high church party, and that he was about, under the cloak of the Protestant religion, to carry into effect his insidious designs for the infringement of our liberties, and the introduction of Popery into every department of the state. This letter the Duke found himself bound to notice; but the earl refused to retract. A correspondence took place, which ended in a duel. Neither party was hurt, and the earl subsequently made a public apology for the original expressions.

In the meanwhile the Emancipation Bill was steadily progressing. On the 19th of February, in introducing the bill for the suppression of dangerous associations, the Duke of Wellington declared that there had been no previous bargain or compact with the Roman Catholic party while the Emancipation Bill was in the House of Commons. Short discussions took place almost every night in the House of Lords upon its merits, in which whenever the Duke joined he did so with the greatest reluctance. At length, on the 2nd of April, he moved the second reading of the bill in the House of Lords, in a speech which reflected credit upon him for moral courage, if not for consistency.

In fact, great moral courage is one of the most striking features in the character of the Duke of Wellington. Some of his supporters will doubt this assertion; and will point to the Emancipation Act as a proof that the Duke wanted the firmness to act up to his avowed principles. This involves a wrong assumption. It is one thing obstinately to adhere to an opinion in defiance of its impracticability: another to retract that opinion so soon as its impracticability is demonstrated. Whether the Duke was right or wrong in his opinions, no one will deny that it required great moral courage for him to stand up in the face of the country, braving the anger of his old associates, and declare that he could no longer resist the force of public opinion.

It was in the course of the speech introducing the Emancipation Bill that the Duke made his well-known declaration "that he would sacrifice his life to prevent one month of civil war."

One fruit of the angry passions excited during the progress of the Emancipation Bill was a series of prosecutions against the *Morning Journal* for libels on the Duke of Wellington, the Lord Chancellor, and the government collectively. These prosecutions were conducted with unusual acrimony by Sir James Scarlet, the Attorney-General; and the Duke of Wellington came in for a very considerable share of public censure for having authorised such prosecutions. Probably the Duke intended to inflict another "great moral lesson," as he has always set his face against the unrestrained license of the press; but, looking back with calmer feelings to the events of that excited period, and admitting that the language used by the editor was certainly too strong, though faithfully representing the feelings of a large class of the public, it is certainly difficult to avoid now coming to the conclusion that Mr. Alexander, when sentenced to twelve months' imprisonment in Newgate and heavy fines, was treated with a severity scarcely justifiable. It is probable that the Duke of Wellington, acting on his rigid notions of the division of responsibility, after ordering the prosecution, left the affair to Sir James Scarlet, and from that moment declined to interfere.

Among the discussions to which the prosecutions gave rise, an amusing speech of Sir Charles Wetherell, on the 2nd of March, 1830, in the House of Commons, will repay perusal.

In a debate which took place in the House of Lords on the first night of the session, upon the state of the country, the Duke of Wellington delivered a speech upon the causes of the existing distress, which proved (allowances being made for differences of opinion) that his qualifications to deal with the most intricate questions involved in civil government were very little inferior to his military talents. Passages from that speech will be found in the following pages. At the time many of his views were ridiculed by those political economists who were destined so soon to rise to power under shelter of the reform question; but it will be seen that the improved experience of the country after ten years' undisputed sway of those gentlemen, confirms many of the chief conclusion to which the astute and practical mind of the Duke of Wellington then led him. That speech, however, raised a hornet's nest around him in the House of Commons. Among others, Sir Francis Burdett made a personal attack on the Duke, in which he said that his administration showed how correct was his estimate of his own powers when he said he would be mad to think of being prime minister. That illustrious individual, he said, had been treated with much tenderness, because he had conferred the greatest benefits on his country; but if his services had been great his recompense had been great also. Mr. Brougham, also, made a most personal attack on the Duke on the day before parliament closed.

In the mean while, George the Fourth died (on the 26th of June), and parliament was dissolved. The new parliament, called by William the Fourth, was opened by the king in person on November the 2nd. It was decidedly unfavourable to the ministry, against whom were arrayed a most talented and unscrupulous opposition. They swayed with almost absolute power the great mass of the people, who hoped everything from parliamentary reform, and had not as yet had experience of the extravagance of such hopes. A part of the tactics of the whig leaders was to excite personal animosity against the Duke of Wellington, who was libelled as a sort of would-be military dictator, seeking to introduce in civil affairs the iron discipline of the camp, and to ride rough shod over a free people.

With the clamour for reform out of doors and in the commons, it was not to be supposed that even the impassible Duke of Wellington could avoid referring to the subject in the debate on the address. This he did, with more candour than prudence, by his well-known declaration against reform, and in favour of the existing system. It will be found at length elsewhere. The excitement it produced was enormous: so great, that in three days afterwards ministers advised William the Fourth not to proceed to the City to visit the Lord Mayor, lest there should be tumults.

On the 15th, they were defeated in the House of Commons, upon a motion of Sir Henry Parnell, for a committee to inquire into the civil list; and on the following day the Duke of Wellington and his colleagues resigned; being apprehensive that the same majority would vote for the principle of parliamentary reform in a day or two after, and not wishing to virtually give up that question by going out after being beaten on it in the House of Commons.

During the year 1831, while the discussions on the Reform Bill were going on, the Duke made frequent speeches against the measure, and led the opposition in the House of Lords in a manner quite consistent with his declaration in November. In a speech he made on the 28th March, explanatory of the causes of his resignation, he distinctly denied that the reform fever was owing to that declaration, and asserted that it was to be attributed to the effect on the public mind of the revolutions in France and Belgium.

On the 10th of October, after the Reform Bill had been thrown out in the House of Lords, the Duke of Wellington was insulted by a mob on his way to the house. In the evening, the windows of his mansion at Hyde Park-corner were broken. It is to be lamented that any class of Englishmen were to be found so degraded as to be guilty of this ingratitude.

Fortunately, the worst of the evil was averted, by the total indifference of the Duke to all such demonstrations. The greatest men have been despisers of mankind, of the swaying multitude, that is to say, the unthinking, the headstrong, and the violent—not of necessity merely, from that intrinsic superiority and natural antagonism which forbid their commingling; but also, and with a more hearty potency, from the experience which they, alternately the adored or the scorned, have had of the inconstancy of the giddy people. In this light estimation, indeed, of the judgment of their less worthy fellows, lies the secret of their greatness and their strength. They ride towards their goal while the stream tends that way, and when the course of the current is diverted, they are not dismayed. Their scorn of the means leads them to pass on by their own strength, or to rest secure on the foundation-rock of our moral nature—principle, and the consciousness of duty done.

In April, 1832, on the motion for the second reading of the new Reform Bill in the House of Lords, the Duke made a speech, characterised by unqualified opposition to the measure, at a time when many of the conservative peers (called "waverers,") were for giving it a qualified support. But, after a defeat of ministers in committee, on Lord Lyndhursts motion of the 7th of May, followed by their resignation, and when the king, rather than agree to create peers, called on the Duke of Wellington to form an administration, he expressed his readiness to do so upon the principle of moderate reform.

This sudden inconsistency the public could not understand; the Duke's avowed reason was that when called on by his sovereign he could not leave him alone in his difficulty. However, the Duke's efforts were brought to a summary conclusion by the refusal of Sir Robert Peel to join in the attempt.

It is amusing to see the opposite Views these two statesmen took of their duties to their king. Sir Robert Peel considered that "his acceptance of office pledged to carry an efficient Reform Bill, he being a determined enemy to such a measure, would be a political immorality which would not allow him to enter on his services with a firm step, a light heart, and an erect attitude." The Duke said, "if he had refused to assist his majesty, because he had hitherto given his opposition to parliamentary reform, he would not have been able to show his face in the streets for shame of having deserted his sovereign in circumstances so painful and alarming." The result of Sir Robert's refusal was, that the Duke gave up the attempt, and Earl Grey was recalled.

During the sessions of 1833 and 1834, the Duke was the leader of the opposition in the House of Lords; always at his post, and always ready to grapple with the different questions brought before the peers. On the 9th of June, 1834, took place his installation as Chancellor of the University of Oxford;—a brilliant scene, at which some of the most distinguished men of the day assisted.

In November, 1834, on the death of Lord Spencer, and the dismissal of the whig ministry, the king called on the Duke of Wellington to form an administration. The Duke recommended his majesty to entrust that office to Sir Robert Peel, who, however, was then at Rome. During the interval that elapsed before his arrival, the Duke accepted, provisionally, the office of First Lord of the Treasury, and the seals of the three secretaryships of state. On Sir Robert Peel's arrival, he gave up the government, with the exception of the office of Secretary for Foreign Affairs, which (December 9th) he retained.

Much clamour was at this time raised against the Duke by the whigs, on the old score of dictatorship, and also as to a supposed insult offered to Lord Melbourne.

On the meeting of parliament in the following February (on the 24th), the Duke gave an explanation of his conduct (inserted in this volume), sufficient to clear him in all impartial eyes of all the charges then urged against him by party spirit.

On the 8th of April following, in consequence of the repeated defeats sustained in the House of Commons by Sir Robert Peel, the conservative ministry resigned, and with them of course the Duke of Wellington. From that time until the re-accession of Sir Robert Peel to power, in 1841, the Duke continued to lead, with his accustomed vigour and unpretending ability, the opposition in the House of Lords. In this position, he exercised the utmost forbearance towards the government; never using his power except when circumstances absolutely required its exercise.

One of these instances occurred at the opening of the session of 1836, when the principles of a particular measure were recommended in a speech from the throne. To the address the Duke moved an amendment, condemnatory of the practice of thus pledging the sovereign in a speech from the throne to the principles of any measure. The amendment was agreed to by the whigs.

During the whole interval between 1833 and 1841, the Duke is to be found occasionally speaking in the upper house, in his capacity of leader of opposition. The same sound practical sense which has been already attributed to him, characterised his whole proceedings. It is needless to particularise the different important debates in which he took part.

In August, 1839, a grand banquet was given to the Duke at Dover, as Lord Warden of the Cinque Ports. A splendid pavilion was erected for the occasion, in which two thousand persons, including some most distinguished men, sat down to dinner. The gallery was filled with ladies. The most interesting point in the day's proceedings, was when Lord Brougham, the most active and distinguished civilian of his age, rose to propose the health of the Duke of Wellington, the most illustrious military commander. Eulogium could scarcely be carried farther than it was by Lord Brougham in these words:—

"Although no man," said the noble and learned lord, "on such an occasion, is entitled to entertain any personal feelings on his own behalf, it would be affectation—it would be insolent ingratitude—were I not to express the sentiments which glow within my bosom, at being made the instrument of making known those feelings which reign predominant in yours. Enough, however, of myself—now for my mighty subject.—But the choice you have made of your instrument—of your organ, as it were, on this occasion—is not unconnected with that subject; for it shows that on this day, on this occasion, all personal, all political feelings are quelled—all strife of party is hushed—that we are incapable, whatever be our opinions, of refusing to acknowledge transcendant merit, and of denying that we feel the irresistible impulse of unbounded gratitude; and I am therefore asked to do this service, as if to show that no difference of opinion upon subjects, however important—no long course of opposition, however contracted upon public principles—not even long inveterate habits of public opposition—are able so far to stifle the natural feelings of our hearts, so far to obscure our reason, as to prevent us from feeling as we ought—boundless gratitude for boundless merit. Neither can it pluck from our minds that admiration proportioned to the transcendant genius, in peace and in war, of him who is amongst us to-day; nor can it lighten or alleviate the painful, the deep sense which the untried mind never can get rid of when it is overwhelmed by a debt of gratitude, too boundless to be repaid. Party—the spirit of party—may do much, but it cannot operate so far as to make us forget those services; it cannot so far bewilder the memory, and pervert the judgment, and eradicate from our bosoms those feelings which do us the most honour, and are the most unavoidable, and, as it were, dry up the kindly juices of the heart; and, notwithstanding all its vile and malignant influence on other occasions, it cannot dry up those juices of the heart so as to parch it like very charcoal, and make it almost as black. But what else have I to do? If I had all the eloquence of all the tongues ever attuned to speak, what else could I do? How could a thousand words, or all the names that could be named, speak so powerfully—ay, even if I spoke with the tongue of an angel, as if I were to mention one word—Sir Arthur Wellesley, Duke of Wellington, the hero of a hundred fields, in all of which his banner was waved in triumph; who never, I invoke both hemispheres to witness—bear witness Europe, bear witness Asia—who never advanced but to cover his arms with glory; the captain who never advanced but to be victorious; the mightier captain who never retreated but to eclipse the glory of his advance, by the yet harder task of unwearied patience, indomitable to lassitude, the inexhaustible resources of transcendant skill, showing the wonders, the marvels of a moral courage never yet subdued. Despising all who thwarted him with ill-considered advice—neglecting all hostility, so he knew it to be groundless—laughing to scorn reviling enemies, jealous competitors, lukewarm friends, ay, hardest of all, to neglect despising even a fickle public, he cast his eye forwards as a man might—else he deserves not to command men—cast forward his eye to a time when that momentary fickleness of the people would pass away, knowing that in the end the people are always just to merit."

 The Duke's acknowledgement, was simple, according to his character, and modest as became his position. He said, "The noble lord, who I hope will allow me to call him my noble friend, has stated to you with great truth, that there are times and circumstances in which, and under which, all feelings of party, all party animosity, all descriptions of political feelings must be laid aside. I must do my noble and learned friend the justice to say, that for years and years there has been nothing of that description in social life as between him and me, notwithstanding which it is certainly true that I have had the misfortune of differing in opinion with my noble and learned friend upon many points of internal and possibly of other descriptions of policy. But I am afraid that, notwithstanding my most anxious wish to co-operate with all of you in the public service in which we have all been employed, I may happen (I know it does happen) to differ with some of you upon subjects of political interest to the country. But my noble and learned friend judges of you correctly when he says that such feelings of difference would not prevent you—as they have not prevented you—from doing me the honour of inviting me to this festival, and of bringing here to meet me not only the whole of this interesting county, but persons from all parts of the kingdom and even from abroad. Therefore my noble and learned friend does you as well as himself justice when he states that there are occasions—occasions in relation to individuals as well as in relation to public interests and services—in which all feelings of party politics and opinions must be laid aside, in order to carry on the public service to the greatest point of advantage to the public interest. I have had sufficient experience in public life to know that this must be the case. I am convinced that it is that feeling which has induced you to pay this tribute of respect to the person holding the situation of Lord Warden of the Cinque Ports, in order that you might encourage others hereafter to perform their duty honestly and conscientiously in the same honourable office."

On the 18th November, the same year, the Duke had an attack of epilepsy, which for a short time alarmed the public greatly for his safety, on account of his advanced age. Sir Astley Cooper and Dr. Hume were down at Walmer with him for a week, at the end of which time he recovered, greatly to the joy of the whole nation. It turned out that the Duke had brought on the attack adopting, to cure himself of a slight illness, a mode of treatment which would not be the most wise in a man of twenty-five, but was most dangerous to one so advanced in years. The Duke is very determined on such points—can never be persuaded that he is not the same man in point of constitution that he was when in the Peninsula; and still preserves all the hardy habits of a soldier's life. On this occasion he had sought to cure himself by fasting and cold bathing: he then, while under this treatment, followed the hounds, the consequence of which was that he fainted, and was soon afterwards seized as described.

On the return of Sir Robert Peel to power, in 1841, the Duke of Wellington again joined him; but this time he took no office, though accepting a seat in the cabinet. He still continued to lead in the lords, where his influence is fully felt, and where he constantly astonishes the house and silences his detractors by displaying a degree of knowledge on all legislative subjects scarcely compatible with his military education, and an activity and attention to business that would be admirable in any one, but which are still more praiseworthy as the voluntary service of a man who has conferred such distinguished benefits on his country.

Few men have been so blessed by fortune as to have been enabled to achieve a first-rate reputation in arms, and afterwards to arrive at as great distinction in the arts of peace. Rarely, at long intervals in the lapse of time, such opportunities have been afforded to great men; but still more rarely have even the greatest men been able to use them. To the Duke of Wellington, in our own time, has this high honour been especially vouchsafed; and no man ever yet lived who shewed himself more worthy the distinction, or more able to fulfill the demands of his country, whether in peace or in war. His youth and prime were spent in achieving victories: to preserve to posterity the fruits of those victories, in steady government, together with free institutions; to make England such an example for foreign nations as would render all such victories unnecessary hereafter; this has been the still more glorious task of his declining years.

The military reputation of the Duke of Wellington rests on so firm a basis, that it will never be shaken. So long as military science is necessary in the world, so long will his system of tactics be followed by commanders responsible in their own hearts for the lives of their soldiers, and to their country for the conduct of their enterprises.

Of the military value of his dispositions and movements, military critics have recorded, almost universally, their unqualified praise. To civilians, it is left to admire the constant and watchful care of the Duke, whether in India or the Peninsula, in securing the due provision for his troops, while he at the same time maintained the strictest honour towards the natives who supplied them; and to respect the clearness of his perception, the sagacity of his decisions, and, above all, the firmness and determination of purpose which sustained him amidst every drawback and difficulty, until by his success he compelled his detractors to yield themselves captive to his judgment. It is only necessary to read the dispatches and general orders of the Duke of Wellington, in order to be convinced that he is not a mere soldier winning battles by superior tactics, but that he is also a man of a very high order of general talent, with an unusual insight into human nature, and possessing almost an instinctive knowledge of how mankind are to be governed. By that wonderful exposition of the comprehensive, wise, and philanthropic mind of the man, even his enemies were subdued.

Much controversy has been spent upon the demeanour of the Duke towards his soldiers, which has been stigmatised as cold, distant, at times harsh, and even selfish. For the charges of coldness and distance there appears to be some foundation. Unlike Napoleon, the Duke of Wellington never appealed to the enthusiasm of his soldiers; but he always relied upon their sense of duty. He regarded his army, organized by discipline, as a perfect machine, upon the performance of which he could calculate with precision, and as he never expected it to do more than it ought, so he never looked to see it do less. The idea of duty, of absolute responsibility and subordination from rank to rank, seems to have been that to which he was always content to appeal. Accordingly, his troops never failed him. Their rock-like steadfastness and constant unimpulsive bravery, it was that enabled him to carry out his plans with such certainty.

The contrast to Napoleon is no Where more seen than in the dispatches of the one and the bulletins of the other. In his demeanour to his men, the Duke was reserved; in his language, curt and laconic. If his troops felt the moral certainty that he was leading them to victory, and honoured him accordingly, it was not from personal enthusiasm, such as the wild love the emperor inspired in those around him, but from a deep respect for his character and a reliance on his talents. Nor did he condescend to charlatanism or bombast, as his great rival too often did. There is not the slightest trace of vanity about him. Compare the speech of the one to his army, beneath the Pyramids, with the simple, "Up, guards, and at them!" of the other. In these trifles, we find the key to the real minds of great men.

The political character of the Duke, and his services as a civilian, have never been sufficiently appreciated by the great mass of his countrymen. His brilliant military reputation cast into the shade his sterling but unobtrusive services as a senator and as a minister. It was even the fashion, for a long time, to assert that his taking office at all was a sign of defective judgment. Indeed, when he declared, in the House of Lords, that he would be "worse than mad to think of such a thing," he gave a colour to the supposition. His subsequent assertion, after he had become prime minister, that he had done so "because nobody else would," conveyed, in all probability, the simple truth. The Duke did not know his own capacity for government, until it was tried.

Another reason why his positive worth, as a politician, has not been so universally admitted as his military merit, is that, in the imaginations of a large portion of the public, he has been identified with a party. This, in a country where party spirit is so strong and so universal, would alone be sufficient to secure his being misunderstood by all those who are not of the party to which he is alleged to be devoted. But it is a mistake to call the Duke of Wellington a party man; that is to say, in the ordinary sense of the word. It is true that, during the greater part of his life he has acted with what is called the conservative party, because in England no man can expect to serve his country efficiently, unless he enlists under some political banner or other. But there is a great difference between acting generally with a party, and the adoption of all its animosities and prejudices: and this difference the Duke of Wellington appears always to have perceived and acted upon. Wherever the choice has lain between the opinions of his party and the general good of his country, the Duke has always preferred his country to his party; and if that is the character of a party man, may all politicians be speedily imbued with the same sentiments!

Notwithstanding this distinction, however, it is certain that the known opinions of the Duke of Wellington, and his ultimately taking office as the prime minister of the tory party, did lead to the belief that he was a party man, and directed towards him all those animosities and all that depreciating rancour which party spirit engenders, and which party tactics perpetuate; so that during a period of some four or five years his distinguished reputation as a soldier was obscured in the minds of many millions of his country, who,—and this remark applies more particularly to the years 1829, 1830, and 1831,—laid themselves open to the charge of being guilty of that meanest and basest of all crimes, ingratitude.

Happily, within the last ten years, a total change has come over the public mind. Those ill-grounded animosities are forgotten: the long and unparalleled services of the Duke are remembered: and a re-action, produced by a sense of shame acting upon early affections, has made him more popular, more beloved, more admired than ever he was before.

Look at the course of business in the House of Lords during the last few years, and you will observe that the Duke of Wellington has been the presiding spirit of that assembly. Nothing was done—nothing could be done without him; for he carries with him the proxies of so many of the thinking, experienced, far-seeing, influential of his countrymen.

It has been argued, that the Duke of Wellington possesses all this influence by virtue of his leadership of a powerful party. Of course this means that any other leader of the conservatives could possess as much, or it means nothing. It is a fallacy. The Duke of Wellington's claims are almost entirely personal. It is to himself alone that all this silent homage is paid. Even were he to retire from active life to-morrow, still would he be followed into his retirement by political pupils, eager to imbibe those distillations of practical wisdom which his sagacity extracts from his vast stores of experience.

The fundamental basis of this power is his high military reputation; though that alone could not have secured it, unless accompanied by his firm principles and habits of observation. England differs from France in this respect,—that while our neighbours are more ready to elevate talent above property than we are, they are less choice as to the degree of the talent which they exalt. But if the English once know that they possess a first-rate man, they place him from that hour securely on an eminence, whence he may look down as from the heavens, upon wealth, rank, blood, and every earthly distinction. The Duke of Wellington is a first-rate man; and his countrymen acknowledge it with pride. But his mind is *sui generis.* His qualities are eminently useful: he could never have condescended to be brilliant. His mind is that of iron mould that defies alike warping, meretricious polish, or demolition.

It is a conviction of the thorough and unflinching honesty of his views and principles, and of the clear perception, the fruitful experience, and sound practical sense which regulate his opinions, that makes the Duke of Wellington the governing spirit in the House of Peers. There is no man in that house, be his talents or his services what they may, whose opinion carries so much weight with it; for there is no other man so independent of party. All the others, however moderate their natures or honest their intentions, have been compelled to give in at some time or other to the spirit of party. But the Duke is above party. He entered the House of Peers with an overpowering reputation, which enabled him from the first to take high ground. He does not need to curry favour with any man; nor does he fear to offend even the most powerful of his supporters, when his cause is just.

But the Duke's ascendancy in the House of Peers is not to be referred to the foregoing causes alone. Had he none of that personal influence derived from services and character to which we have referred, his abilities and information alone would enable him to take high rank. His claims in these respects are much, underrated by those who are opposed to him in politics. His reasoning is so simple, clear and palpable—so much in the character of what is called common sense—and his style of speaking so unpretending and free from ornament, that superficial observers have set him down as a mere blunt soldier, with a few fixed ideas, and a disposition dogmatically to insist on their adoption. This is altogether a mistake. The Duke of Wellington has as much of the true spirit of the statesman as any man who now affects the destinies of this country. There is scarcely a subject that has come before parliament since the commencement of his political career into which he has not fully entered. The character of his mind is to grasp every question. Less than mastery of it—so far as the formation of a decided opinion according to the lights afforded to or by his mind—will not satisfy him. With the exception of one or two questions of high constitutional principle, the "*cui bono?*" is the view his mind naturally takes. He is a practical utilitarian, seeking in every measure the utmost quantity of good of which it is capable; not always as much as he would perhaps wish to see, but as much as circumstances allow the hope of securing.

This mode of dealing with subjects is not well calculated for oratorical display, or for the parade of extensive information, even if the unaffected character of the Duke of Wellington would allow him to avail himself of them. They are cast aside, in pursuit of a less brilliant, but more useful, mode of treatment. Accordingly, the speeches of the Duke are brief, clear, pointed, and in one sense dogmatical. After having canvassed details, and brought to bear upon them his long and varied experience, he states his conclusions, accompanying them with the general principles that have guided their formation, in a few brief authoritative sentences. He is very careless about catching stray listeners, or drawing in his train the prejudiced or the inexperienced; but rather addresses himself to those whose age and wisdom entitle them to anticipate consequences, or to those to whom experience of the value of his opinions may have taught a pre-disposed deference.

At other times, however—for instance, when making ministerial statements on matters connected with finance, or foreign policy, or important changes in the law—this short, abrupt, devil-may-care style is changed for one eminently adapted to the object. No one can then complain of a want of the proper information. All the historical facts, or figures, or principles, or general details, are then marshalled forward with a regularity and precision only to be equalled by the military arrangements of the Duke. There is not a word too much or too little: you are made thoroughly to comprehend the whole bearings of the question, without being overburthened with the useless details that so often figure in the speeches of orators of the red-tape school. The natural superiority of the Duke's mind is never more exhibited than in the masterly way in which he separates the wheat from the chaff, and weaves a clear and connected statement from masses of facts, on subjects so foreign to the military pursuits of his youth and manhood.

To many, this praise of the Duke of Wellington, in a character in which he is so little known to the great mass of the public, will appear exaggerated; but those who have been accustomed to observe him in the House of Peers, will not be surprised to hear the estimation in which he is held by his political contemporaries of all parties. Those who have not heard and seen him in his character of politician and statesman, will scarcely continue sceptical (even if they are so), after having read the extracts contained in the following pages.

Much, however, as the independent spirit of self-reliance of the Duke, fortified by his character and experience, has secured him sway in the House of Lords, we must not blind ourselves to the fact, that this illustrious man has sometimes, in the assertion of his opinions (unconsciously, we believe, and unintentionally) fallen into a practice of dogmatising, of calling on the House of Peers and the public to adopt his views, not so much on account of reasons urged in their support, as because they are stated by him. Rarely, however, have such instances occurred, and in extenuation of what, in a country of free discussion, would justly be deemed a dangerous innovation, we must bear in mind that where a man's opinions are the result of vary long experience and very extensive observation, it is not always possible to make the general mind aware of the process by which particular principles or views have been arrived at. The greatest men have often been compelled to content themselves with the simple assertion of opinions not pleasing to the multitude, and to appeal to time as the only test of their truth.

The Duke of Wellington looks to the practical common-sense bearing of every subject brought under his notice. His first aim is the public good; his next, how to attain that good with the least departure from established principles of policy. This practical turn of mind, joined as it is to a far-seeing and prophetic spirit, has contributed to confirm in the minds of his countrymen the admiration and influence which his military genius and success first created. They repose the utmost confidence in his sagacity; he is a party in himself. Whatever is essential to the national reputation, the welfare of the whole people, and, above all, to the stability of property, is sure to be originated, or, at all events, warmly supported by him.

For this reason a revolution never could have occurred under the government of the Duke; he has too intense a horror of the evils of civil contention, ever to have allowed matters to come to that pass. This, it will be admitted, is a quality rarely to be found in a soldier, and a soldier, too, of such an inflexible cast as the Duke. Not less intense is his regard for national faith and honour. He would maintain the honour of the state at any expense, even of his own personal prejudices on home politics; for the Duke, like all strong-minded men, has his prejudices. He has vanquished, and obtained the mastery of the spirit of change, by showing that he can curb it, while he does not affect to play the tyrant over it. He knows when to be firm and when to yield. Many acts of the Duke of Wellington, in the course of his political career, that have called forth unlimited censure, have been based upon calculations which only so well-tutored and so well-stored a mind could have made.

It is an intellectual treat of the highest order to see the Duke of Wellington's demeanour in the House of Lords. It is essentially different from that of every other man there. He is almost the only unfettered man in the house. Others are fettered by obstacles which they create for themselves, in various ways, by the too eager pursuit of personal or party objects. But the Duke of Wellington's high reputation and standing place him above all such considerations. He can afford to speak the truth, and he does speak it on all occasions fearlessly. While other speakers, on either side of the house, have been wasting their powers in fruitless eloquence (mere personal display), or in perverting the truth for the purpose, either of unfair attack or unfair defence, the Duke of Wellington has appeared to be paying not the slightest attention to the proceedings. He has sat absorbed in thought, or at least in seeming indifference. You would almost suppose that, overcome by fatigue, or indisposition, he was sleeping, so perfectly motionless and silent is he, reclining, with folded arms, his legs stretched out to their full length, and his hat over his brow. The question has been discussed, argued, disputed upon for hours. No result seems to have been come to, and you are as ignorant of the object and scope of the measure as when the debate began; nor have you any clear idea what will become of the bill.

At length, the Duke of Wellington rises, advances abruptly to the table, wraps the tails of his coat, like a dressing-gown, over his legs, and plunges at once *in medias res*. There is an undivided attention while he speaks, indeed, it is sometimes absolutely necessary, for, when indisposed, he is often with difficulty heard, even by those near to him, as, indeed, he himself hears with difficulty, from being deaf on one side. But in a moment you see that his mind is still as vigorous as ever. His keen intelligence pierces at once to the very core of the subject; no fallacy can blind or deceive the Duke of Wellington. He knows why the measure was introduced, what it is, what it will do, and what will become of it. He grapples with it in the spirit of a statesman. He is a guardian of the interests of the nation; he is the parliamentary trustee of the people; he is bound to look to their interests as a whole, for by the people he understands, not those who bawl the loudest about their rights, but those also who trust the maintenance of their privileges and their interests to parliament, in silent faith. He never forgets the *salus populi*.

On the other hand, the chap-trap maxims of liberalism, foreign or domestic, meet from him with just as much credence and attention as they deserve; he never allows enthusiasm to intrude among political considerations. He measures the length, breadth, and thickness of the bill before him; calculates with his unerring precision and practical wisdom, the effect which it will have, either on the happiness of the people, or on the social or political constitution of the country. According to its value for good or for evil, does the Duke of Wellington support or oppose it; and from that hour its fate is usually decided. Why? because the unbending unflinching honesty of the man, and his political sagacity, have created him a character unprecedented in the annals of his country.

The Duke's style of speaking is what might be expected from his character, plain, simple, straightforward. His sentences are short and pithy, his language clear and lucid; his delivery abrupt. When he makes a point, it falls on the mind with the force of a sledge-hammer. His voice reminds one of that of an officer giving the word of command; he lays emphasis, short and somewhat harsh, on the leading words of the sentence, and speaks the rest in an under tone.

Although, however, in consequence of his age and the gradual approach of infirmity, his utterance is not so clear as it used to be, yet you can always understand immediately his whole meaning. He uses the plainest language of every-day colloquy. His style is impressive from its doric simplicity. You never entertain a doubt of his sincerity; and although you may not always agree with him in opinion, you have, at least, the satisfaction of knowing that his propositions are the true result of his feelings or his thoughts; and are not merely put forward to answer the purposes of party, or to secure a triumph in debate.

For the same reason, the Duke never attempts to impose on the house a fictitious enthusiasm, or a pretended excitement. If he gets excited, (and he will sometimes get into a terrible passion at any infringement of constitutional integrity or breach of discipline), there is no mistaking it for a mere prepared climax to a speech; he is completely possessed by the demon. The only action he ever uses is on such occasions, and then it is almost convulsive. His arms and legs seem no longer to be under control, they quiver, and shake, and tremble: and the clenched fist, violently and frequently struck upon the table, denotes that some very potent feeling of indignation is, for the time, mastering the usual calmness of this self-possessed man.

Yet though at times he is thus carried away by his feelings, his ultimate judgment of a measure is not impaired by it. He can cauterise or cut out the cankered part, and yet preserve all that was not offensive to his sense of right and wrong.

Those who have read the speeches of the Duke, will have remarked the intensely British feeling that pervades them. He is like the old Romans in his admiration and love for his country and her institutions. The same feeling breathes in all his speeches. The same magnanimous brevity that marked the public declarations of that haughty people, dignifies the addresses of the Duke of Wellington. Some of his sayings, as, for instance, "that a great nation can never wage a little war," will he embalmed in history. His denunciations are like the alarum of a war trumpet. The same character of simplicity which marks the Duke's speeches pervades his whole conduct, public and private. Though no man is more capable of enjoying the refinements of modern society, luxury has not enervated his mind or his manners. His dress, his equipage, his habits, all partake of the same indifference to effect—all have a cast of the hardy self-denial of the camp. A mattress bed, constant horse exercise, rising with the lark, not unfrequently remaining up twenty hours out of the twenty-four, and the daily use of cold shower baths, winter and summer,—these contradictions to the usual habits of men, when their age approaches to fourscore, bespeak no ordinary carelessness of ease, and a singular determination of purpose. Well, indeed, has he been named the Iron Duke.

MAXIMS AND OPINIONS OF HIS GRACE THE DUKE OF WELLINGTON.

INDIA.

To offer a public reward, by proclamation, for a man's life, and to make a secret bargain to have it taken away, are very different things; the one is to be done, the other, in my opinion, cannot by an officer at the head of the troops.

Dispatch, July 8, 1800.

As for the wishes of the people, particularly in this country (India), I put them out of the question. They are the only philosophers about their governors that ever I met with, if indifference constitutes that character.

Dispatch, August 20, 1800.

In military operations time is everything.

Dispatch, June 30, 1800.

Articles of provision are not to be trifled with, or left to chance; and there is nothing more clear than that the subsistence of the troops must be certain upon the proposed service, or the service must be relinquished.

Dispatch, Feb. 18, 1801.

Indignant rejection of a proffered Bribe.

You inform me that the Rajah, or Dessaye of Kittoor, has expressed a wish to be taken under the protection of the British Government; and has offered to pay a tribute to the company, and to give you a bribe of 4000 pagodas, and me one of 10,000 pagodas, provided this point is arranged according to his wishes.

I cannot conceive what can have induced the Rajah of Kittoor to imagine that I was capable of receiving that or any other sum of money, as an inducement to do that which he must think improper, or he would not have offered it. But I shall advert to that point more particularly presently.

The Rajah of Kittoor is a tributary of the Mahratta Government, the head of which is an ally, by treaty, of the honourable company. It would be, therefore, to the full as proper, that any officer in command of a post within the company's territories, should listen to and enter into a plan for seizing part of the Mahratta territories, as it is for you to listen and encourage an offer from the Rajah of Kittoor to accept the protection of, and transfer his allegiance and tribute to the honourable company's government. In case you should hear anything further upon this subject from the Rajah of Kittoor, or in future from any of the chiefs of the Mahrattas on the frontier, I desire that you will tell them what is the fact, that you have no authority whatever to listen to such proposals, that you have orders only to keep up with them the usual intercourse of civility and friendship, and that if they have any proposals of that kind to make, they must be made in a proper manner to our superiors. You may, at the same time, inform them that you have my authority to say that the British government is very little likely to take advantage of the misfortunes of its ally, to deprive him, either of his territories or of the allegiance or tribute due to him by his tributaries.

In respect to the bribe offered to you and myself, I am surprised that any man in the character of a British officer should not have given the Rajah to understand that the offer would be considered as an insult; and that he should not have forbidden its renewal, than that he should have encouraged it, and even offered to receive a quarter of the sum proposed to be given him for prompt payment. I can attribute your conduct on this occasion, to nothing excepting the most inconsiderate indiscretion, and to a desire to benefit yourself, which got the better of your prudence. I desire, however, that you will refrain from the subject with the Rajah of Kittoor at all, and that if he should renew it, you will inform him, that I and all British officers consider such offers as insults on the part of them by whom made.

Letter to an officer in India, January 20, 1803.

Principle of Warfare in India.

We must get the upper hand, and if once we have that, we shall keep it with ease, and shall certainly succeed. But if we begin by a long defensive warfare, and go looking after convoys that are scattered over the face of the earth, and do not attack briskly, we shall soon be in distress.

Dispatch, Aug. 17, 1803.

How to avoid Party Spirit in the Army.

It occurs to me that there is much party in the army in your quarter; this must be put an end to. And there is only one mode of effecting this, and that is for the commanding officer to be of no side excepting that of the public; to employ indiscriminately those who can best serve the public, be they who they may, or in whatever service; the consequence will be that the service will go on, all parties will join in forwarding it, and in respecting him; there will be an end to their petty disputes about trifles; and the commanding officer will be at the head of an army instead of a party.

Letter to an officer, Sept. 16, 1803.

The power of the Sword necessary in India.

It is necessary that the political agents at the durbars of the native princes should be supposed to have a considerable degree of power. In this part of the world there is no power excepting that of the sword; and it follows that if these political agents have no authority over the military, they have no power whatever.

The natives would soon find out this state of weakness, and the residents would lose their influence over their councils. It may be argued if that is the case, the military commanding officer ought to be the resident, or political agent. In answer to this argument, I say, that the same reasoning applies to every part of the executive government; and that, upon this ground, the whole ought to be in the hands of the military. In short, the only conclusion to be drawn from all reflection and reasoning upon the subject is, that the British government in India is a phenomenon; and that it will not answer to apply to it, in its present state, either the rules which guide other governments, or the reasoning upon which these rules are founded.

Dispatch, Oct. 13, 1803.

Reason for the ambiguity of Treaties.

It is impossible to frame a treaty of peace in such a manner as to find in it a decision of all questions which can arise between the parties concerned; particularly when the parties have frequently been at war, and have preserved a recollection of a variety of contradictory claims arising out of the events of their wars, which they are ready to bring forward on all occasions.

Dispatch, Jan. 7, 1804.

Foundation of British Power in India in 1803.

The British government has been left by the late Mahratta war in a most glorious situation. They are the sovereigns of a great part of India, the protectors of the principal powers, and the mediators by treaty of the disputes of all. The sovereignty they possess is greater, and their power is settled upon more permanent foundations, than any before known in India; all it wants is the popularity which, from the nature of the institutions and the justice of the proceedings of the government, it is likely to obtain, and which it must obtain, after a short period of tranquillity shall have given the people time and opportunity to feel the happiness and security which they enjoy.

Dispatch, Jan. 16, 1804.

British "Moderation" in India.

I declare that, when I view the treaty of peace,[2] and its consequences, I am afraid it will be imagined that the moderation of the British government in India has a strong resemblance to the ambition of other governments.

[Footnote 2: After the Mahratta war.]

Jan. 29, 1804.

Contrast between European and Asiatic Policy.

European governments were, till very lately, guided by certain rules and systems of policy so accurately defined and generally known, that it was scarcely possible to suppose a political event, in which the interest and conduct of each state would not be as well known to the corps diplomatique, in general, as to the statesmen of each particular state. The Asiatic governments do not acknowledge, and hardly know of, such rules and systems. Their governments are arbitrary; the objects of their policy are always shifting; they have no regular established system, the effect of which is to protect the weak against the strong; on the contrary, the object of each of them separately, and of all of them taken collectively, is to destroy the weak; and if by chance, they should, by a sense of common danger, be induced for a season to combine their efforts for their mutual defence, the combination lasts only so long as it is attended with success; the first reverse dissolves it; and, at all events, it is dissolved long before the danger ceases, the apprehension of which originally caused it. The company's government in India, the other contracting party to their alliance, is one bound by all the rules and systems of European policy. The company's power in India is supposed to depend much upon its reputation; and although I do not admit that it depends upon its reputation, as distinguished from its real force, as appears to be contended by some, I may say that it is particularly desirable for a government, so constituted as the company's, never to enter upon any particular object, the probable result of which should not be greatly in favour of success.

Besides this, the company's government in India is bound by acts of parliament not to undertake wars of aggression, not to make any but defensive alliances, and those only in cases in which the other contracting party shall bind itself to defend the possessions of the company actually threatened with hostilities.

The company's government in India is also connected with his majesty's government, and, as an Asiatic power, is liable to be involved in wars with European powers possessing territories in India, whenever his majesty shall be at war with those powers.

The picture above drawn of the state of politics among Asiatic powers, proves that no permanent system can be adopted which will preserve the weak against the strong, and will keep all for any length of time in their relative situations, and the whole in peace; excepting there should be one power, which, either by the superiority of its strength, its military system, or its resources, shall preponderate, and be able to protect all.

1804.

It is necessary for a man who fills a public situation, and who has great public interests in charge, to lay aside all private considerations, whether on his own account or that of other persons.

March 2, 1804.

When war is concluded, all animosity should be forgotten.
March 12, 1804.

The British character for good faith must be preserved in India.

I would sacrifice Gwalior, or every portion of India, ten times over, in order to preserve our credit for scrupulous good faith, and the advantages and honour we gained by the late war and the peace: and we must not fritter them away in arguments, drawn from overstrained principles of the laws of nations, which are not understood in this country. What brought me through many difficulties in the war, and the negociations for peace? The British good faith, and nothing else.

Dispatch, March 17, 1804.

Civil Government in India must follow immediately on Military Conquest.

I rather think that you and the Governor-General agree in opinion on the subject of the affairs of Malabar. He says, "examine and report the state of the province before you commence your military operations; define the evils, and propose a system of government which shall afford a remedy, towards the establishment of which system military operations may be directed."

It would be useless to commence military operations upon any great scale, unless the civil officers should be prepared to take possession of the country, and to re-establish the civil government as the troops shall conquer it. If the civil government were not re-established in this manner, the rebels would rise again as soon as the troops would pass through the districts; and the effect of the operations of a large body of troops would be much the same as that of a small body. But if the civil government is to be re-established in this manner, it would be better to establish that system which is found to be good, and is to be permanent, than that which is known to be had, and which is intended should not last. Supposing that the bad system were first introduced, it must be followed afterwards by the good one; and, supposing that the bad system did not produce a rebellion of itself (which I acknowledge I do not think it would, as rebellion in Malabar is to be traced to causes entirely independent of all systems of civil government, excepting as they are connected with a strong or weak military force), the change from the bad to the good system would produce a degree of convulsion, and, possibly, momentary weakness, which it is always desirable to avoid. It is particularly desirable to avoid it in this instance, as it will not be difficult, by an examination of all that has passed in Malabar, to fix upon the general principles according to which that province ought to be governed, and to form a system accordingly, in the time which must elapse before the troops can he employed in settling the province.

March 20, 1804.

Principle of Relief to the Poor.

The principle, of the mode in which I propose to relieve the distresses of the inhabitants, is not to give grain or money in charity.

Those who suffer from famine may properly be divided into two classes: those who can, and those who cannot, work. In the latter class may be included old persons, children, and the sick women; who, from their former situation in life, have been unaccustomed to labour, and are weakened by the effects of famine.

The former, viz., those of both sexes who can work, ought to be employed by the public; and in the course of this letter I shall point out the work on which I should wish that they might be employed, and in what manner paid. The latter, viz., those who cannot work, ought to be taken into an hospital and fed, and receive medical aid and medicine at the expense of the public.

According to this mode of proceeding, subsistence will be provided for all; the public will receive some benefit from the expense which will be incurred, and, above all, it will be certain, that no able-bodied person will apply for relief, unless he should be unwilling to work for his subsistence, that none will apply who are able to work, and who are not real objects of charity; and that none will come to Ahmednuggur for the purpose of partaking of the food which must be procured by the labour, or to obtain which they must submit to the restraint of an hospital.

Dispatch, April 11, 1804.

Tactics to be pursued against Predatory Troops.

I have served a good deal in this part of India against this description of freebooter; and I think that the best mode of operating, is to press him with one or two corps capable of moving with tolerable celerity, and of such strength as to render the result of an action by no means doubtful, if he should venture to risk one. There is but little hope, it is true, that he will risk an action, or that any one of these corps will come up with him. The effect to be produced by this mode of operation is to oblige him to move constantly, and with great celerity. When reduced to this necessity, he cannot venture to stop to plunder the country, and he does comparatively but little mischief; at all events the subsistence of his army becomes difficult and precarious, the horsemen become dissatisfied, and they perceive that their situation is hopeless, and they desert in numbers daily; the freebooter ends by having with him only a few adherents, and he is reduced to such a state as to be liable to be taken by any small body of country horse, which are the fittest troops to be then employed against him.

In proportion as the body of our troops, to be employed against a freebooter of this description, have the power of moving with celerity, will such freebooter be distressed. Whenever the largest and most formidable bodies of them are hard pressed by our troops, the village people attack them upon their rear and flanks, cut off stragglers, and will not allow a man to enter their villages;

because their villages being in some degree fortified, they know well that the freebooters dare not wait the time which would be necessary to reduce them. When this is the case, all their means of subsistence vanish, no resource remains excepting to separate, and even this resource is attended by risk, as the village people cut them off on their way to their homes.

Dispatch, May 27, 1804.

Importance of Secresy in Public Affairs.

There is nothing more certain than that of one hundred affairs ninety-nine might be posted up at the market-cross, without injury to the public interests; but the misfortune is that where the public business is the subject of general conversation, and is not kept a secret, as a matter of course, upon every occasion, it is very difficult to keep it secret upon that occasion on which it is necessary. There is an awkwardness in a secret which enables discerning men (of which description there are always plenty in an army) invariably to find it out; and it may be depended upon that, whenever the public business ought to be kept secret, it always suffers when it is exposed to public view. For this reason secresy is always best; and those who have been long trusted with the conduct of public affairs are in the habit of never making known public business of any description that it is not necessary that the public should know. The consequence is that secresy becomes natural to them, and as much a habit as it is to others to talk of public matters; and they have it in their power to keep things secret or not, as they may think proper.

Remember that what I recommend to you is far removed from mystery; in fact, I recommend silence upon the public business upon all occasions, in order to avoid the necessity of mystery upon any.

Dispatch, June 28, 1804.

In all retreats, it must be recollected that they are safe and easy, in proportion to the number of attacks made by the retreating corps.

Dispatch, Sept. 12, 1804.

Neglect of his Services in India.

In regard to staying longer (in the Deccan), the question is exactly whether the court of directors, or the king's ministers, have any claim upon me, strong enough to induce me to do anything so disagreeable to my feelings (leaving health out of the question) as to remain, for a great length of time, in this country. I have served the company in important situations for many years, and have never received anything but injury from the court of directors, although I am a singular instance of an officer who has served under all governments, and

in communication with all the political residents, and many civil authorities; and there is not an instance on record, or in any private correspondence, of disapprobation of any of my acts, or a single complaint, or even a symptom of ill-temper from any one of the political or civil authorities in communication with whom I have acted. The king's ministers have as little claim upon me as the court of directors. I am not very ambitious, and I acknowledge that I never have been very sanguine in my expectations that military services in India would be considered in the scale in which are considered similar services in other parts of the world. But I might have expected to be placed on the staff in India; and yet if it had not been for the lamented death of General Fraser, General Smith's arrival would have made me supernumerary. This is perfectly well known to the army, and is the subject of a good deal of conversation.
Jan. 4, 1805.

I mistrust the judgment of every man in a case in which his own wishes are concerned.
Feb. 3, 1805.

Advice to a Native Ruler in India.
Let the prosperity of the country be your great object; protect the ryots and traders, and allow no man, whether invested with authority or not, to oppress them with impunity. Do justice to every man.
March 2, 1805.

Without distinction of religion every man ought to be called upon to do service to the state, wherever he is particularly qualified to do that service.
House of Commons, May 11, 1808.
Control of the Navy and Army.
The navy is the characteristic and constitutional force of Britain, and may therefore be governed by regulations of the legislature; but the army is a new force, arising out of the extraordinary exigencies of modern times, and from every consideration of expediency and necessity, must be left under the control of the crown.
House of Commons, June 3, 1808.

The Law-breaker always Wrong.
It frequently happens that the people who do commit outrages and disturbances have some reason to complain; but he who breaks the law must be

considered in the wrong, whatever may have been, the nature of the provocation which he has received.[3]

[Footnote 3: This remark, though it applies generally, was made with respect to Ireland.]

Ibid, July 7, 1808.

THE PENINSULA.
The Battle of Vimeiro.

The action of Vimeiro is the only one I have ever been in (1808), in which everything passed as was directed, and no mistake was made by any of the officers charged with its conduct.

Dispatch, Aug. 22, 1806.

Distinction between Civil and Military Responsibility.

There is a great distinction of duty between military and civil inferior situations. If, in a civil officer, the inferior differs materially from the superior, he ought to resign, but in military appointments, it is the duty of the inferior officer to assist his commander in the mode in which that commander may deem his services most advantageous.

Defence of his conduct with regard to the Convention of Cintra. House of Commons, Feb. 21, 1809.

Rapidity of the French Retreats accounted for.

It is obvious, that if an army throws away all its cannon, equipments, and baggage, and everything which can strengthen it, and can enable it to act together as a body; and abandons all those who are entitled to its protection, but add to its weight and impede its progress;[4] it must be able to march by roads through which it cannot be followed, with any prospect of being overtaken by an army which has not made the same sacrifice.

[Footnote 4: Alluding to the rapidity of the French retreat.]

Dispatch, May 18, 1809.

I have long been of opinion that a British army could bear neither success nor failure.[5]

[Footnote 5: Referring to their habits of plunder.]

Dispatch, May 31, 1809.

Inefficiency of Spanish Officers.

Nothing can be worse than the officers of the Spanish army, and it is extraordinary that when a nation has devoted itself to war, as this nation has by the measures which it has adopted in the last two years, so little progress has been made in any one branch of the military profession by any individual, and that the business of an army should be so little understood. They are really children in the art of war, and I cannot say they do anything as it ought to be done, with the exception of running away, and assembling again in a state of nature.

Dispatch, Aug. 1809.

Terrorism and Force, not Enthusiasm, enabled the French Revolutionary Armies to conquer.

People are very apt to believe that enthusiasm carried the French through their revolution, and was the parent of those exertions which have nearly conquered the world; but if the subject is nicely examined, it will be found that enthusiasm was the name only, but that force was the instrument which brought forward those great resources under the system of terror which first stopped the allies; and that a perseverance in the same system of applying every individual and every description of property to the service of the army, by force, has since conquered Europe.

Dispatch, Aug. 25, 1809.

The Spaniards and Portuguese want the true spirit of Soldiers.

We are mistaken if we believe that what these Portuguese and Spanish armies require is discipline, properly so called. They want the habits and spirit of soldiers—the habits of command on one side, and of obedience on the other—mutual confidence between officers and men; and above all, a determination in superiors to obey the spirit of the orders they receive, let what will be the consequence, and the spirit to tell the true cause if they do not.

Dispatch, Sept. 8, 1809.

Importance of good understanding between Negotiating Parties.

Half the business of the world, particularly that of our country, is done by accommodation, and by the parties understanding each other, but when rights are claimed they must be resisted, if there are no grounds for them; when appeal must be made to higher powers there can be no accommodation, and much valuable time is lost in reference which ought to be spent in action.

Dispatch, Sept. 20, 1809.

Popular Assemblies unmanageable.

I acknowledge that I have a great dislike to a new popular assembly; even our own ancient one would be quite unmanageable, and in three days, would ruin us, if the present generation had not before its eyes the example of the French revolution; and if there were not certain rules and orders for its guidance and government, the knowledge and use of which render safe, and successfully direct, its proceedings.
Dispatch, Sept. 22, 1809.

Distracted State of Spain.
I declare that if I were in Buonaparte's situation, I should leave the English and the Cortes to settle Spain in the best manner they could; and I should entertain very little doubt but that in a very short space of time Spain must fall into the hands of France. At the same time I must agree with you in thinking that affairs are now in so desperate a situation that they cannot be worse; that there is a real want of men of common capacity in Spain, in whose hands any form of government, intended for vigorous action, could be placed with any hope that their powers could he used to the public advantage; and that the Cortes, with all their faults, and the dangers attendant upon such an assembly, will have at least this advantage, that they will have the confidence of the country, and the prejudices of their countrymen of the lower class in our favour, and against France; the remark being perfectly well founded, that there is no prejudice or jealousy of us any where in Spain excepting by the government.

But in order to enjoy common safety under such an assembly as the Spanish Cortes, the rules and orders for their proceedings and internal government ought to be well defined, and to be, if possible, a part of the constitution of the assembly. Great care should also be taken in their formation to protect them from the effects of popular fury in the place of their sitting; but still with all these precautions I should prefer a wise Bourbon, if we could find one, for a regent, to the Cortes.
Dispatch, Sept. 22, 1809.

Whatever may be eventually the fate of Spain, Portugal must be a military country.
Dispatch, Sept. 24, 1809.

Military Value of an Armed and Friendly People.
In respect to the army and armament of the people in Spain and Portugal, there is no man more aware than I am of the advantage to be derived from these measures; and if I had not reflected well upon the subject, my experience of the war in Portugal and in Spain—(in Portugal, where the people are in some degree

armed and arrayed; and in Spain, where they are not)—would have shewn me the advantage which an army has against the enemy when the people are armed and arrayed, and are on its side in the contest. But reflection, and, above all, experience have shewn me the exact extent of this advantage in a military point of view; and I only beg that those who have to contend with the French, will not be diverted from the business of raising, arming, equipping, and training regular bodies, by any notion that the people, when armed and arrayed, will be of, I will not say any, but of much use to them.
Dispatch, Oct. 11, 1809.

Difficulties in the Peninsular War. The Battle of Talavera.
You will have heard of all that has passed in this country, and I will not therefore trouble you with a repetition of the story. The battle of Talevera was certainly the hardest fought of modern days, and the most glorious in its results to our troops. Each side engaged lost a quarter of their numbers.

It is lamentable that, owing to the miserable inefficiency of the Spaniards, to their want of exertion, and the deficiency of numbers, even, of the allies, much more of discipline and every other military quality, when compared with the enemy in the Peninsula, the glory of the action is the only benefit we have derived from it. But that is a solid and substantial benefit, of which we have derived some good consequences already; for, strange to say, I have contrived with the little British army to keep everything in check since the month of August last; and if the Spaniards had not contrived, by their own folly and against my entreaties and remonstrances, to lose an army in La Mancha about a fortnight ago, I think we might have brought them through the contest; as it is, however, I do not despair. I have in hand a most difficult task, from which I may not extricate myself; but I must not shrink from it, I command an unanimous army; I draw well with all the authorities in Spain and Portugal; and I believe I have the good wishes of the whole world. In such circumstances, one may fail, but it would be dishonourable to shrink from the task.
Letter to Col. Malcome, Dec. 3, 1809.

Buonaparte's System Hollow.
The Austrian marriage is a terrible event, and must prevent any great movement on the continent for the present. Still I do not despair of seeing, at some time or other, a check to the Buonaparte system. Recent transactions in Holland shew that it is all hollow within; and that it is so inconsistent with the wishes, the interests, and even the existence of civilized society, that he cannot trust even his brothers to carry it into execution.
Dispatch, April 4, 1810.

Military Law the will of the General.

Military law, as applied to any persons excepting the officers, soldiers, and followers of the army, for whose government there are particular provisions of law in all well regulated countries, is neither more nor less than the will of the general of the army. He punishes either with or without trial, for crimes either declared to be so, or not so declared, by any existing law, or by his own orders. This is the plain and common meaning of the term military law. Besides the mode of proceeding above described, laws have been made in different countries at different times to establish and legalize a description of military constitution.

The commander-in-chief, or the government, has been authorized to proceed by military process—that is, by court martial or council of war—against persons offending against certain laws, or against their own orders, issued generally for the security of the army; or for the establishment of a certain government or constitution odious to the people among whom it is established.

Of both descriptions of military law, there are numerous instances in the history of the operations of the French army during the revolution; and there is an instance of the existence both of the first-mentioned description and of the last-mentioned in Ireland, during the rebellion of 1798, when the people were in insurrection against the government, and were to be restrained by force.

Dispatch, April 19, 1810.

Letter to a Portuguese of Rank on the Position and Duties of Persons in his station.

I have received your letter containing a complaint against——, of the quarter-master general's department, that he had ill-treated one of your servants, into which I shall make inquiry, and let you know the result.

It is impossible, however, for me to interfere in any manner with a billet, given by the magistrates of Coimbra, for an officer and his family to be quartered in your house. I must at the same time inform you, that I am not a little surprised that a person of your rank and station, and quality in the country, should object to give accommodation in your house, and should make a complaint of this officer, that he had asked you for additional accommodation, when it appears by the letter which you enclosed, and which I now return, that when you objected to give him this additional accommodation for which he asked, he acquiesced in your objection, and did not any longer require this accommodation.

The unfortunate situation in which Portugal is placed, and the desire of the insatiable enemy of mankind to force this once happy and loyal people to submit to his iron yoke, to plunder them of their properties to destroy their religion and to deprive them of their monarch, has rendered it necessary to collect in this country a large army, in order, if possible, to defeat and frustrate the designs of the enemy. It is the duty of those whose age, whose sex, or whose profession, do not permit them to take an active part in the defence of their country, to assist those employed in its defence with provisions, lodgings for officers and troops, means of transport, &c., and at all events not to oppose themselves to the granting of this description of assistance. These duties are more particularly incumbent upon the rich and high in station, who would be the first victims of, and greatest sufferers from, the enemy's success, unless, indeed, they should be of the number of those traitors who are aiding to introduce the common enemy into the country, to destroy its happiness and independence.

Under these circumstances I am not a little astonished to receive these frivolous and manifestly unfounded complaints from you, and that you should be the person to set the example of objecting to give quarters to an officer, because he is married and has children.

It is not very agreeable to anybody to have strangers quartered in his house; nor is it very agreeable to us strangers, who have good houses in our own country, to be obliged to seek for quarters here. We are not here for our pleasure; the situation of your country renders it necessary: and you, a man of family and fortune, who have much to lose, should not be the first to complain of the inconvenience of our presence in the country.

I do everything in my power to alleviate the inconvenience which all must suffer. We pay extravagant prices with unparalleled punctuality for everything we receive; and I make it a rule to inquire into and redress every injury that is really done by the troops under my command, as I shall that to which I have above referred, of which you complain, in the conduct of——towards your servant.

Dispatch, August 23, 1810.

Croaking Spirit in the British Army in Portugal.

It appears that you have had a good smart contest with the government respecting our plan of operations. They will end in forcing me to quit them, and then they will see how they will get on. They will then find that I alone keep things in their present state. Indeed the temper of some of the officers of the British army gives me more concern than the folly of the Portuguese government. I have always been accustomed to have the confidence and support of the officers of the armies which I have commanded; but for the first time, whether owing to the opposition in England, or whether the magnitude of the concern is too much for their minds and their nerves, or whether I am mistaken and they are right, I cannot tell; but there is a system of croaking in the army which is highly injurious to the public service, and which I must devise some means to put an end to, or it will put an end to us. Officers have a right to form their own opinions upon events and transactions, but officers of high rank or situation ought to keep their opinions to themselves; if they do not approve of the system of operations of their commander, they ought to withdraw from the army. And this is a point to which I must bring some, if I should not find that their own good sense prevents them from going on as they have done lately.

Believe me that if any body else, knowing what I do, had commanded the army, they would now have been in Lisbon, if not, in their ships.

Dispatch, September 11, 1810.

Note—This passage from a letter to the British minister at Lisbon is one of many, which explain the difficulties Lord Wellington had to encounter from the Portuguese Government, from the opposition and the press in England, and from the want of proper military spirit in his own officers.

Conduct of the Portuguese.

If we are to go on as we have hitherto; if Great Britain is to give large subsidies, and to expend large sums in the support of a cause in which these most interested sit by and take no part; and those at the head of the government, with laws and power to force the people to exertion in the critical circumstances in which the country is placed, are aware of the evil, but neglect their duty and omit to put the laws into execution, I must believe their professions to be false; that they look to a little dirty popularity instead of to save their country; that they are unfaithful servants to their master, and persons in whom his allies can place no confidence.

Oct. 28, 1810.

The National Disease of Spain.

The national disease of Spain, that is, boasting of the strength and power of the Spanish nation, till they are seriously convinced that they are in no danger, then sitting down quietly and indulging their national indolence.

Dec. 2, 1810.

Apathy of the Portuguese.

There exists in the people of Portugal, an unconquerable love of their ease, which is superior even to their fear and detestation of the enemy. Neither will they, or their magistrates, or the government, see that the temporary indulgence of this passion for tranquillity must occasion the greatest misfortunes to the state and hardships to the individuals themselves; and no person in the country likes to have his tranquillity and habits disturbed for any purpose, however important, or to be the instrument of disturbing those of others. Thus every arrangement is defeated, and every order disobeyed with impunity. The magistrate will not force the inhabitants to adopt a measure, however beneficial to the state and himself, which will disturb his old habits; and the government will not force the magistrate to do that which will be disagreeable to him and to the people: thus we shall go on till the end of time.

January 3, 1811.

Takes no Notice of Newspapers.

I hope that the opinions of the people in Great Britain are not influenced by paragraphs in newspapers, and that those paragraphs do not convey the public opinion or sentiment upon any subject: therefore I (who have more reason than any other public man of the present day to complain of libels of this description) never take the smallest notice of them; and have never authorized any contradiction to be given, or any statement to be made in answer to the innumerable falsehoods, and the heaps of false reasoning, which have been published respecting me and the operations which I have directed.

January 7, 1811.

Indolence of the Natives of the Peninsula.

There is something very extraordinary in the nature of the people of the Peninsula. I really believe them, those of Portugal particularly, to be the most loyal and best disposed, and the most cordial haters of the French, that ever existed; but there is an indolence and a want even of the power of exertion in their disposition and habits, either for their own security, that of their country, or of their allies, which baffle all our calculations and efforts.

January 16, 1811.

Different Constitution of the French and English Armies.

It may also be asked why should we spend our money, and why these troops should not go on as the French troops do, without pay, provisions, magazines, or any thing? The French army is certainly a wonderful machine; but if we are to form such a one, we must form such a government as exists in France, which can with impunity lose one-half of the troops employed in the field every year, only by the privations and hardships imposed upon them. Next, we most compose our army of soldiers drawn from all classes of the population of the country; from the good and middling, as well as in rank as education, as from the bad; and not as all other nations do, and we in particular, from the bad only. Thirdly, we must establish such a system of discipline as the French have; a system founded on the strength of the tyranny of the government, which operates upon an army composed of soldiers, the majority of whom are sober, well disposed, amenable to order, and in some degree educated.

When we shall have done all this, and shall have made these armies of the strength of those employed by the French, we may require of them to live as the French do, viz., by authorised and regular plunder of the country and its inhabitants, if any should remain; and we may expose them to the labour, hardships and privations which the French soldier suffers every day; and we must expect the same proportion of loss every campaign, viz., one-half of those who take field.

January 26, 1811.

Character of the Marques de la Romana.

In him the Spanish army have lost their brightest ornament, his country their most upright patriot, and the world the most strenuous and zealous defender of the cause in which we are engaged; and I shall always acknowledge with gratitude the assistance which I received from him, as well by his operations as by his counsel, since he had been joined with this army.

January 26, 1811.

None but the worst men enter the Army as Privates.

In respect to recruiting the army, my own opinion is, that the government have never taken an enlarged view of the subject. It is expected that people will become soldiers in the line, and leave their families to starve, when, if they become soldiers in the militia, their families are provided for. This is an inconsistency that must strike the mind of even the least reflecting of mankind. What is the consequence? That none but the worst description of men enter the regular service.

But admitting the truth of the expense, I say that the country has not a choice between army and no army, between peace or war. They must have a large and efficient army, one capable of meeting the enemy abroad, or they must expect to meet him at home; and then farewell to all considerations of measures of greater or lesser expense, and to the ease, the luxury, and happiness of England. God forbid that I should see the day on which hostile armies should contend within the United Kingdom; but I am very certain that I shall not only see that day, but shall be a party in the contest, unless we alter our system, and the public feel in time the real nature of the contest in which we are at present engaged, and determine to meet its expense. I have gone a little beyond the question of recruiting; but depend upon it that you will get men when you provide for the families of soldiers in the line and not in the militia, and not before.

January 28, 1811.

Buonaparte's "disgusting Tyranny."

I am glad to hear such good accounts of affairs in the North. God send that they may prove true, and that we may overthrow this disgusting tyranny: however, of this I am certain, that whether true or not at present, something of the kind must occur before long, and, if we can only hold out, we shall yet see the world relieved.

March 23, 1811.

A French army in England would be the consequence of our withdrawal from the Peninsula.

I shall be sorry if government should think themselves under the necessity of withdrawing from this country, on account of the expense of the contest. From what I have seen of the objects of the French government, and the sacrifices they make to accomplish them, I have no doubt that if the British army were for any reason to withdraw from the Peninsula, and the French government were relieved from the pressure of military operations on the Continent, they would incur all risks to land an army in his majesty's dominions. Then indeed would commence an expensive contest; then his majesty's subjects discover what are the miseries of war, of which, by the blessing of God, they have hitherto had no knowledge; and the cultivation, the beauty, and prosperity of the country, and the virtue and happiness of its inhabitants, would be destroyed: whatever might be the result of the military operations; God forbid that I should be a witness, much less an actor, in the scene.[6]

[Footnote 6: At this time the clamours of the opposition regarding the expense of the war induced a fear that the government might determine to discontinue it.]

March 23, 1811.

The Peninsular Governments must not mind unpopularity.

I recommend to them (the Spaniards and Portuguese) to advert seriously to the nature of the task which they have to perform. Popularity, however desirable it may be to individuals, will not form, or feed, or pay an army; will not enable it to march and fight; will not keep it in a state of efficiency for long and arduous services. The resources which a wise government must find for these objects must be drawn from the people, not by measures which will render those unpopular who undertake to govern a country in critical circumstances, but by measures which must for a moment have a contrary effect. The enthusiasm of the people in favour of any individual never saved any country. They must be obliged by the restraint of law and regulation, to do those things and to pay those contributions, which are to enable the government to carry on this necessary contest.

April 9, 1811.

Coolness in action, not headlong bravery, is required in the Army.

The desire to be forward in engaging the enemy is not uncommon in the British array; but that quality which I wish to see the officers possess, who are at the head of the troops, is a cool, discriminating judgment in action, which will enable them to decide with promptitude how far they can and ought to go, with propriety; and to convey their orders, and act with such vigour and decision, that

the soldiers will look up to them with confidence in the moment of action, and obey them with alacrity.
May 15, 1811.

The battle of Albuera one of the most glorious in the War.
You will have heard of the Marshal's (Beresford) action on the 16th. The fighting was desperate, and the loss of the British has been very severe; but, adverting to the nature of the contest, and the manner in which they held their ground against all the efforts the whole French army could make against them, notwithstanding all the losses which they had sustained, I think this action one of the most glorious, and honourable to the character of the troops, of any that has been fought during the war.
May 20, 1811.

Portuguese Troops, better than Spanish.
What a pity it is that the Spaniards will not set to work seriously to discipline their troops! We do what we please now with the Portuguese troops; we manoeuvre them under fire equally with our own, and have some dependence on them; but these Spaniards can do nothing but stand still, and we consider ourselves fortunate if they do not run away.
May 25, 1811.

Disorganized state of the Peninsular Governments.
Those unfortunate governments in the Peninsula have been reduced to such a state of decrepitude, that I believe there was no authority existing within Spain or Portugal before the French invaded these countries. The French invasion did not improve this state of things; and, since what is called in Spain the revolution, and in Portugal the restoration, no crime that I know of has been punished in either, excepting that of being a French partisan. Those malversations in office—those neglects of duty; the disobedience of orders; the inattention to regulation, which tend to defeat all plans for military operation, and ruin a state that is involved in war, more certainly than the plots of all the French partisans, are passed unnoticed; and, notwithstanding the numerous complaints which Marshal Beresford and I have made, I do not know that one individual has yet been punished, or even dismissed from his office. The cause of this evil is the mistaken principle on which the government have proceeded. They have imagined that the best foundation for their power was a low, vulgar popularity; the evidence is the shouts of the mob of Lisbon, and the regular attendance at their levees, and the bows and scrapes of people in office, who ought to have other modes of spending their time; and to obtain this babble the government of

Portugal, as well as the successive governments in Spain, have neglected to perform those essential duties of all governments, viz., to force those they are placed over to do their duty, by which, before this time, these countries would have been out of danger.

The other evil is connected very materially with the first. The government will not regulate their finances, because it will interfere with some man's job. They will not lay on new taxes, because in all countries those who lay on taxes are not favourites with the mob. They have a general income-tax, called 10 per cent., and, in some cases, 20 per cent., which they have regulated in such a manner as that no individual, I believe, has paid a hundredth part of what he ought to have paid. Then, for want of money, they can pay nobody, and, of course, have not the influence which they ought to have over the subordinate departments.

In addition to embarrassments of all descriptions surrounding us on all sides, I have to contend with an ancient enmity between these two nations, which is more like that of cat and dog than anything else, of which no sense of common danger, or common interest, or anything, can get the better, even in individuals.

June 12, 1811.

To write an anonymous letter is the meanest action of which any man can be guilty.

Dispatch, July 3, 1811.

British Officers, as well as Soldiers, require to be kept in order.

I must also observe that British officers require to be kept in order, as well as the soldiers under their command, particularly in a foreign service. The experience which I have had of their conduct in the Portuguese service has shown me that there must be authority, and that a strong one, to keep them within due bounds, otherwise they would only disgust the soldiers over whom they should be placed, the officers whom they should be destined to assist, and the country in whose service they should be employed.

October 1, 1811.

Money in aid of Labour better than Charity.

That which would be desirable is, if possible, to aid laborious exertions to procure a subsistence by small advances of money; and I propose to keep this principle in view in the distribution of the money entrusted to me, by which not only it will subsist those to whom it will be given for a longer period, but it may be hoped that the people will resume their habits of industry, and that they will soon again be able to provide for their own subsistence.

Oct. 11, 1811.

A General Re-action against Buonaparte predicted.

I have, however, long considered it probable, that even *we* should witness a general resistance throughout Europe to the fraudulent and disgusting tyranny of Buonaparte, created by the example of what has occurred in Spain and Portugal; and that *we* should be actors and advisers in these scenes; and I have reflected frequently upon the measures which should be pursued to give a chance of success.

Those who embark in projects of this description should be made to understand, or to act as if they understood, that having once drawn the sword they must not return it, till they shall have completely accomplished their object. They must be prepared, and must be forced, to make all sacrifices to the cause. Submission to military discipline and order is a matter of course; but when a nation determines to resist the authority, and to shake off the government of Buonaparte, they must be prepared and forced to sacrifice the luxuries and comforts of life, and to risk all in a contest, which it should be clearly understood before it is undertaken, has for its object to save all or nothing.

The first measure for a country to adopt is to form an army, and to raise a revenue from the people to defray the expense of the army: above all, to form a government of such strength, as that army and people can be forced by it to perform their duty. This is the rock upon which Spain has split; and all our measures in any other country which should afford hopes of resistance to Buonaparte should be directed to avoid it. The enthusiasm of the people is very fine, and looks well in print; but I have never known it to produce any thing but confusion. In France, what was called enthusiasm was power and tyranny, acting through the medium of popular societies, which have ended by overturning Europe, and in establishing the most powerful and dreadful tyranny that ever existed. In Spain, the enthusiasm of the people spent itself in *vivas* and vain boasting. The notion of its existence prevented even the attempt to discipline the armies; and its existence has been alleged, ever since, as the excuse for the rank ignorance of the officers and the indiscipline and constant misbehaviour of the troops.

I therefore earnestly recommend you, wherever you go, to trust nothing to the enthusiasm of the people. Give them a strong and a just, and, if possible, a good government; but, above all, a strong one, which shall enforce upon them to do their duty by themselves and their country; and let measures of finance to support an army go hand in hand with measures to raise it.

I am quite certain that the finances of Great Britain are more than a match for Buonaparte, and that we shall have the means of aiding any country that may be disposed to resist his tyranny. But those means are necessarily limited in every country by the difficulty of procuring specie. This necessary article can be obtained in sufficient quantities only by the contributions of the people; and although Great Britain can and ought to assist with money, as well as in other modes, every effort of this description, the principal financial as well as military effort, ought to be by the people of the resisting country.

Dec. 10, 1811.

The French System of Predatory War.

In the early days of the revolutionary war, the French, at the recommendation, I believe, of Brissot, adopted a measure which they called a *levée en masse*; and put every man, animal, and article, in their own country, in requisition for the service of the armies. This system of plunder was carried into execution by the popular societies throughout the country. It is not astonishing that a nation, among whom such a system was established, should have been anxious to carry on the war beyond their own frontiers. This system both created the desire and afforded the means of success; and with the war, they carried, wherever they went, the system of requisition; not, however, before they had, by these and other revolutionary measures, entirely destroyed all the sources of national prosperity at home.

Wherever the French armies have since gone, their subsistence, at least, the most expensive article in all armies, and means of transport, have been received from the country for nothing. Sometimes, besides subsistence, they have received clothing and shoes; in other instances, besides these articles, they have received pay; and from Austria and Prussia, and other parts of Germany and Italy, they have drawn, besides all these articles of supply for their troops, heavy contributions in money for the supply of the treasury at Paris. To this enumeration ought to be added the plunder acquired by the generals, officers, and troops; and it will be seen that the new French system of war is the greatest evil that ever fell on the civilised world.

The capital and industry of France having been destroyed by the revolution, it is obvious that the government cannot raise a revenue from the people of France adequate to support the large force which must be maintained in order to uphold the authority of the new government, particularly in the newly-conquered or ceded states; and to defend the widely-extended frontier of France from all those whose interest and inclination must lead them to attack it. The French government, therefore, under whatever form administered, must seek for support for their armies in foreign countries. War must be a financial resource; and that appears to me to be the greatest misfortune which the French revolution has entailed upon the present generation.

Jan. 31, 1812.

I consider the Portuguese troops, next to the British, the best in the Peninsula.

May 3, 1812.

It is very difficult to manage the defence of the kingdom of Portugal, the whole country being frontier.

June 11, 1812.
How to establish National Credit.

When a nation is desirous of establishing public credit, or, in other words, of inducing individuals to confide their property to its government, they must begin by acquiring a revenue equal to their fixed expenditure; and they must manifest an inclination to be honest, by performing their engagements in respect to their debts.

June 25. 1812.

The Spaniards cry "Viva!" but don't act.

I do not expect much from the exertions of the Spaniards, notwithstanding all that we have done for them. They cry *viva!* and are very fond of us, and hate the French; but they are, in general, the most incapable of useful exertion of all the nations that I have ever known; the most vain, and at the same time the most ignorant, particularly of military affairs, and above all of military affairs in their own country.

August 18, 1812.

Imbecility of the Spanish Leaders.

It is extraordinary that the revolution in Spain should not have produced one man with any knowledge of the real situation of the country. It really appears as if they were all drunk, and thinking, and talking of any other subject but Spain.

November 1, 1812.

Evils of uncontrolled popular Legislatures.

The theory of all legislation is founded in justice; and, if we could be certain that legislative assemblies could on all occasions act according to the principles of justice, there would be no occasion for those checks and guards which we have seen established under the best systems. Unfortunately, however, we have seen that legislative assemblies are swayed by the fears and passions of individuals; when unchecked, they are tyrannical and unjust; nay, more, it unfortunately happens too frequently, that the most tyrannical and unjust measures are the most popular. Those measures are particularly popular which deprive rich and powerful individuals of their properties under the pretence of the public advantage; and I tremble for a country in which, as in Spain, there is no barrier for the preservation of private property, excepting the justice of a legislative assembly possessing supreme powers.

January 29, 1813.

Ingratitude of the Portuguese to the British Army.

I must say, that the British army, which I have the honour to command, have met with nothing but ingratitude from the government and authorities in Portugal for their services; and that everything that could be done has been done by the civil authorities, lately, to oppress the officers and soldiers on every occasion in which it has by any accident been in their power. I hope, however, that we have seen the last of Portugal.
July 20, 1813.

Jealousy of the interference of foreigners in their internal concerns, is the characteristic of all Spaniards.
July 12, 1813.

Sound sense is better than abilities.
August 8, 1813.

Basis of military operations against the United States from the side of Canada.
Any offensive operation founded upon Canada must be preceded by a naval superiority on the lakes. But even if we had that superiority, I should doubt our being able to do more than secure the points on those lakes at which the Americans could have access. In such countries as America, very extensive, thinly peopled, and producing but little food in proportion to their extent, military operations by large bodies are impracticable, unless the party carrying them on has the uninterrupted use of a navigable river, or very extensive means of land transport, which such a country can rarely supply.

I conceive, therefore, that were your army larger even than the proposed augmentation would make it, you could not quit the lakes; and, indeed, would be tied to them the more necessarily in proportion as your army would be large.[7]

[Footnote 7: The letter from the Duke the above is taken was written in reply to an application by the home government for his opinion. We frequently find the Duke applied to for his opinion on political matters at home, while serving in the Peninsula.]
February 22, 1814.

The Morale of an Army important to Discipline.
No reliance can be placed on the conduct of troops in action with the enemy, who have been accustomed to plunder, and those officers alone can expect to derive honour in the day of battle from the conduct of the troops under their command, who shall have forced them, by their attention and

exertions, to behave as good soldiers ought in their cantonments, their quarters, and their camps.
March 5, 1814.

English officers are very strictly instructed, and those who mean to serve their country well must obey their instructions, however fearless they may be of responsibility. Indeed, I attribute this fearlessness very much to the determination never to disobey, as long as the circumstances exist under which an order is given.
April 16, 1814.

French Feelings about the Slave Trade.
You (Mr. Wilberforce) judge most correctly regarding the state of the public mind here upon this question. Not only is there no information, but, because England takes an interest in the question, it is impossible to convey any through the only channel which would be at all effectual, viz., the daily press. Nobody reads anything but the newspapers; but it is impossible to get anything inserted in any French newspaper in Paris in favour of the abolition, or even to show that the trade was abolished in England, from motives of humanity. The extracts made from English newspapers upon this, or any other subject, are selected with a view, either to turn our principles and conduct into ridicule, or to exasperate against us still more the people of this country; and therefore the evil cannot be remedied by good publications in the daily press in England, with a view to their being copied into the newspapers here.

I must say that the daily press in England do us a good deal of harm in this as well as in other questions. We are sure of the king and his government, if he could rely upon the opinion of his people. But as long as our press teems with writings drawn with a view of irritating persons here, we shall never be able to exercise the influence which we ought to have upon this question, and which we really possess.
Letter to Mr. Wilberforce, October 8, 1814.

The real power in Spain is in the clergy.
October 20, 1814.

Les choses neuves, surtout quand elles sont compliquées, ne vont pas bien.

Letter to Doumouriex, November 3, 1814.
FRANCE.
Effects of Buonaparte's Government of France.
Ce qu'il y a de pis c'est le mécontentement général, et la pauvreté universelle. Cette malheureuse révolution et ces suites ont ruiné le pays, de fond en comble. Tout le monde est pauvre, et, ce qui est pis, leurs institutions empêchent qu'aucune famille devienne riche et puissante. Tous doivent donc nécessairement viser à remplir des emplois publics, non, comme autrefois, pour l'honneur de les remplir, mais pour avoir de quoi vivre. Tout le monde donc cherche de l'emploi public.

Buonaparte laissa une armée de million d'hommes en France, outres les officiers prisonniers en Angleterre et en Russie. Le roi ne peut pas en maintenir le quart. Tous ceux non employées sont mécontens. Buonaparte gouvernait directement la moitié de l'Europe, et indirectement presque l'autre moitié. Pour des causes à présent bien develloppées et connues, il employait une quantité infinie de personnes dans ses administrations; et tous ceux employés, ou dans les administrations extérieures, civiles, ou dans les administrations militaires des armées, sont renvoyés, et beaucoup des ceux employés dans les administrations intérieures; à cette classe nombreuse ajouter la quantité d'émigrés, et de personnes rentrés, tous mourant de faim, et tous convoitant de l'emploi public afin de pouvoir vivre, et vous trouverez que plus des trois quarts de la classe de la société, non employée à la main d'oeuvre ou à labourer la terre, sont en état d'indigence, et, par conséquence, mécontens. Si vous considerez bien ce tableau, qui est la stricte vérité, vous y verrez la cause et la nature du danger du jour. L'armée les officiers, sourtout, sont mécontens. Ils le sont pour plusieurs raisons inutiles à detailler ici, mais ce mécontentement pourra ce vaincre en adoptant des mesures sages pour améliorer l'esprit.

Letter to Doumouriex, November 26, 1814.

Re-establishment of the Bourbons necessary to the Peace of Europe.
I have frequently told your highness, and every day's experience shews me that I am right, that the only chance of peace for Europe consists in the establishment in France of the legitimate Bourbons. The establishment of any other government, whether in the person of——, or in a regency in the name of young Napoleon, or in any other individual, or in a republic, must lead to the maintenance of large military establishments, to the ruin of all the governments of Europe, till it shall suit the convenience of the French government to commence a contest which can be directed only against you, or others for whom we are interested. In this contest we shall feel the additional difficulty, that those who are now on our side will then be against us, and you will again find yourself surrounded by enemies. I am convinced that the penetration of your highness will have shewn you the danger of all these schemes to the interests of the emperor, and that you will defeat them all by adhering to that line of conduct (in

which you will find us likewise) which will finally lead to the establishment in France of the legitimate government, from which alone can Europe expect any genuine peace.

May 20, 1815.

Effects of Waterloo.

I may be wrong, but my opinion is, that we have given Napoleon his death-blow: from all I hear, his army is totally destroyed, the men are deserting in parties, even the generals are withdrawing from him. The infantry throw away their arms, and the cavalry and artillery sell their horses to the people of the country, and desert to their homes. Allowing for much exaggeration in this account, and knowing that Buonaparte can still collect, in addition to what he has brought back with him, the 5th corps d'armée, under Rapp, which is near Strasbourg, and the 3rd corps, which was at Wavre during the battle, and has not suffered so much as the others, and probably some troops from La Vendée, I am still of opinion that he can make no head against us—qu'il n'a qu'à se pendre.

June 23, 1815.

Some of the regiments (the new ones I mean) are reduced to nothing; but I must keep them as regiments, to the great inconvenience of the service, at great expense; or I must send them home, and part with the few British soldiers I have.

I never was so disgusted with any concern as I am with this; and I only hope that I am going the right way to bring it to an early determination some way or other.

June 25, 1815.

Waterloo described to a Soldier.

Notre Bataille du 18 a été une de géans; et notre succès a été complet, comme vous voyez. Que Dieu me favorise assez pour que je n'en aie plus, parceque je suis désolé de la perte de mes anciens amis et comrades.

Mon voisin et collaborateur (Blücher) est en bonne santé quoique un peu souffrant d'une chute qu'il a faite d'un cheval blessé sous lui dans la bataille du 16.

Letter to Doumouriex, June 26, 1815.

If Buonaparte is to be put to Death, he will not be his Executioneer.

General——has been here this day to negociate for Napoleon's passing to America, to which proposition I have answered, that I have no authority. The

Prussians think the Jacobins wish to give him over to me, believing that I will save his life.—— wishes to kill him; but I have told him I shall remonstrate, and shall insist upon his being disposed of by common accord. I have likewise said that, as a private friend, I advised him to have nothing to do with so foul a transaction; and that he and I had acted too distinguished parts in these transactions to become executioners, and that I was determined that, if the sovereigns wished to put him to death, they should appoint an executioner, which should not be me.
June 26, 1815.

The "Pounding Match."
You will have heard of our battle of the 18th. Never did I see such a pounding match. Both were what the boxers call "gluttons." Napoleon did not manoeuvre at all. He just moved forward in the old style, in columns, and was driven off in the old style. The only difference was that he mixed cavalry with his infantry, and supported both with an enormous quantity of artillery.

I had the infantry for some time in squares, and we had the French cavalry walking about as if they had been our own. I never saw the British infantry behave so well.
Letter to Marshal Beresford, July 9, 1815.

Blucher's Vandalism averted.
To Marshal Prince Blucher.—Several reports have been brought to me during the evening and night, and some from the government, in consequence of the work carrying on by your highness on one of the bridges over the Seine, which it is supposed to be your intention to destroy.

As this measure will certainly create a good deal of disturbance in the town, and as the sovereigns when they were here before, left all these bridges, &c., standing, I take the liberty of suggesting to you to delay the destruction of the bridge, at least till they should arrive; or, at all events, till I can have the pleasure of seeing you to-morrow morning.
July 8, 1815.

The destruction of the bridge of Jena is highly disagreeable to the king and to the people, and may occasion disturbance in the city. It is not merely a military measure, but is one likely to attach to the character of our operations, and is of political importance. It is adopted solely because the bridge is considered as a monument of the battle of Jena, notwithstanding that the government are willing to change the name of the bridge. Considering the bridge as a monument, I beg leave to suggest that its immediate destruction is inconsistent with the promise made to the commissioners on behalf of the part of the army, during the negociation of the convention, viz., that the monuments, museums, &c., should be reserved for the decision of the allied sovereigns.

All that I ask is, that the execution of the orders given for the destruction of the bridge may be suspended till the sovereigns shall arrive here, when, if it should be agreed by common accord that the bridge ought to be destroyed, I shall have no objection.

July 9, 1815.[8]

[Footnote 8: The Duke rarely writes or speaks twice, when once will do. On this occasion he was anxious; and—successful.]

Summary Justice.

To the Sous-Préfet de Pontoise.—J'ai ordonné qu'on vous fasse prisonnier, parceque, ayant envoyé une réquisition à Pontoise pour des vivres, vous avez répondu que vous ne les donneriez pas, sans qu'on envoie une force militaire assez forte pour les prendre.

Vous vous êtes mis dans les cas des militaires, et je vous fais prisonnier de guerre, et je vous envoie en Angleterre.

Si je vous traitais comme l'usurpateur et ses adherens ont traité les habitans des pays ou ils ont fait la guerre, je vous ferais fusiller; mais, comme vous vous êtes constitué guerrier, je vous fais prisonnier de guerre.

July 13, 1815.

Characteristic Letter to Marshal Beresford.

The battle of Waterloo was certainly the hardest fought that has been for many years, I believe, and has placed in the power of the allies the most important results. We are throwing them away, however, by the infamous conduct of some of us; and I am sorry to add that our own government also are taking up a little too much the tone of their rascally newspapers. They are shifting their objects; and, having got their cake, they want both to eat it and keep it.

As for your Portuguese concerns, I recommend you to resign, and come away immediately. It is impossible for the British government to maintain British officers for the Portuguese army, at an expense even so trifling as it is, if the Portuguese government are to refuse to give the service of the army in the cause of Europe in any manner. Pitch them to the devil, then, in the mode which will be most dignified to yourself, and that which will have the best effect in opening the prince's eyes to the conduct of his servants in Portugal; and let the matter work its own way. Depend upon it, the British government must and will recall the British officers.

August 7, 1815.

SPEECHES IN PARLIAMENT.
Praise of Lord Hastings and the Indian Army.
He professed his entire concurrence in the tribute of approbation bestowed on the Marquis of Hastings, for his conduct of the late war in India. There could not remain a doubt in the minds of those acquainted with the facts, but that the wisdom of the plan on which it was commenced, and the vigour of its execution, merited the highest praise. The noble Duke said, he was pleased that an opportunity, like the present, had occurred to do justice to the services and gallantry of our troops in India, which were often neglected or disallowed. No troops in the world performed their duty better, or observed a more steady discipline. They had evinced their good qualities in all their late transactions, whether acting in great masses or small detachments. In all situations they had nobly performed their duty.
House of Lords, March 9, 1819.
Impossibility of granting Catholic Emancipation.
The whole question turned upon the degree of security which could be given to the Protestant religion as by law established in Ireland. To consider this, it was necessary to consider how the reformation had been established in Ireland. It was not necessary for him to recall to their lordships remembrance that the unreformed religion had been established in Ireland at the point of the sword, and by means of confiscations. All this was repeated at the revolution, and was fresh in the recollection of the people of Ireland. Keeping in view that the Irish Roman Catholic church, under all oppressions, continued in the same state—the pope having the same influence over the clergy, the clergy the same power over the people; in this state of things, he would ask, whether it was possible that Roman Catholics could be safely admitted to hold seats in parliament? The influence of the priesthood over the people was fostered by the remembrance of the events to which he had alluded; and the idea of unmerited and mutual suffering; and no doubt could be entertained, from their present feelings, that if the Roman Catholics were admitted to the enjoyment of political power, their first exertion would be to restore their religion to its original supremacy; and to recover the possessions and property of which they had been stripped by the reformation. It was, however, said, that securities were offered on the part of the Roman Catholics.

The pope, it seemed, had in the appointment of bishops, relinquished all to the crown, except the mere conferring of a spiritual blessing. But how had that concession been received by the people of Ireland? It had excited the utmost discontent, and was regarded as an abandonment of the essential principles of their religion, and an attack on their national independence. Did that arise from the people of Ireland having a less clear idea of national independence than other people? No; but they felt if the executive power possessed any control over the appointment of the Roman Catholic bishops, some security would be thereby obtained for the Protestant church. Considering, then, that the whole

question turned on the degree of security which could be given, and looking at the various securities which had at several times been proposed, he had never yet seen anything that came up to his notion of that which ought to be required. As to what had been said of the domestic nomination of bishops, he did not see how the laws of the country could operate upon it, so as to make it an adequate security. Then as to the oath of allegiance which the bishop was to take, of what avail could it be, that the law required this oath from a bishop, appointed God knows how, or by whom? When all these circumstances were considered, the state of the Irish Catholic church, the way in which the reformation had been effected, the rivalry and enmity between the Catholics and the established church, and the inadequacy of all securities which had been proposed, there was in his opinion, enough to decide the question; for, the first and greatest duty of the legislature was, to secure the establishments as settled at the revolution.
House of Lords, May 17, 1819.

County meetings if properly regulated, are a fair constitutional mode of taking the sense of the county; but this cannot be the case if they are attended by a mob for the express purpose of supporting one side.
House of Lords, January 26, 1821.

The Porte our ancient Ally.
The Ottoman Porte is the ancient ally of this country. It forms an essential part of the balance of power in Europe. The preservation of the Ottoman Porte has been an object of importance not merely to England but also to the whole of Europe; and the changes of possession which have taken place in the east of Europe within the recollection of all who hear me, render its existence as an independent and powerful state, necessary to the well being of this country.

In the late war, had it not been for the influence of the councils of England over the Porte, I may safely say that the disaster which finally led to the establishment of Europe as it now is, would not have occurred to the extent it did in 1812. Under these circumstances I think we may term the Ottoman Porte the "ancient ally" and friend of this country, even though the treaties upon which our alliance is founded are not of a hundred years standing.
House of Lords, Jan. 29, 1828.

Battle of Navarino an untoward Event. Sir E. Codrington acquitted of all blame.
There is one other subject to which I shall address myself, I mean the sense in which the word "untoward" has been used. It was intended by "untoward" to convey, that the event referred to was unexpected—was unfortunate. The sense in which the word was used was this: in the treaty which is not yet before the

house, and which cannot, therefore, regularly come under discussion, though all of us have read it, it is mentioned as one stipulation, that the execution of it, if possible, shall not lead to hostilities; and therefore, when the execution of it did lead to hostilities, it was a consequence which the government did not anticipate, and which it has, therefore, a right to call untoward.

It was hoped by the former government, that the treaty could be executed without risk of commencing hostilities; and that is rendered quite indisputable, not merely by the treaty, but by the force which the contracting parties sent into the Mediterranean to superintend its operation.

The late administration entertained hopes that those treaties could be carried into execution without hostilities, as your lordships must have perceived from what you have seen of those treaties themselves, as well as from the nature of the force sent to see them carried into execution; and when it was ultimately found that hostilities were likely to ensue, every one must look upon it as an untoward event which could give rise to such a state of things.

When the news of the affair which took place at Navarino reached Constantinople, it was apprehended that a war would ensue, and therefore every one was justified in looking upon it as an untoward event.

It is gratifying, however, to find from his majesty's speech, that those appearances of hostility have ceased to exist, and that hopes are entertained that no impediment will present itself to an amicable adjustment of the question; this, however, does not deprive the transaction of the character of "untowardness" which it originally possessed.

But in making this statement, do I make the slightest charge, do I cast the most distant imputation upon the gallant officer who commanded at Navarino? Certainly not. That gallant officer, in doing as he has done, discharged what he felt to be his duty to his country. His majesty's government have taken that gallant officer's conduct into consideration, and have acquitted him of all blame; and, therefore, it would ill become me to cast the slightest imputation on the distinguished action he performed. It should be recollected, that the gallant admiral was placed in a situation of great delicacy as well as difficulty. He was placed in the command of a combined squadron, in conjunction with two foreign admirals; and his conduct was such, that they placed the most implicit confidence in him, and allowed him to lead them to victory. My lords, I should feel myself unworthy of the situation which I hold in his majesty's councils, if I thought myself capable of uttering a single syllable against that gallant admiral, admiring, as I do, the intrepid bravery with which he conducted himself in a moment of much danger and difficulty.

House of Lords, January 29, 1828.

Reason for being Prime Minister.
When I received his majesty's commands to give my opinion respecting the formation of a ministry, it was far from my wish to place myself at its head, or to

take any office, other than that which I already held; but finding, in the course of the negotiation which arose out of the commands of his majesty, a difficulty in getting another individual to fill the place, and that it was the unanimous wish of those who are now my colleagues, that I should take it, I determined to accept it; but having so determined, I resigned the office of commander-in-chief.

House of Lords, January 29, 1828.

The Doctrine of Non-interference.

Much has been said here and elsewhere, at various times, on the question of interference by one state in the affairs of another. I do not admit the right of one country to interfere with the internal affairs of another country, except where the law of necessity or great political interests may render interference absolutely necessary. But I say that non-interference is the rule, and interference the exception. This is the ground of the policy on which this country acts. She disdains a daily interference with the affairs of other countries.

House of Lords, February 11, 1828.

No Personal or Political Hostility to Canning.

I rise to protest against any such imputation being cast upon me, as that I ever entertained any personal hostility to Mr. Canning. On a former occasion I stated distinctly to your lordships, why I did not think proper to remain in the government of which Mr. Canning was the head. The communications that passed between me and Mr. Canning have, unfortunately, I must be allowed to say, been made public enough, and I defy any man to point out anything like personal feelings in those communications. It is true, that when I found it necessary to withdraw from the government, I also thought it my duty to lay down the military office which I hold; but I beg leave to call your lordships' recollection to the explanation which I gave at that time, and to my subsequent conduct. After I left the government, I always met Mr. Canning in the way in which I had been accustomed to meet him, and did not depart from those habits which had marked our previous intercourse. But I will go further and say, that I had no hostility towards Mr. Canning's government. I did, it is true, propose that a clause should be added to the corn-bill, but did I not at the same time beg of the government to adopt that clause, or something like it, and not to abandon the bill? I must again repeat, that to the day of his death I felt no personal hostility to Mr. Canning; and that I am equally free from the imputation of having entertained any political hostility towards him. To whatever persons the declaration of the right honourable gentleman (Mr. Huskisson) was intended to apply.[9] I claim to myself the right of not being included in the number of Mr. Canning's enemies.

[Footnote 9: Referring to an angry speech of that gentleman in the Commons.]

House of Lords, February 25, 1828.

Corn Law of 1828, Principle on which founded.
Your lordships are all aware that a variety of opinions exist throughout the country respecting the introduction of foreign corn; one class of persons maintaining that its importation should be prohibited; while others contend for its free introduction into the markets of the country. I have considered it my duty, and my colleagues also have considered it theirs, in the measure which they are about to propose to parliament, to endeavour to steer their course between the two extremes, and to propose a measure which shall have the effect of conciliating all parties, be at the same time favourable to the public, and shall be permanent. Your lordships will recollect, notwithstanding the difference of opinion which exists on this subject, all parties agree, generally, that the corn growers of this country ought, in some measure, to be protected.

The number of individuals, either in parliament or out of it, who maintain that foreign corn should be altogether free of duty, are very few indeed. Some persons, undoubtedly, think that a small fixed duty ought to be imposed; and I, my lords, should certainly say here, that if any such fixed duty were imposed, it ought to be a very small one; but I repeat, that whatever may be the particular doctrines or opinions of one class of persons or another, all agree that some protection ought to be afforded to the agriculture of this country. This opinion is founded on the great burden of taxation upon the country generally, as well as on the particular burdens on the land; and on the fact that the labouring classes here are better fed, clothed, and lodged, than the people of the same class in other countries. It is admitted by those who entertain this opinion in favour of a low duty, that their expectation and intention are, that the poorer lands of this country, which have been brought into cultivation by the application of great labour, and by the expenditure of large capital, should at once be thrown out of cultivation; and even the richer lands would become, comparatively, unprofitable in consequence of the adoption of their system. I will maintain that this country has been brought to its present high state of cultivation, and consequent internal wealth, by the fostering protection which has invariably been given to agriculture, and which has induced gentlemen to lay out their capital in redeeming waste lands and bringing them into cultivation. The result of such a system would be—to throw out of cultivation the land thus redeemed from waste; to reduce the extent of cultivation of the richer lands, consequently to lessen the productive power of the country; and finally to throw us for subsistence and support on the resources of foreign nations. My lords,—I will not exaggerate the effects likely to be produced by the pursuing of a system such as that to which I have alluded; but I beg your lordships to reflect on the consequences which must result, if the powers, from whose dominions these resources are generally drawn, should think proper to lay a heavy tax on the export of such corn, or that it should be subject to such an operation by any other state, in its transit to this country. I entreat your lordships to consider what must be the consequences of such a measure in its results to this country; a measure, too, in which I may say, that foreign states might, from circumstances, be highly justified. But supposing such moderation on the part of those states, that they should continue to allow us to draw our supplies from their dominions; supposing we could be supplied from other countries—America, for instance; yet I entreat your lordships to observe, that this country would be constantly, under the proposed system of fixed duty, placed in the state in which it found itself in years of famine and scarcity, which occurred in both the last and present century, and would of consequence be exposed to the highest possible prices for wheat. This, my Lords, I say, would be the inevitable consequence.

The cost of production, in Poland, for instance, would not be increased; but the prices would be regulated here, not by the prices of that country, but by the scarcity price of this country, and by the profits of all those who might be, directly or indirectly, concerned in the contemplated importation of corn, in such a state of things as that to which I have alluded. Under these circumstances, a low duty would not be productive of a reduction in price; indeed, so far from diminution, I am confident it would produce an enormous increase. But, my Lords, I would ask, even supposing it were otherwise, whether it would be proper to adopt such a measure, in reference to its probable effect in other respects? My Lords, look to Ireland, and consider what must by the inevitable consequence if agriculture is not to be encouraged in that country—a country, which, during the last year supplied England with more than 2,000,000 quarters of grain. The quantity of wheat alone imported from Ireland last year, was no less than 400,000 quarters. I do therefore, beg your Lordships to consider what must be the consequence of cutting off from that country nearly the only source of industry—the only manufacture, with one exception, which is established in that country. No man, whether connected with that country or not, can for a moment think of imposing such a sacrifice on that country. On the contrary, I am disposed to think, that many of your Lordships will be ready to make considerable sacrifices to procure for the people of Ireland a share of that plenty their industry affords us. But, my Lords, I speak not only with reference to Ireland, but with reference to this country. I am ready to state that the gentlemen of this country have, by the extent of their capital, and the labour which they have employed on their estates, raised the agriculture of this kingdom to its present prosperous condition; and nothing would be more unjust than to take from them that protection by which they have been enabled to bring cultivation to the state in which it now is, and to deprive them of those profits which are so justly their due, on account of the capital laid out by them.

I will say, that the merchant, that the manufacturer, the poor, and the whole public, are interested in the maintenance of the independent affluence of the nobility and gentry of this country,—that the Government are interested in supporting their influence, on account of the assistance which has always been derived from them in every branch of internal government, and on account of the support which they have afforded to Government under every circumstance.

If it were in my power to make corn cheaper by diminishing the protection which the landed gentry have always received, I would not do it at the expense of Ireland, and of all the evils which the measure must inflict upon the essential interests of this country.

My Lords, having expressed my opinion upon the system of importation at a low duty, I will now offer a few observations with respect to the other system,—that of entire prohibition; and which, I must say, has been greatly and justly complained of. The truth is, that such a system could not be carried into execution without exposing the country to the greatest possible evils:—first of all, from want—next from high prices, and also from a superabundance of corn, arising from the introduction of a greater quantity of wheat than required being in the country at a period when the scarcity might have been relieved by an abundant harvest; and, lastly, from the depression of prices, affecting not only the producers of corn in this country, but also the importers of foreign grain. My Lords, evils like these can only be relieved by the illegal interference of the Government, or by ministers coming to Parliament, in order to induce it to consent to a suspension of the law.

Such, my Lords, is the history of the corn question as regards prohibition; and there is not the least doubt that the system has produced all the evils to which I have alluded at one period or another.

March 31, 1828.

Reason for repealing the Test and Corporation Acts.

I fully agree that the security of the Church of England, and the union existing between it and the state, depend neither on the law about to be repealed by the present bill, nor upon the provisions of this measure itself. That union and security, which we must all desire to see continued, depend upon the oath taken by his Majesty, to which we are all, in our respective stations, parties, and not only on that oath, but on the Act of Settlement, and the different acts of union from time to time agreed to; all of which provide for the intimate and inseparable union of church and state, and for the security of both.

The question is, what security does the existing system of laws, as they now stand, afford the church establishment? My lords, I am very dubious as to the amount of security afforded through the means of a system of exclusion from office, to be carried into effect by a law which it is necessary to suspend by an annual act, that admits every man into office whom it was the intention of the original framers of the law to exclude. It is perfectly true it was not the intention of those who brought in that suspension law originally, that dissenters from the church of England should be permitted to enter into corporations under its provisions. The law was intended to relieve those whom time or circumstances had rendered unable to qualify themselves according to the system which government had devised. However, the dissenters availed themselves of the relaxation of the law, for the purpose of getting into corporations, and this the law allowed. What security, then, I ask, my Lords, is to be found in the existing system? So far from dissenters being excluded by the corporation and test acts, from all corporations, so far is this from being the fact, that, as must be well known to your Lordships, some corporations are absolutely and entirely in the possession of dissenters. Can you suppose that the repeal of laws so inoperative as these, can afford any serious obstacle to the perfect security of the church, and the permanent union of that establishment with the state? The fact is, that the existing laws have not only failed completely in answering their intended purpose, but they are anomalous and absurd—anomalous in their origin, absurd in their operation.

If a man were asked the question, at his elevation to any corporate office, whether he had received the sacrament of the church of England, and if he said "No," he lost every vote that had been tendered on his behalf, and there was an end of his election, but if, on the contrary, by accident or design, he got in without the question relative to the sacrament being put to him, then the votes tendered for him were held good, and his election valid; so that no power could remove him from the office which he held. I ask, is there any security in that? My noble friend says, that the original intention of the framers of these acts, was that the sacrament should not be taken by dissenters; but the law requires that a man, on entering into any corporation, shall receive the sacrament, without regard to his religious belief. Thus an individual whose object it is to get into a particular office, may feel disposed, naturally enough, to take the sacrament before his election, merely as a matter of form, and thus a sacred rite of our church is profaned, and prostituted to a shameful and scandalous purpose. I confess my Lords, I should have opposed this bill, if I thought it calculated to weaken the securities at present enjoyed by the church. However, I agreed not to oppose the bill; though I consented in the first instance to oppose it, in order to preserve the blessings of religious peace. I was willing to preserve the system which had given us this peace for forty years, for during that time the name and the claims of the dissenters not been heard of. But now they have come forward, and their claims are approved of by a great majority of the House of Commons, and the bill has come up to this house. If it be opposed by the majority of this house, it is to be feared, now that the claims are made, that such an opposition will carry hostility throughout the country, and introduce a degree of rancour into every parish of the kingdom, which I should not wish to be responsible for.

April 17, 1828.

Additional reasons for repealing the Test Act.

I have not called on your lordships to agree to this bill because it has been passed by the House of Commons; I merely assigned that as one of the reasons which induced me to recommend the measure to your Lordships. I certainly did allude to the feeling in favour of the bill which has for some time been growing up in the House of Commons, as a good reason for entertaining it in your

Lordships' house,—but other reasons also operated on my mind. Many individuals of high eminence in the church and who are as much interested as any other persons in the kingdom in the preservation of the Constitution, have expressed themselves as being favourable to an alteration of the law. The religious feelings of those venerable persons disposed them to entertain this measure, because they felt strong objections to the sacramental test. Under these circumstances, wishing to advance and preserve the blessings of religious peace and tranquillity; conceiving the present a good opportunity for securing to the country so inestimable an advantage,—I felt it to be my duty to recommend this measure to your Lordships. It is on all these grounds that I support the bill, and not on the single ground, the circumstance of its having been carried in the House of Commons, as a noble Lord has stated. I am not one of those who consider that the best means of preserving the constitution of this country, is by rigidly adhering to measures which have been called for by particular circumstances, because those measures have been in existence for two hundred years; for the lapse of time might render it proper to modify, if not to remove them altogether.

I admit my Lords, that for about two hundred years, the religious peace of the country has been preserved under these bills; but, when Parliament is discussing the best means of preserving the constitution of the country, it is surely worth while to inquire whether any and what changes, in what have been deemed the securities of the church, can safely be made, so as to conciliate all parties.

All I hope is, that your Lordships will not unnecessarily make any alteration in the measure, that would be likely to give dissatisfaction; that your Lordships will not do anything which may be calculated to remove that conciliating spirit which is now growing up,—a spirit that will redound to the benefit of the country, and which, so far from opposing, we ought, on the contrary, to do everything to foster and promote.

April 21st 1828.

Emancipation.—*Will oppose it, (April 1828,) unless he sees a great change in the government.*

There is no person in this house, whose feelings and sentiments, after long consideration, are more decided than mine are, with respect to the subject of the Roman Catholic claims; and I must say, that until I see a very great change in that question, I certainly shall continue to oppose it.

April 28th, 1828.

State of the Poor in Ireland.

I am thoroughly convinced that no part of his Majesty's dominions so imperiously requires the constant and particular attention of his Majesty's servants as Ireland does. A noble earl has stated that there are in Ireland 8,000,000 of people, the situation of 6,000,000 of whom demands inquiry. He has told your Lordships likewise, that all the wealth of Ireland is not sufficient to give employment to those people. Now, certainly, I cannot but think that this is an exaggerated statement on the part of the noble earl.

It cannot be supposed that there are 6,000,000 of the Irish population who require employment—I cannot admit that the whole of those people are unemployed. It is not true that they suffer this distress at all times,—it is not true that they suffer the same degree of distress in different years; but it is unquestionably true, that they do suffer great distress at various periods, owing to the casualties of the seasons, and to the particular species of food on which they subsist. Such is the plain fact. The noble earl has stated, that the people are able to procure that sort of food on which they chiefly live, at the rate of three-farthings a stone. Now, really, if those people do not suffer distress, except that which is occasioned by the untowardness of the seasons; if those 6,000,000 of people can get provisions at the price mentioned by the noble earl, in favourable seasons,—it does appear to me that the case hardly calls for inquiry, except at a time when their food has failed in consequence of an unproductive season. But then the noble earl has asserted that the distress arises from want of work, and that it would take more than all the wealth of Ireland to procure employment for the people. "Let us then," said the noble earl, "relieve the sick, the lame, the aged, and the impotent." The noble earl has said, that one of the great evils of Ireland is want of capital; but I must beg leave to tell the noble earl, that profusion of capital alone will not prevent the existence of a numerous body of poor, and to prove the fact let the noble earl look to the situation of England. There is no want of capital in this country; the noble earl has told your lordships that there are invested here £9,000,000 of capital belonging to Ireland alone; and yet, with all this capital, the support of the poor required last year amounted to no less than £7,000,000 of rates.

May 21st. 1828.

Catholic Emancipation.

A noble friend of mine has stated to the house, that the proposed measure is inconsistent with the constitution, as established at the revolution; and another noble lord has concurred in that statement. If I had been going to propose a measure which would introduce a predominant Catholic power into Parliament, I should then be doing that which is clearly inconsistent with the constitution. But I am not going to do any such thing. There are degrees of power at least. Will any man venture to say, that Catholic power does not exist at present, either here or in Ireland? I will address myself more particularly to the noble Lords who have so pointedly opposed me, and I will ask them whether Roman Catholic power was not introduced into Ireland by measures of their own? Did not some noble lords exert their influence to the utmost to produce that very power, which has rendered a measure like that which I have announced to Parliament absolutely necessary? As such is the case, I implore noble Lords to look at the situation of the country, and the state of society which it has produced. Whether it has been brought about by the existence of these disabilities, or by the Catholic Association, I will not pretend to say; but this I will say, that no man who has looked at the state of things for the last two years, can proceed longer upon the old system, in the existing condition of Ireland, and of mens' opinions on the subject, both in that country and in this. My opinion is, that it is the wish of the majority of the people, that this question should be settled one way or other. It is upon that principle, and in conformity to that wish, that I and my colleagues have undertaken to bring the adjustment of it under the consideration of Parliament.

February 5, 1829.

Defence of his Conduct with respect to Emancipation.

I have repeatedly declared my earnest wish to see the Roman Catholic question settled. I believe nothing could ever have been more distinct or explicit than my expression of that wish; and is it a matter of surprise that the person entertaining it should avail himself of the first opportunity of proposing the adoption of that which, over and over again, he declared himself anxiously to wish? On this particular question I had long ago made up my mind, as a member of this house, to take a particular course. It may be thought peculiar as a matter of taste; but, for many years, I have acted upon the determination never to vote for the affirmation of this question until the Government, acting as a Government, should propose it to the legislature. My noble relation (Lord Longford) knows, that ever since the year 1810, the several successive Governments of this country have been formed upon a principle which prevented their ever proposing, as a Government, the adoption of any measure of relief in regard to the Catholics. In order to the formation of a cabinet which, acting as a Government, could propose this measure, it was, in the first place, necessary to obtain the consent of that individual, the most interested by his station, his duty, and the most sacred of all obligations, of any individual in the empire. It was necessary, I say, that I should obtain the consent of that individual, before the members of the Government could consider the question as a Government one. Now, under such circumstances as these, would it have been proper in me to have breathed a syllable on the subject, until I had obtained the consent of the illustrious personage to whom I have alluded?[10] I call upon my noble relative to answer this question, if he can, in the negative. I beg of my noble relative to ask himself this question, whether I was wrong in having kept secret my views, since the month of July or August, not talking to any man upon the subject, until I had the consent of that exalted personage, to form a Government upon the principle of taking the question to which I have alluded into consideration? My noble relative ought to place himself in my situation—he ought to see what was expected of me; and then, instead of blaming me for acting as I have done, he would see that, if I had acted otherwise, I should have been highly blameable. When the question had been decided—when I received the permission, so as to be enabled to make the declaration—on not having made which, alone the accusation of surprise can be founded—the opening of the session was so near, that it was impossible to make known what had occurred earlier, or in any other manner than by the speech from the Throne.

[Footnote 10: Lord Longford had accused him of concealment.]

February 10, 1829.

The Emancipation Bill not the result of Fear.

He would positively reject the charge which had been so positively made, that those measures had been suggested to his Majesty's ministers, or that their minds had been at all influenced by the fear of anything that would occur in this or any other country. He totally denied the truth of such an assertion. There never was a period during the last twenty years in which, looking to the circumstances and relations of this country, there was a more total absence of all cause for fear than the present; and whatever might be the consequences of this measure, he would maintain, that the period at which it was introduced, showed sufficiently that its introduction did not proceed from fear; and that such was the fact, he was ready to prove to any man upon the clearest possible evidence. But, though these measures had not been suggested by fear nor by intimidation, it would be found, when they were brought forward, that they were founded upon the clear and decided opinion, that this question ought to be settled, and that considerable sacrifices had been made by himself and his colleagues in this, and in the other House of Parliament, with a view to the final adjustment of it. In doing so, he begged the noble Lord on the cross bench to believe, that not the least considerable or the least disagreeable sacrifice on his part, was the necessity imposed on him of differing from the noble lord on this subject. But he would not talk of his own sacrifices—they were trifling, when compared with the sacrifices which had been made by some of his noble friends near him, and by his right honourable friend in another place. He could not conceive a greater sacrifice than must have been made by his right honourable friend, to bring his mind to the determination of carrying this measure. It was obvious that nothing but an imperious sense of duty had induced his right honourable friend to make such a sacrifice; but the inconveniences and dangers which had arisen from the present state of things in this country and in Ireland, had left no alternative but the adoption of this measure; and now that he had adopted it, he would use his best endeavours, in concert with his colleagues, to carry it into effect. Under such circumstances, he would entreat their lordships to wait until the whole question should have come before them. When the measure should have been well considered by them, they would then see whether it would be attended with

the dangerous consequences ascribed to it—and whether the carrying it would not place the Protestant Constitution of these realms upon a better footing than it had been since the union with Ireland. He would not now enter into the discussion, whether the consequences of this measure would be injurious to that Throne, for the maintenance of which he was ready to sacrifice his life, or whether the measure was likely to produce those effects which were apprehended by his noble friend on the cross bench. Of this he was certain, that the existence of the dangers which some noble lords seemed to apprehend from the adjustment of this question, they were never able to establish; and whenever the discussion of the measure came before their lordships, he would be ready to prove, that the Protestant institutions of this country were exposed to more dangers at present, than they would be exposed to after the adoption of the measure that would be proposed.
February 16, 1829.

Former Associations in Ireland could not be put down.—Mr. Pitt for Emancipation.

He must say, he apprehended from the number of persons in the habit of attending that Association, the nature of the speeches there delivered, and the measures to which all alike appeared parties, that the people of Ireland at large had been parties to the Association.

He proposed the present bill as a preliminary measure; the necessity for which was founded on the statements already made to their Lordships. He considered any other mode of proceeding as inconsistent with the dignity of the Crown, and of Parliament; and as absolutely necessary, in order to reconcile to the ulterior measure which he intended to propose, the good and worthy men in this country, who viewed with dismay and disgust the violent and unconstitutional acts of the Association. He entreated their Lordships to consider, that the eyes of all Europe were upon them; and that they should do nothing which could give any man ground to believe that, in the steps they were about to take, they were guided by any other motive than that of expediency and good policy.

If they looked to the state in which the Roman Catholic question stood in Parliament, from the period of the Union down to the present, they would see the prevalence of a growing opinion in its favour. Mr. Pitt had, in his time, considered it necessary to admit, that the laws enforcing eligibility upon Catholics ought to be reviewed, for the purposes of modification; and, under the repeated assurances of different eminent statesmen, a Roman Catholic influence had undoubtedly grown up in Ireland, which it was high time to satisfy by a reasonable change of policy. For some years after this subject had attracted parliamentary attention, there were reasons of a highly creditable nature, both to individual ministers and to Parliament, why it would have been improper and impolitic to have brought the measure forward as a measure of government; but, since the year 1811, these particular reasons had not been in full operation; and the subject, notwithstanding the divided state of the Cabinet upon it, had been constantly discussed, and during all that time, had been gaining ground. He was not prepared to describe here the mode in which the principle of a divided government had operated upon the Catholic question; but he defied any member of the government, at the period to which he referred, to deny that, whether the question before them was one of education for Ireland, one for the alteration of the Criminal Law, or one for the regulation of tithes, this division was felt to affect one and all of these topics; in fact, that none of them could come to be discussed, without some reference to the great subject which was so long in agitation. The time had, he hoped, now arrived, when Parliament was prepared to settle it.

February 19, 1829.

Unparalleled State of Ireland in 1829.

From all he had seen and read relative to Ireland, during the last two years, he was forced to arrive at this conclusion, namely, that he did not believe there was on the face of the globe any country claiming the denomination of a civilized country, situated as that country now was, under the Government of his Majesty and the Imperial Parliament.

February 19, 1829.

The Roman Catholic Association dangerous.

The true description of this Association was, in his opinion, to be found stated in the speech which had been delivered from the Throne, on the first day of the session. In that speech, after observing that the state of Ireland had been "the object of his Majesty's continued solicitude," it was further observed, "his Majesty laments that in that part of the United Kingdom, an association should still exist which is dangerous to the public peace, and inconsistent with the spirit of the Constitution— which keeps alive disorder and ill-will amongst his Majesty's subjects, and which must, if permitted to continue, effectually obstruct every effort permanently to improve the condition of Ireland." The speech proceeded to say—"His Majesty confidently relies on the wisdom and on the support of his Parliament; and his Majesty feels assured, that you will commit to him such powers as may enable his Majesty to maintain his just authority." Such was a just description of the recent state of the Roman Catholic Association; but he believed he was justified in stating, that in the original institution and formation of the society, on the subject of which it was his duty to address their lordships, there was nothing strictly illegal. The illegality subsequently complained of, and which it was the object of this, as well as of a former bill, to suppress, proceeded from its acts. Those acts consisted principally in levying a tax upon certain of his Majesty's subjects, called Catholic Rent; and this, by means and acts of extreme violence, which occasioned constant heart-burnings and jealousies amongst his Majesty's subjects—by appointing persons to collect the rent—by appointing other individuals to be treasurers of it; farther, by adopting measures for organising the Catholic population—by appointing persons to superintend that organisation—and by assuming to themselves the government of the country, and still more, affecting to assume it. Besides, they expended this rent in a manner contrary to, and utterly inconsistent with, all law and order, and the Constitution of the country. But this was not the least material part of the danger occasioned by the Catholic Association. Part of the money thus improperly obtained was spent for election purposes. And here he called the attention of the noble and learned lord, to acts proving the existence in Parliament of a Roman Catholic influence, and of an influence directly derived from this Association. He would not discuss that subject further at the present moment; but he begged noble lords not to forget it, in discussing the details of a measure which he should have to propose hereafter for their Lordships' adoption. Besides the money spent in elections, there were other sums (also arising out of the rent) spent in endeavours to contravene the due administration of justice in Ireland. When he made this observation, he fully and freely admitted the right, and, indeed, duty of every man, to watch closely and vigilantly the administration of law and justice in this country; but, at the same time, he was prepared to maintain, that that right and duty could not be conveniently and justly exercised by the members of a self-elected Association, having large sums at their command, and employing the money which they possessed for the purpose of exciting a spirit of litigation and dissatisfaction among his Majesty's subjects—employing it for the purpose of defending some individuals—for the purpose of prosecuting others— for the purpose of prejudicing the first inquiries in cases of criminal procedure, and unduly interfering with the administration of justice by the magistracy.

February 10, 1829.

The people were insidiously led to believe that the proposed measures were for the establishment of popery, and the destruction of the protestant establishment of the country; and, acting very properly on this unfounded delusion, petitioned against them. But while he admired and rejoiced in the excellent motives which induced the people of this country, in many places, to protest against the intended measures of government; he hoped that when they saw that those measures were not of the dangerous nature ascribed to them, and that they tended, so far from establishing popery, to check and prevent its growth, and to promote the influence of the protestant religion in Ireland,—he hoped, he said, the people of England would, in their conduct, evince that loyalty to the crown, whence the recommendation of the measure had emanated, and that confidence in the wisdom of parliament, which had ever honourably distinguished them. Indeed, he was convinced, that when the people of England saw there was no fear of the extension of popery from the measure which ministers felt it to be their duty to recommend to their sovereign, but that, on the contrary, they would tend to strengthen the protestant interests of the state, they would hail those measures as beneficial to all classes.[11]

[Footnote 11: This, and the foregoing extracts on the subject of Catholic Emancipation, are from short speeches made by the Duke in the House of Lords after the intentions of the government had been made known, but before the Emancipation Bill came up to that house. Although the Duke earnestly deprecated these preliminary discussions, he was called up almost every night by some peer or other.]

March 2, 1829.

No Compact with Rome would add to the security of the church of Ireland.

I know that there are many in this house, and many in this country, who think—and I am free to admit that I was formerly of the same opinion myself—that the state ought to have some security for the church against the proceedings of the Roman Catholic clergy, besides the oaths imposed on them by the Act of Parliament I confess that on examining into the question, and upon looking more minutely than I had before leisure to do, at the various acts of Parliament by which the church of England is constituted, and which form the foundation on which it rests, I can think of no sort of arrangement capable of being carried into execution in this country which can add to the security of the established church. I beg your Lordships to attend for a moment whilst I explain the situation of the kingdom of Prussia with respect to the Roman Catholic religion. The King of Prussia exercises the power which he does over the Roman Catholic church, in her various dominions, under different concordats made with the Pope: in Silesia, under a concordat made by Buonaparte with the Pope; and in the territories on the right bank of the Rhine, under the concordat made by the former sovereigns of those countries with the Pope. Each of these concordats supposes that the Pope possesses some power in the country, which he is enabled to concede to the sovereign with whom the concordat is made. That is a point which we can never yield to any sovereign whatever. There is no sovereign, be he who he may, who has any power in this country to confer upon his majesty. We must keep our sovereign clear from such transactions. We can, therefore, have no security of that description,—not even a veto, on the appointment of a Roman Catholic bishop, without detracting, in some degree, from the authority and dignity of the sovereign, and without admitting that the Pope has something to concede to his Majesty.

Now let us suppose another security. Suppose it were arranged that his Majesty should have the nomination of the Catholic bishops. If he nominated them, he must also give them a jurisdiction—he must give them a diocese. I should like to know in what part of Ireland or England the king could fix upon a spot where he could, consistently with the oath he has taken, nominate a Catholic bishop, or give him a diocese? The king is sworn to maintain the rights and privileges of the bishops, and of the clergy of this realm, and of the churches committed to their charge. Now, consistently with that oath, how could the king appoint a bishop of the Roman Catholic religion; and would not the Established church lose more than it gained by the assumption of such a power on the part of his Majesty? Then, my Lords, there is another security, which some noble Lords think it desirable to have,—namely, the obtaining, by government, of copies of all correspondence between the Catholic clergy and the Court of Rome; and the supervising of that correspondence, in order to prevent any danger resulting to the Established church. Upon that point I must say I feel the greatest objection to involve the government of this country in such matters. That correspondence, we are told, turns on spiritual affairs. But I will suppose for the sake of argument, that it turns on questions of excommunication. Is it, then, to be suffered, that the Pope, and his Majesty, or his Majesty's secretary of state acting for him, should make law for this country? for that would be the result of communications between the Catholic clergy of this realm and the Pope being submitted to his Majesty's inspection, or to the inspection of his Majesty's secretary of state. Such a security amounts to a breach of the constitution, and it is quite impossible that it could be made available. It would do more injury to the constitution and the church, than any thing which could be done by the Roman Catholics themselves, when placed by this bill in the same situation as dissenters.

With respect to communication with the Court of Rome, that has already been provided against and prevented by laws still in existence. Your Lordships are aware that those laws, like many others regarding the Roman Catholic religion, are not strictly enforced, but still, if they should be abused,—if the conduct of those persons whose actions those laws are intended to regulate should be such as to render necessary the interference of government, the very measure which is now before your lordships will enable government to interfere in such a manner as not only to answer the object of its interference, but also to give satisfaction to this house, and to the country.

April 2, 1829.

Anticipation of success for the Measure. The parallel case of the Scotch Church instanced.

When I recommend this measure to your Lordships attention, you have, undoubtedly, a right to ask what are the reasons I have for believing that it will effect the purpose for which it was intended.

Note—The above extract and those which follow of the same date, are from the Duke's speech in introducing the Catholic Relief Bill.

My Lords, I believe it will answer its object, not only from the example of all Europe, but from the example of what occurred in a part of this kingdom on a former occasion. If I am not mistaken, at the time of the dispute between the Episcopalians and the Kirk of Scotland; the state of society in Scotland was as bad then as the state of society in Ireland is at the present moment. Your

Lordships know that abroad, in other parts of Europe, in consequence of the diffusion of civil privileges to all classes, the difference between Protestant and Catholic is never heard. I am certain I can prove to your Lordships what I stated when I said, that the state of society in Scotland, previous to the concession of civil privileges to the Episcopalians, was as bad as the present state of society in Ireland.

I hope your Lordships will give me leave to read a petition which has been sent to me this day, and which was presented to the Scottish Parliament at the period when those concessions were about to be made, and your Lordships will perceive that the petition is almost a model of many petitions which have been read in this house respecting the question under discussion. I am, therefore, in expectation that should the present bill pass this house, there will be no longer occasion for those complaints which have been expressed to your Lordships, and that the same happy and peaceful state of things which has for the last century prevailed in Scotland will also prevail in Ireland. I will, with your Lordships' permission, read the petition I have alluded to, and I think that after you have heard it, you will be of the same opinion as I am with respect to the similarity it bears to many petitions which have been presented to your Lordships on the Catholic question. The petition states, that "to grant toleration to that party (the Episcopalians) in the present circumstances of the Church, must unavoidably shake the foundation of our present happy constitution; overthrow those laws on which it is settled, grievously disturb that peace and tranquillity which the nation has enjoyed since the late revolution, disgust the minds of his Majesty's best subjects; increase animosity; confirm discord and tumult; weaken and enervate the discipline of the church; open the door to unheard of vices, and to Popery as well as to other errors; propagate and cherish disaffection to the government, and bring the nation under the danger of falling back into those mischiefs and calamities, from which it had lately escaped by the divine blessing. We, therefore, humbly hope, that no concessions will be granted to that party which would be to establish iniquity by law, and bring upon the country manifold calamities and disasters, from which we pray that government may preserve the members of the high court of Parliament."

I sincerely hope, that as the prophecy contained in this petition has not been fulfilled, that a similar prophecy respecting the passing of the present bill, contained in many petitions presented to your Lordships, will not be fulfilled. But, my Lords, I have other grounds besides those which I have already stated for supposing that the proposed measure will answer the object in view. There is no doubt, that after this measure shall be adopted, the Roman Catholics can have no separate interest as a separate sect,—for I am sure that neither this house, nor the other house of parliament, will be disposed to look upon the Roman Catholics, or upon anything that respects Ireland, with any other eye than that with which they regard whatever affects the interests of Scotland, or of this country. For my own part, I will state, that if I am disappointed in the hopes which I entertained that tranquillity will result from this measure, I shall have no scruple in coming down and laying before Parliament the state of the case. I shall act with the same confidence that parliament would support me then, as I have acted in the present case.

April 2, 1829.

Abolition of the Jesuits and other Monastic Orders.

Another part of this bill has for its object, the putting an end to the order of the Jesuits and other monastic orders in this country. If your Lordships will look at the act passed in the year 1791, you will probably see that at that time, as well as in this, it was possible for one person to make laws through which another might drive a coach and four. My noble and learned friend (Lord Eldon) will excuse me for saying, that notwithstanding all the pains which he took to draw up the act of 1791, yet the fact is,—of which there cannot be the smallest doubt,—that large religious establishments have been regularly formed, not only in Ireland, but also in this country. The measure which I now propose for your Lordships adoption will prevent the increase of such establishments, and, without oppression to any individuals, without injury to any body of men, will gradually put an end to those which have already been formed. There is no man more convinced than I am of the absolute necessity of carrying into execution that part of the present measure, which has for its object the extinction of monastic orders in this country. I entertain no doubt whatever, that if that part of the measure be not carried into execution, we shall very soon see this country and Ireland inundated by Jesuits and regular monastic clergy, sent out from other parts of Europe, with means to establish themselves within his Majesty's kingdom.

April 2, 1829.

Rationale of Roman Catholic Exclusion.

My Lords in the Bill of Rights there are some things permanently enacted, which I sincerely hope will be permanent; these are, the liberties of the people, the security for the Protestantism of the person on the throne of these kingdoms, and that he shall not be married to a Papist. There is an oath of allegiance and supremacy to be taken by all those of whom that oath of allegiance is required, which is also said to be permanent; but it contains no declaration against transubstantiation. There is also an oath of allegiance different from that which is to be taken by a member of Parliament. I beg your Lordships will observe, that although this oath of allegiance was declared permanent, it was altered in the last year of King William. This shews what that "permanent" act was. Then, with respect to the oaths to be taken by members of Parliament. I beg your Lordships to observe that these oaths, the declaration against transubstantiation, and the sacrifice of the mass, are not originally in the act of William III., they are in the act of 30th Charles II. During the reign of Charles II. there were certain oaths imposed, first on dissenters from the church of England, by the 12th or 13th Charles II., and to exclude Roman Catholics by the 25th Charles II., and 30th Charles II. At the period of the Revolution, when King William came, he thought proper to extend the basis of his government, and he repealed the oaths affecting the dissenters from the church of England, imposed by the 13th and 14th Charles II. and likewise that affirmative part of the oath of supremacy, which dissenters from the church of England could not take. That is the history of the alteration of these oaths by William III., from the time of Charles II.

But my Lords, the remainder of the oath could be taken by Dissenters, but could not be taken by Roman Catholics. The danger with respect to Roman Catholics, had arisen in the time of Charles II., and still existed in the time of William III.; but the oath was altered because one of the great principles of the Revolution was to limit the exclusion from the benefits of the constitution as far as it was possible. Therefore we have this as one of the principles I before stated, derived from the Bill of Rights. The noble Lords state, that what they call the principles of 1688,—that is to say, these oaths excluding Roman Catholics, are equally permanent with the Bill of Rights by which the Protestantism of the crown is secured. If they will do me the favour to look at the words of the act, they will see that the difference is just the difference between that which is permanent and that which is not permanent. The act says that the Protestantism of the Crown shall last for ever; but, as for these oaths, they are enacted in exclusive words, and there is not one word about how long they shall last. Well then, my Lords, what follows? The next act we have is the act of Union with Scotland; and what does that act say? That the oaths to be taken by the members of Parliament, as laid down by the 1st of William and Mary shall continue and be taken till Parliament shall otherwise direct. This is what is called a permanent act of Parliament, a permanent provision for all future periods, to exclude Catholics from seats in Parliament. My Lords, I beg to observe that, if the act which excludes Roman Catholics from seats in Parliament, is permanent, there is another clause, (I believe the 10th of cap 8. 1st William and Mary) which requires officers of the army and navy to take those very oaths previous to the acceptance of their commissions. Now if the act made in the first year of William and Mary, which excludes Roman Catholics from Parliament, is permanent, I should like to ask noble Lords, why the clause in that act is not equally permanent? I suppose that the noble and learned Lord will answer my question by saying, that one act was permanent and ought to be permanently maintained, but that the other act was not permanent, and the Parliament did right in repealing it in 1817. But the truth of the matter is, that neither act was intended to be permanent; and the Parliament of Queen Anne recognised by the Act of Union that the first act, relating to seats in Parliament, was not permanent; and the noble and learned Lord (Eldon) did right when he consented to the act of 1817, which put an end to the 10th clause of the 1st William III., cap. 8. Then, my Lords, if this principle of exclusion—if this principle of the constitution of 1688, as it is called, be not permanent,—if it be recognised as not permanent, not only by the act of union with Scotland, (in which it was said that the exclusive oath should continue till Parliament otherwise provided,) but also by the late act of Union with Ireland, I would ask your Lordships, whether you are not at liberty now to consider the expediency of doing away with it altogether, in order to relieve the country from the inconveniences to which I have already adverted? I would ask your Lordships, whether you are not called upon to review the state of the representation of Ireland,—whether you are not called upon to see, even supposing that the principle were a permanent one, if it be fit that Parliament should remain, as it has remained for some time, groaning under Popish influence exercised by the Priests over the elections in Ireland. I would ask your Lordships, I repeat, whether it is not right to make an arrangement, which has for its object, not only the settlement of this question, but at the same time to relieve the country from the inconveniences I have mentioned. I have already stated the manner in which the organization I have alluded to, works upon all the great interests of the country; but I wish your Lordships particularly to attend to the manner in which it works upon the church itself. That part of the church of England which exists in Ireland is in a very peculiar situation; it is the church of the minority of the people. At the same time, I believe that a more exemplary, a more pious, or a more learned body of men, than the members of that church do not exist. The members of that church certainly enjoy and deserve the affections of those whom they are sent to instruct, in the same degree as their brethren in England enjoy the affections of the people of this country; and I have no doubt that they would shed the last drop of their blood in defence of the doctrines and discipline of their church. But violence, I apprehend, is likely to affect the interests of that church; and I would put it to the House, whether that church can be better protected from violence by a government united in itself, united with Parliament and united in sentiment with the great body of the people, or by a government disunited in opinion, disunited from Parliament, and by the two houses of Parliament disunited. I am certain that no man can look to the situation of Ireland, without seeing that the interest of the church as well as the interest of every class of persons under government, is involved in such a settlement of this question, as will bring with it strength to the government, and strength to every department of the state.

The bill before the House concedes to Roman Catholics the power of holding any office in the state, excepting a few connected with the administration of the affairs of the church; and it also concedes to them the power of becoming members of Parliament. I believe it goes further, with respect to the concession of offices, than any former measure which has been introduced into the other House of Parliament. I confess that the reasons which induced me to consider it my duty to make such large concessions now, arose out of the effects which I observed following the acts proposed in the years 1782 and 1793. I have seen that any restriction upon concession has only had the effect of increasing the demands of the Roman Catholics, and at the same time giving them fresh power to enforce those demands. I have, therefore, considered it my duty, in making this act of concession, to make it as large as any reasonable man can expect it to be; seeing clearly that any thing which might remain behind would only give ground for fresh demands, and being convinced that the settlement of this question tends to the security of the state, and to the peace and prosperity of the country. I have already stated to your lordships my opinion respecting the expediency of granting seats in Parliament to Roman Catholics; and I do not conceive, that the concession of seats in Parliament, can in any manner effect any question relative to the church of England. In the first place, I beg your Lordships to recollect, that at the time those acts, to which I have before alluded,—the one passed in the 30th of Charles II., and the other at the period of the Revolution, were enacted—it was not the church that was in danger—it was the state. It was the state that was in danger; and from what? Not because the safety of the church was threatened. No; but because the Sovereign on the throne was suspected of Popery, and because the successor to the throne was actually a Papist. Those laws were adopted, because of the existence of a danger which threatened the state, and not of one which threatened the church. On the contrary, at that period danger to the church was apprehended, not from the Roman Catholics, but from the Dissenters from the church of England. I would ask of your Lordships, all of whom have read the history of those times, whether any danger to the church was apprehended from the Roman Catholics? No! Danger to the church was apprehended from the Dissenters, who had become powerful by the privileges granted to them under the act of Parliament passed at the period of the Revolution. I think, therefore, that it is not necessary for me to enter into any justification of myself for having adopted this measure, on account of any danger which might be apprehended from it to the church. Roman Catholics will come into Parliament under this bill, as they went into Parliament previous to the act of 30th Charles II. They sat in Parliament up to that period, and were not obliged to take the oath of supremacy. But by this bill they will be required to take the oath of allegiance, in which a great part of the oath of supremacy is included—namely, that part which refers to the jurisdiction of foreign potentates; and, I must say, that the church, if in danger, is better secured by the bill than it was previous to the 30th of Charles II. The object for which that act was recognised at the period of the Revolution—namely, to keep out the house of Stuart from the throne—has long ceased to exist, by the extinction of that family. It is the opinion of nearly every considerable man in the country (of nearly all those who are competent to form a judgment on the question), that the time has now arrived for repealing these laws. Circumstances have been gradually tending towards their repeal since the extinction of the house of Stuart; and at last the period has come, when it is quite clear that the repeal can be no longer delayed with safety to the state.

April 2, 1829.

State of Ireland, a Reason for Emancipation.

I know that, by some, it has been considered that the state of Ireland has nothing to do with this question—that it is a subject which ought to be left entirely out of our consideration. My Lords, they tell us that Ireland has been disturbed for the last thirty years—that to such disturbance we have been accustomed—and that it does not at all alter the circumstances of the case, as they have hitherto appeared. My Lords, it is perfectly true that Ireland has been disturbed during the long period I have stated, but within the last year or two, there have been circumstances of particular aggravation. Political circumstances have, in a considerable degree, occasioned that aggravation; but, besides this, my Lords, I must say, although I have no positive legal proof of the fact, that I have every reason to believe that there has been a considerable organization of the people for the purpose of mischief. My Lords, this organization is, it appears to me, to be proved, not only by the declarations of those who formed, and who arranged it, but likewise by the effects which it has produced in the election of churchwardens throughout the country; in the circumstances attending the election for the county of Clare, and that preceded and followed that election; in the proceedings of a gentleman who went at the head of a body of men to the north of Ireland; in the simultaneous proceedings of various bodies of men in the south of Ireland, in Templemore, in Kilenaule, Cahir, Clonmel, and other places; in the proceedings of another gentleman in the King's county; and in the recall of the former gentleman from the north of Ireland by the Roman Catholic Association. In all these circumstances it is quite obvious to me, that there was an organization and direction by some superior authority. This organization has certainly produced a state of society in Ireland which we have not heretofore witnessed, and an aggravation of all the evils which before afflicted that unfortunate country.

My Lords, late in the year, a considerable town was attacked, in the middle of the night by a body of people who came from the neighbouring mountains—the town of Augher. They attacked it with arms, and were driven from it with arms by the inhabitants of the town. This is a state of things which I feel your Lordships will admit ought not to exist in a civilized country. Later in the year still, a similar event occurred in Charleville; and, in the course of the last autumn, the Roman Catholic Association deliberated upon the propriety of adopting, and the means of adopting, the measure of ceasing all dealings between Roman Catholics and Protestants. Is it possible to believe supposing these dealings had ceased, supposing this measure had been carried into execution—as I firmly believe it was in the power of those who deliberated upon it to carry it into execution—is it possible to believe that those who would cease those dealings would not likewise have ceased to carry into execution the contracts into which they had entered? Will any man say that people in this situation are not verging towards that state, in which it would be impossible to expect from them that they would be able to perform the duties of jurymen, or to administer justice between man and man, for the protection of the lives and properties of his Majesty's subjects? My Lords, this is the state of society to which I wished to

draw your attention, and for which it is necessary that Parliament should provide a remedy.
April 2, 1829.

Emancipation claimed as the Price of the Union.
I am old enough to remember the rebellion in 1798. I was not employed in Ireland at the time—was employed in another part of his Majesty's dominions; but, my Lords, if I am not mistaken, the Parliament of Ireland, at that time, walked up to my Lord Lieutenant with an unanimous address, beseeching his Excellency to take every means to put down that unnatural rebellion, and promising their full support, in order to carry those measures into execution. The Lord Lieutenant did take measures, and did succeed in putting down that rebellion. Well, my Lords, what happened in the very next session? The Government proposed to put an end to the Parliament, and to form a Legislative Union between the two kingdoms, for the purpose, principally, of proposing this very measure; and, in point of fact, the very first measure that was proposed after this Legislative Union, after those successful endeavours to put down this rebellion, was the very measure with which I am now about to trouble your Lordships. Is it possible noble Lords can believe that, supposing there was a renewal of the contest to which I have referred—is it possible noble Lords can believe that such a contest could be carried on without the consent of the other House of Parliament? I am certain, my Lords, that, when you look at the division of opinion which prevails in both Houses of Parliament; when you look at the division of opinion which prevails in every family of this kingdom, and of Ireland—in every family, I say, from the most eminent in station, down to the lowest in this country;—when you look at the division of opinion that prevails among the Protestants of Ireland on this subject; I am convinced you will see that there would be a vast difference in a contest carried on now, and that which was carried on on former occasions.
April 2, 1829.

No Remedy for the State of Ireland but Emancipation.
Neither the law, nor the means in the possession of Government, enabled Government to put an end to the state of things in Ireland. Therefore, we come to Parliament. Now let us see what chance there was of providing a remedy for this state of things by coming to Parliament. My Lords, we all recollect perfectly well, that the opinion of the majority in another place is, that the remedy for this state of things in Ireland is a repeal of the disabilities affecting his Majesty's Roman Catholic subjects. We might have gone and asked Parliament to enable us to put down the Roman Catholic Association; but what chance had we of prevailing upon Parliament to pass such a bill, without being prepared to come forward and state that we were ready to consider the whole condition of Ireland,

with a view to apply a remedy to that which Parliament had stated to be the cause of the disease? Suppose that Parliament had given us a bill to put down the Roman Catholic Association, would such a law as that be a remedy for the state of things which I have already described to your Lordships as existing in Ireland? Would it do any one thing towards putting an end to the organization, which I have stated to your Lordships exists—towards putting down the mischiefs which are the consequences of that organization—towards giving you the means of getting the better of the state of things existing in Ireland, unless some further measure were adopted? But, my Lords, it is said, if that will not do, let us proceed to blows. What is meant by proceeding to "blows," is civil war. Now, I believe that every Government must be prepared to carry into execution the laws of the country by the force placed at its disposition, not by the military force, unless it should be absolutely necessary, but by the military force in case that should be necessary; and, above all things, oppose resistance to the law, in case the disaffected, or ill-disposed, are inclined to resist the authority, or sentence of the law; but, in this case, as I have already stated to your Lordships, there was no resistance of the law—nay, I will go further, and will say that I am positively certain that this state of things existing in Ireland, for the last year and a half, bordering upon civil war (being attended by nearly all the evils of civil war), might have continued a considerable time longer, to the great injury and disgrace of the country, and, nevertheless, those who managed this state of things—those who were at its head—would have taken care to prevent any resistance to the law, which must have ended, they knew as well as I did, in the only way in which a struggle against the King's Government could end. They knew perfectly well they would have been the first victims of that resistance; but knowing that, and knowing, as I do, that they are sensible, able men, and perfectly aware of the materials upon which they have to work, I have not the smallest doubt that the state of things which I have stated to your Lordships would have continued, and that you would now have had an opportunity of putting it down in the manner some noble Lords imagined. But, my Lords, even if I had been certain of such means of putting it down, I should have considered it my duty to avoid those means.

April 2, 1829.

Would sacrifice his Life to prevent one Month of Civil War.

I am one of those who have, probably, passed a longer period of my life engaged in war than most men, and principally in civil war; and, I must say this, that if I could avoid, by any sacrifice whatever, even one month of civil war in the country to which I was attached, I would sacrifice my life in order to do it. I say, there is nothing which destroys property, eats up prosperity by the roots, and demoralizes the character, to the degree that civil war does; in such a crisis, the hand of man is raised against his neighbour, against his brother, and against his father; servant betrays master, and the whole scene ends in confusion and devastation. Yet, my Lords, this is the resource to which we must have looked—these are the means which we must have applied, in order to have put an end to this state of things, if we had not made the option of bringing forward the measures, for which, I say, I am responsible. But let us look a little further. If civil war is so bad, when it is occasioned by resistance to the Government, if it is so bad in the case I have stated, and so much to be avoided, how much more is it to be avoided, when we are to arm the people, in order that we may conquer one part of them, by exciting the other part against them?

April 2, 1829.

Defence of the Government from the Charge of Inconsistency.

Another subject to which I wish to advert, is a charge brought against several of my colleagues, and also against myself, of a want of consistency in our conduct. My Lords, I admit that many of my colleagues, as well as myself, did on former occasions, vote against a measure of a similar description with this; and my Lords, I must say, that my colleagues and myself felt, when we adopted this measure, that we should be sacrificing ourselves, and our popularity to that which we felt to be our duty to our sovereign and our country.

We knew very well that if we put ourselves at the head of the Protestant cry of "No Popery," we should be much more popular even than those who have excited that very cry against us. But we felt that, in so doing, we should have left on the interests of the country a burden, which must end in bearing them down; and further, that we should deserve the hate and execration of our countrymen. The noble Earl on the cross bench (Winchelsea) has adverted particularly to me, and has mentioned in terms of civility the services which he says I have rendered to the country; but I must tell the noble Earl that be those services what they may, I rendered them through good repute, and through bad repute, and that I was never prevented from rendering them by any cry which was excited against me at the moment. Then, I am accused by a noble and learned friend of mine, (the Earl of Eldon) of having acted with great secresy respecting this measure. Now I beg to tell my noble and learned friend—and I am sorry that, in the course of these discussions, anything has passed which has been unpleasant to my noble and learned friend,—I beg to tell him, I say, that, he has done that to me in the course of this discussion which he complains of others having done to him;—in other words, he has, in the words of a right honourable friend of his and mine, thrown a large paving stone, instead of throwing a small pebble stone. I say, that if my noble and learned friend accuses me of acting with secresy on this question, he does not deal with me altogether fairly. He knows, as well as I do, how the Cabinet was constructed on this question; and I ask him, had I any right to say a single word to any man whatsoever on this measure, until the person most interested in the kingdom upon it had given his consent to my speaking out? I say, that before my noble and learned friend accused me of secresy, and improper secresy too, he ought to have known the precise day upon

which I received the permission of the highest personage in this country; and he ought not to have accused me of improper conduct, until he knew the day on which I had leave to open my mouth upon this measure. There is another point also upon which the noble Earl accused me of misconduct, and that is that I did not at once dissolve the parliament. Now, I must say, that I think noble Lords are mistaken in the notion of the benefits which they think they would derive from a dissolution of parliament at this crisis. I believe that many of them are not aware of the consequences and of the inconveniences of a dissolution of parliament at any time. But when I knew, as I did know, and as I do know, the state of the elective franchise in Ireland in the course of last summer,—when I knew the consequences which a dissolution would produce on the return to the house of commons, to say nothing of the risk which must have occurred at each election,—of collisions that might have led to something little short of civil war,—I say, that knowing all these things, I should have been wanting in duty to my Sovereign, and to my country, if I had advised his Majesty to dissolve his parliament.
April 4, 1829.

No Danger to the Church from the Emancipation Bill.
It has been repeatedly assumed by many of your Lordships in the course of the discussion, but particularly by the right reverend Prelates who have spoken, that the church of Ireland (or, as I have recently been reminded, the church of England in Ireland) is in danger. I call on those who apprehend that danger to state clearly whether that danger, on this particular occasion, is more to be expected as resulting from legislation, or from violence. If they say it is resulting from legislation, I answer that their apprehensions are puerile. It is impossible to suppose that a small number of persons admitted into this house, and a small number admitted into the other house, while we have a Protestant Sovereign upon the throne, should be productive of legislative danger to the church of England in Ireland. I beg to observe, with respect to the point relating to the union of the two countries, that a fundamental article of the union is the junction of the two Churches, called the United Churches of England and Ireland. It is impossible, therefore, that any mischief can occur to the Church of Ireland, without a breach in the union of the two countries. There is another point to which I beg leave to advert for a moment. Although it is true that we do admit into parliament members of the Roman Catholic persuasion, yet, at the same time, by another measure brought forward with it, and on which we equally rely, we propose regulations which will have the effect of destroying the influence of the Catholic priesthood in the election of members of parliament. We have carefully examined the measure, and do expect that it will give additional security to all the interests of the state.
April 4, 1829.

English Soldiers respect the Religion of other Nations.

Although I have served in my profession in several countries, and among foreigners, some of whom professed various forms of the Christian religion, while others did not profess it at all; I never was in one in which it was not the bounden duty of the soldier to pay proper deference and respect to whatever happened to be the religious institutions or ceremonies of the place where he might happen to be. We soldiers do not go into these foreign countries to become parties to the religious differences of the people, or to trouble ourselves with their notions upon matters of faith. We go to perform a very different kind of duty,—one which is purely military, and has no reference to the people's religion. I confess I never heard, however, that it was our custom to take any part in their religious rites, nor do I believe we have taken any such part. Indeed, I have never heard of anything like any co-operation by our soldiers of military parade, except at Malta, where I know it has long been the practice of the garrison to direct some artillery officers to cause a few small guns to be fired, as some particular procession passes the platform. And I know that certain officers of the artillery, or military, three of them, I believe, thought proper on military grounds, and not upon religious scruples, to refuse to fire, according to the usual order of their commandant—for such refusal they were brought to a court-martial, and sentenced to be cashiered, not because they would not form a part of any religious procession to which they were hostile—not because they would not conform to the rites of the natives, and worship any relic that was honoured by them; but for this plain and intelligible reason,—that they had taken upon themselves to refuse obedience to the orders of the commander-in-chief on the spot.

April 8, 1829.

The real meaning of Irish Agitation.

If you glance at the history of Ireland during the last ten years, you will find that agitation really means something just short of rebellion; that, and no other, is the exact meaning of the word. It is to place the country in that state in which its government is utterly impracticable, except by means of an overawing military force.

May 4, 1829.

Theory of a Metallic Currency.

The restoration of the currency, my Lords, has, in truth, but little to do with the distress of the country. Since the restoration of the currency, the revenue has risen to the amount which has been stated to your Lordships, notwithstanding the repeal of taxes to the amount of 27,000,000 l., since 1814. The fact is, that at the present moment, the revenue produces, in real currency, much more than it produced when the war was terminated. Is not that circumstance alone, I ask your Lordships, a proof of the increasing prosperity of the country? But, my Lords, I did not rest my argument on that fact only. Notwithstanding, there is, at present, much distress, still, in the last year, there was an increase of produce in every branch of manufacture, in every branch of industry, beyond what was apparent in the three preceding years. Under these circumstances, your Lordships must ascribe the distress of the country to something else, rather than to the alteration of the currency. My opinion is, that the people, during the lengthened war which existed previously to the peace of 1815—during that period, when there was an enormous expenditure—acquired habits which they cannot readily throw aside. During that time, any man, of whatever description of credit, could obtain money, or the semblance of money, to carry on any speculation. The people then employed a fictitious wealth; they proceeded on a system, which could not be continued, without mining and destroying the country; and that system having been destroyed, that fictitious wealth having been removed, they cannot immediately come down to those quiet habits, which are required from them under that state of things now prevailing in the empire. That, my Lords, is the real cause of the distress under which they are at present suffering. Besides, your Lordships will recollect, that the population of the country has enormously increased; and it should also be taken into the calculation, that the power of production by machinery has increased in an incalculable degree. As much can now be produced in one year, as formerly could be produced in five years; and the produce of one year now amounts to more than can be taken off our hands in a year and a half, or even two years. Distress, therefore, has occurred, notwithstanding that the utmost exertions have been made to repel it; and notwithstanding the great and general prosperity of trade throughout the world. My Lords, the plain fact is, that owing to the alterations of trade—a great demand at one time, and a want of demand at another—the manufacturers, and those engaged in commercial pursuits, must sustain considerable distress at different periods. It has been recommended as a remedy, that Government should go back to the system of the circulation of the notes. Now, my Lords, with respect to the one-pound bank notes—it will be well to recollect what has been the proceeding of Parliament on that subject. In 1826, Parliament having seen the facility with which speculations could be undertaken by persons possessing no capital, in consequence of the circulation of those one-pound bank-notes—looking to the evils that resulted from those speculations, and finding that a great number of banks in the country had failed in consequence of such speculations—thought proper to pass a law to prevent the circulation of this species of paper, after the lapse of three years. A noble Lord has said, that this measure of Parliament occasioned the failure of a great number of country bankers. But, I beg the noble Lord's pardon, he has not stated the fact correctly. Most of the banks which about that period failed, it ought to be recollected, broke previously to the meeting of Parliament. The fact is, that it was the breaking of the banks which occasioned the measure, and not the measure the breaking of the banks. But we have now accomplished the measure adopted in 1826; that measure is now carried into execution; the currency of the country is now sufficient; bank notes, 5l., and above 5l., in value, are in circulation; and I will assert this fact, that there is at present more of what

I may call State currency in circulation—more notes of the Bank of England and sovereigns—a greater quantity of circulating medium of those two denominations, than there has been at any former period before the late war, or before the Bank Restriction Act was passed. I beg leave, my Lords, to ask, what want is there of any additional circulation, when the circulation is at present greater than it ever was? Is it necessary to have a more extended circulation, to afford the means of procuring loans of money to those who have no capital and no credit? I contend that this is a state of things that ought not to exist in any country. Persons who really possess credit, can raise money at the present moment with every facility that is reasonable or proper. But, undoubtedly, those who have no credit, are deprived of the facilities of borrowing money, which they formerly enjoyed, because there is no longer a large class of persons dealing in one-pound notes, to assist them in carrying on their speculations. This is the real state of the case. It was this situation of affairs that gave rise, and justly gave rise, to the measure of 1826—a measure which, I trust, that Parliament will persevere in, for the purpose of placing the country in a proper state. It has been said truly, that nothing is so desirable as to see the country carrying on its mercantile transactions with a paper currency founded on, and supported by, a metallic basis. Now, your Lordships must be aware, that is exactly the sort of currency which the country has got at present; and, in proportion as the country goes on conquering its difficulties—the existence of that currency still being continued—we shall see prosperity daily revive, and we shall see mercantile transactions carried on as they ought to be, without any mixture of those ruinous speculations, to which so much of the prevailing distress must be attributed. But, my Lords, the noble Lord in tracing out the sources of this distress, has omitted one of the great causes of it. He has not adverted to the immense loss of capital which has been sustained by the country during the last six or eight years, in consequence of loans to foreign powers—of which neither principal or interest has been paid, nor ever will, in my opinion, be paid. The noble Lord has not adverted to the effect which that loss of capital must have produced, with respect to the employment of industry in all parts of the country. In the next place, the noble Lord has not adverted to the effect which those loans must have had on the trade and manufactures of the country, in consequence of the glut in foreign markets, occasioned by the forced exportation of goods on account of such transactions. In most instances, my Lords, no returns were made on account of those goods, and even when returns were made, they were of the most unsatisfactory description. The noble Lord has not adverted to the fact, that these returns, when any were received, came home in the shape of interest, and did not, of course, require any demand or export from this country. Surely all these things should be considered, when the noble Lord speaks of the distress the country is labouring under. That distress has fallen not only on the manufacturing and commercial interests, but also on those who have encouraged and embarked in the various schemes and speculations which have done the country so much mischief.

May 26, 1829.

Extended Currency means unlimited creation of Paper Money by Individuals.
   I will now say a few words upon the remedy proposed by the noble Lord (the Earl of Carnarvon), who has totally misunderstood the argument of the noble Viscount (Goderich). My noble Friend stated that the revenue, in 1815, was 80,000,000 l. sterling, in paper currency; that taxes were first of all repealed to the amount of 18,000,000 l., and afterwards to the amount of 9,000,000 l., making in all 27,000.000 l.; and he says that the revenue now produces, in a sound currency, as great an amount as it produced in a depreciated currency; that is to say, that it produces now a sum, in sound currency, which, in paper currency, would amount to 80,000,000 l. sterling. Those persons who consume the articles which produce the revenue, must be able to purchase them, or the revenue could not exist. The increase of the revenue is a proof, then, that consumption has increased full one-third since the time when the taxes were reduced. It is utterly impossible that a country in which, within a period of fifteen years, the revenue has risen one-third, can be suffering universal and unexampled distress. The noble Lord has thought proper to refer the distress to a deficient circulation, and he recommends a system which he thinks would remedy the evil. Now, I will tell the noble Earl that the largest amount of currency in circulation, at any time during the Bank Restriction Act, was 65,000,000 l. sterling. The Bank of England notes were 20,000,000 l.; country bank paper, 23,000,000 l.; gold, 4,000,000 l.; and, silver, 7,000,000 l. But, in 1830, the amount of Bank of England paper in circulation is 19,900,000 l.; and, of country bank paper, 9,200,000 l.; of gold, 28,000,000 l.; and, of silver. 8,000,000 l.; making a total of 65,000,000 l. It is certain, therefore, that there is more money in circulation now, than there was at any period of the Bank restriction. There can be no want, therefore, of more currency. The noble Earl says he wants an extended currency; but what he, in fact, wants, is not an extended currency, but an unlimited currency. He would give an unlimited power to certain individuals, not to the Crown, to coin as much money as they please. The noble Lord wants to give them the power of lending capital to whomsoever they might think proper thus to indulge. That is what the noble Lord recommends, but that is what, I say, cannot be allowed, without bringing the country again to the brink of ruin, from which it was extricated in the year 1826.
   The noble Lord tells you that, heretofore, a farmer, with a good stock, was able to borrow capital to carry on his business; but that now, let his corn-yard be ever so full, he cannot borrow a shilling, because the banker has not the power of giving him one-pound notes. The noble Lord says—the banker gets no interest upon his own capital, and therefore will not lend it. My Lords, the banker who lends his capital to a farmer, or trader, does obtain interest for the use of it, in the shape of discount upon the bill, or other security, which the borrower gives him. The question with him, at present, is one of security, and not of profit. If the banker should lend, under existing circumstances, he must lend his own real capital, and not a fictitious capital in the shape of one pound

notes, created for the purpose. He must be certain that the security given to him is good and available, as it ought to be; and if he is not satisfied with the profits arising from the use of his capital, it is because he thinks the risk is so great as not to be covered by the profits. The noble Lord would wish to pledge your Lordships, by your votes this night, to give the country bankers additional profits, by enabling them to coin money, or to create fictitious paper to any extent, and thus to create a fictitious capital.

February 4, 1830.

Taxes reduced under a Metallic Currency.

In answer to all the declamations we have heard this night respecting the evils resulting from a metallic currency, I beg leave to remind the House of some facts; since the year 1815, and principally since the Bank restriction was taken off, measures have been adopted to relieve the country of taxes to the amount of 27,000,000 l. sterling; and measures have been also adopted which have reduced the charges of the national debt between 3,000,000 l. and 4,000,000 l. a year, that being the interest on nearly 100,000,000 l. sterling. I beg your Lordships will bear this circumstance in mind; and let me tell you, that all the advantages of a so-called equitable adjustment will never equal the advantage already obtained from an adherence to the principles of justice and good faith.

February 4, 1830.

Causes of Manufacturing Distress.

I wish to know whether the competition of machinery and the universal application of steam which has been generally introduced since the peace, have not occasioned a decrease in the demand for labour, and have not lowered the wages of labour in manufactures? Must we not take into consideration the general spirit of manufacture abroad, the competition of foreign nations in foreign markets, and the universal use of machinery worked by steam? How can we control the subjects of foreign powers? We must seek foreign markets for our surplus produce. How can we prevent steam from creating competition abroad in the sale of that produce, as well as a fall in the wages of manufactures, and thus occasioning a part of the distress complained of?

Feb. 4, 1830.

Distress exaggerated.

If the exports of Great Britain have gone on increasing for some years—if they were greater last year than in any former year—if the amount of our exports is now greater than ever it was,—I say, not only that these are the strongest symptoms of the prosperity of the country increasing, but that the distress cannot be so great and unexampled as the noble Earl (Carnarvon) would make it. There is not a rail-road, or a common road, or a canal in the country, on which the traffic has not increased every year during the last few years, and particularly in the last year. It may be true that there is a diminution of profit in commercial transactions in general; but profit there must be, or men would not devote themselves for years to these pursuits. Money would not be laid out in the conveyance from place to place of the produce and manufactures of the country. The traffic being greater than ever it was before, it is impossible but what it must be to the advantage of somebody. The distress then cannot be so universal as represented. The profit and advantage may not be so great as they were some years back; but still advantage there is.

There are other circumstances well worthy the attention of the House in the consideration of this subject. The retail dealers are a very numerous body in this country. Consider of their profits. Look at nearly every market town in the kingdom, and many villages in progress towards being rebuilt. Who pays the money for re-building these houses? Who pays the increased rents for them? Are the people ruined who require and can pay for these new houses? My Lords, these are facts which do shew that, notwithstanding the existing distress which every man must deplore, the country, in spite of the pressure upon it, is upon the whole, rising.

Feb. 4, 1830.

Proofs of National Improvement in 1830.

Among other topics of accusation, I have been arraigned for my assertion on the first day of the session, that the distress of the country was not of that magnitude which some persons have affirmed. The noble Lord (Stanhope) is quite at liberty to indulge in such invectives if it pleases him to do so, but if he supposes I do not feel for the distresses of the people, he is utterly mistaken, as I can sincerely aver that I have as strong sympathies on the subject as any noble member of this house. But I am resolved to tell plainly and honestly what I think, quite regardless of the odium I may incur from those whose prejudices my candour and sincerity may offend. I am here to speak the truth and not to flatter the prejudices and prepossessions of any man. In speaking the truth, I shall utter it in the language that truth itself most naturally suggests.

I request your Lordships to look at the state of the savings banks. A measure was sometime back adopted to prevent the investment of money in these banks beyond a certain amount for each person, in order that the parties not entitled to it should not derive the advantage which is intended for the poorer classes. Large sums were drawn out of those banks soon after; but they have since revived in some degree. Whence has the money come? From the lower classes. This cannot be considered as a proof of general distress. Your Lordships ought likewise not to omit from your consideration the increased traffic carried on the railroads and canals in the country. The noble Earl (Roseberry) has told your Lordships, that I have availed myself of the increased traffic upon the roads and canals by merchants and manufacturers—in despair seeking a market—in order to represent the country in a state of prosperity; whereas it is an additional symptom of distress. My Lords, I said that this traffic had been increasing for years; and that it had, in some cases, doubled in ten years. In one of the recent discussions in this House, upon the currency, the noble Marquis opposite (the Marquis of Lansdowne) very truly remarked,—that a large quantity of currency might be found in a country in which there should be little riches and prosperity; and that the facility and rapidity of the circulation of the currency were signs of the prosperity of a country, rather than the quantity of that currency. I entirely concur in the truth and justice of this observation. But I would beg to ask the noble Marquis whether it is possible that transactions can increase and multiply as they have done in this country, in the last few years, without giving fresh scope for the circulation of the currency of the country, fresh employment for labour, and occasioning, in some degree, the augmentation of general prosperity.

Feb. 25, 1850.

Causes of Manufacturing Distress, over which Parliament can have no Control.

There can be no doubt that there has been, of late years, a great increase of manufactures and manufactured produce in this country. It is true, that this produce has given to the manufacturer but little profit, and that the wages of the manufacturing labourer are low; but, as I will show presently, the circumstance, equally with the cause of the agricultural distress, is beyond legislative control.

My Lords, it is impossible to consider this branch of the subject without adverting likewise to the state of the commerce of the country. The produce of the manufactures of the country is greater than the country can consume; and, consequently, the price and the reward of the labourer must depend upon the foreign demand, as well as upon the demand at home.

In respect to the distress felt by manufacturing labourers, there can be no doubt that the wages of manual labour have been lowered by the successful application of steam to the movement of machinery for the purpose of manufacture. Here, my Lords, is a cause of distress over which the Legislature has no practical control. As I go further in my observations upon the speech of the Noble Earl (Stanhope) who made the motion,[12] I will point out other causes of distress equally beyond the control of the Legislature.

[Footnote 12: For an inquiry into the state of the nation.]

My Lords, let me beg to call to the recollection of the House the state in which the world was at the end of the war in the years 1814 and 1815. Europe was absolutely overrun with armies, and had been so for about twenty years. There was absolutely nothing but armies in the world, and nothing was thought of but the means of sustaining them. Except in France and this country, there were but few manufacturers in Europe; but when the peace took place, all the world became manufacturers. I have already stated, that the country manufacturing more than it consumes, is under the necessity of resorting to foreign countries, and foreign markets with its produce, where this produce necessarily comes in competition with the manufactured produce of foreign countries, brought there by cheaper labour, and by machinery worked by steam. The prices in those foreign countries, of necessity, govern the prices in this country. Here again is a cause of the existing distress, over which it will be admitted, that the Legislature can have no control. Nothing that it is in our power to do, will raise prices abroad; and till these prices shall be raised, the prices of our produce must continue low, and profits and wages must be low likewise.

But, my Lords, low as the prices of our produce are, compared with those of former years, those of other countries have fallen in a still greater proportion. My Lords, I will read, from a paper I hold in my hand, a few extracts of prices in different parts of the country, since the peace of 1814. Raw cotton in England, in 1814 and 1815, sold at 2s. 2d. the pound, or with duty included at 2s. 4d. In 1816 and 1817 it sold at 1s. 8d1/2., and in 1829, at 6d. This was a fall in price greater than had taken place in any other article. Silk, in 1814, sold for 1l. 4s., or with duty included, 1l. 9s.; whilst in 1829 it sold for 8s. 10d., or with the duty, 8s. 11d. the pound. Spanish wool, in 1814, sold for 8s. 2d., or with the duty, at 8s. 3d.; whilst in 1829 it sold for only 2s. 3d., or with the duty at 2s. 4d. Another article, that of fir-timber, fell in proportion. It was then 3l. 14s. 11d. the load, and with the duty, 10l. 5s.; it is now 2l. 5s., and with the duty, 4l. 19s. This fall in the price of foreign produce, and in our domestic manufactures, added to the advantage which the master manufacturers derived from the use of machinery moved by steam, and from the lowness of wages, have given them a greater advantage; and have enabled them to make a profit, notwithstanding the fall of prices of the produce of their manufactures since the war.

On articles of manufacture the prices are still lower than those of corn and other agricultural produce. Cotton yarn, which sold for 4s. 4-1/2d. the pound in 1814, in 1830 sells for 1s. 5-1/2d.; and cotton manufactured goods have altered in price within the same period from 1s. 5d. to 1s. 8d. and 2s. 0-1/2d., to 6-1/4d., 8-3/4d., and 8-1/2d., or nearly a third. Irish linens have fallen from 1s. 7d. to 1s. 0-3/4d.; woollen cloths in the same proportion. Other articles have been reduced enormously in price by the competition with foreigners. In those articles in which there is no competition with foreigners, prices have been reduced, but not in the same proportion; such, for instance, as in the iron, the pottery, and other trades. Here, then, are causes evidently beyond the control of Parliament. Parliament cannot raise the price of manufactured goods—the thing is impossible.

February 25, 1830.
Principle of Reduction in the Public Service.
When offices become vacant, the Government always consider whether the public service could not go on without their being filled up; the next point is, to consider whether the place could not be filled up by some persons who already receive half-pay or pensions, so that the half-pay or pension might be saved to the public. We have tried to reduce the list of pensions of the army and navy, by

keeping men in the service the full time they ought to serve, according to the original institutions of the army. I should deceive the House by saying that savings could be beneficial if made at the expense of individuals who must be thrown on the public as soon as they were made.

February 23, 1830.

The Corn Law of 1828 worked well.

The measure of 1828 has worked well to promote the objects which the Legislature had in view in passing it, by preventing the price of corn from rising so high in a season of scarcity as to be injurious to the country at large, and particularly to that part of the population engaged in manufacture; whilst, both in that season and the season which followed, the price has been sufficient to give the agriculturist a fair value for his commodity. In the second year of the existence of that law, a greater import of corn took place than ever, to the extent of 5,000,000 of quarters, of which 2,500,000 were from Ireland, and the prices have not been lowered in this country, beyond what is deemed a remunerating price to the agriculturists. With reference to another branch of Agriculture, I have means of proving that the prices received for other articles of agricultural produce, such as meat, timber, &c. are equal to what they were in times when the country paid a very large amount of taxes, and the Bank Restriction Act was in force.

Feb. 26, 1830.

I am convinced the corn laws cannot be repealed without injury to the country.

Feb. 25, 1830.

Establishments necessary to maintain the National Honour.

It is perfectly true, that this island is but a small portion of the globe, yet its interests are extended over all the world, and must be maintained, though at a great expense. Now the expense necessary for the maintenance of the honour and interests of this country (and over that alone have we any control), is at present only 12,000,000 l. of money; for there has been a decrease, in the present and last sessions of Parliament of not less than 2,000,000 l. on this part of the expenditure; and your Lordships must know that there are other portions of the national expenditure, which cannot be touched at all. With respect to that part which cannot be touched, his Majesty's Government have effected all that they possibly could. Having said this, I must claim for myself and my colleagues in office, credit for an anxious desire to do everything in our power to diminish the expenditure. With respect to the amount of expenses incurred on account of our

Colonies, I believe that the number of troops in the old colonies and places occupied by a military force previously to 1792, is now reduced lower than it was in that year. This country, however, in the course of the last war, made very considerable conquests; those conquests require for their maintenance large bodies of men, and, consequently, create a great additional expense. They require for their protection very nearly as many troops as the old colonies. Before the war we were not masters of the Cape of Good Hope, of the Mauritius, or of Ceylon. In the Mediterranean, we had no station, unless Gibraltar can be deemed one, which is not the case now. My Lords, it is obvious, that all the new stations which we have acquired, demand a larger force for their protection. These things considered, it appears to me, that the military establishment has been reduced as far as it can be reduced, a proper regard being had to the interests of the empire.

March 4, 1830.

Difficulty of Legislating on the Poor Laws.

It should be recollected that some of the greatest men that ever lived in England—including Mr. Pitt and Mr. Whitbread—attempted to deal with the difficult subject of the poor laws, and failed. It is a subject equally important, difficult, and complicated. The system, as far as local practice and arrangements go, varies in almost every parish of England more or less; and, I repeat, it is almost impossible to deal with it successfully. We ought not to enter into the subject of the poor laws hastily, or at an inopportune period like the present. It will be better to wait till the country is restored to a state of complete prosperity, and then investigate the subject with a proper degree of attention.

March 18, 1830.

The Home Market is the best.

The greatest difficulty is experienced by our manufacturers in exporting their manufactures. In some countries there is a total prohibition of them; in others there is an extremely high duty; and in all there is much competition and jealousy. The Government, in every one of those foreign countries, seems to do everything in its power to prevent the sale of British manufactures. I am convinced, if we went to the Continent, and purchased all the corn in Poland, not an additional article should we be able to force into France, Germany, Prussia, or Russia, If the merchants of this country were allowed freely to purchase grain, foreign subjects would get as much for their corn as they possibly could; but their rulers would not allow a single article of our manufactures to be imported in consequence of our being obliged to buy, or in return for our buying the grain of those countries. There is, undoubtedly, a certain quantity of manufactures in this country more than the population itself can consume, which it would be very desirable to get rid of. But, my Lords, is it exactly true, that taking foreign corn would have the effect of enabling other countries to purchase them? And even if such were the case, what are we to do with our own corn?

Now, my Lords, if the buying corn of the Pole, the Russian, or the Prussian, enable them to give high prices for our manufactures, why do not you give the same advantages to those nearer home? For my own part, I believe, after all, that the home market is our best resource, and that there we dispose of the greatest proportion of our manufactured articles. It has, and I think with truth, been stated, that two-thirds of the whole quantity of our manufactures are disposed of in this country. The whole of our woollen and the whole of our silk manufactures are consumed here; and of iron and other manufactures, a very considerable portion. I ask, then, if such profits are to be derived from an exchange with a foreign market, why do you not cultivate the home, which is admitted to be decidedly the best market of all. I think the more this matter is discussed, the more will the country see that the interests of one class of the community involve the interests of all. We are not to look merely to the interests of the cotton manufacturers, or of the iron manufacturers. That which we are bound to consider is the benefit of all; and, in my opinion, the common good will be most effectually secured, by getting the greatest quantity of provisions for the whole community,—by giving a proper remuneration to those who produce such provisions,—and thus encouraging them to do that which is most beneficial to the community at large.

March 29, 1830.

How far the principle of Equitable Adjustment should be carried.

The noble Lord (Viscount Goderich), speaking with his usual candour on the subject of the equitable adjustment, admitted the existence of an increase of price during some years of the war generally, and consequently of public expense and of debt, to the amount of 20 per cent, in consequence of the depreciation of the currency; and he has made a calculation of a supposed equitable adjustment, founded upon his estimate of the expense of the war for some years, and of the debt created by the excess of price. It is true that there was a very large increase of prices in England during the war; that this increase of prices increased the expense of the war; and the amount of debt successively raised. But it is not true that the excess of prices was occasioned solely by the paper currency. Many other circumstances occasioned it; and in my opinion, my noble friend has admitted too much in admitting that the annual payment on account of the debt has been increased to the amount of 3,500,000 l. in consequence of the paper money circulated during the war.

Having frequently heard of an equitable adjustment, which, however, is absolutely impracticable as a measure to be applied solely to the national creditor, it has always appeared to me, that such an arrangement could be calculated only on the foundation of the difference between the currency, or the market price of gold, and the mint price of gold, at the period at which the Bank restriction was repealed, or in the year 1812. That difference was at that period about 4 per cent; or the difference between 3l. 17s. 10-1/2d., and 4l. 1s. The annual payment on account of the debt at that time, amounted to about 30,000,000 l. sterling; upon which what is called an equitable adjustment might, at that time, have been made to the amount of 5 per cent., or 1,200,000 l. In making this supposed equitable adjustment, we should have betrayed the honour of the country; we should have destroyed its credit and reputation for fair dealing, justice, and honesty; and, for this paltry diminution of the annual expense of the debt in 1819, we should have lost the advantages since acquired, as detailed to the House by my noble friend, amounting to a diminution of the annual charge of the debt, not of 1,200,000 l., but nearly of 5,500,000 l. or the interest of 150,000,000 l. of capital at 3 per cent. This is a fair calculation of the comparative advantage of what has been done, and what might have been done, by a supposed equitable adjustment.

May 6th, 1830.

The Shipping Interest has not been Neglected.

These reciprocity treaties were adopted with a view to decrease the price of freight in this country to our merchants, and with a view to their taking in abroad, and bringing home, their commodities at a cheaper cost of transit. These treaties were, my Lords, framed with a foresight of the state of commerce which was likely to ensue in the world in future times which were then immediately before us. We were, therefore, to diminish the expense of shipping to meet the new contingencies; and to enable those engaged in commerce to carry on their trade under all the difficulties of a new situation; and the object of those laws was to lower the price of commodities for that purpose. What was the result?— profits upon specific articles became reduced; but since the year 1814 the trade in them has nearly doubled. What the shipping interest then lost in the reduced amount of freight per tonnage, they regained in the greater number of voyages which commerce opened to them.

May 13th, 1830.

Eulogium on George IV.

My lords, our late Sovereign received the best education which this country affords. He had, also, the singular advantage of having passed all the earlier period of his life, and the greater part of his manhood, under the superintendence of the King, his father, and subsequently in the society of the most eminent men whom this country possessed; and he likewise enjoyed the society of the most distinguished foreigners who resorted to this country. His Majesty's manners accordingly received a polish, his understanding acquired a degree of cultivation, almost unknown in any other individual. My Lords, he carried those advantages to the Government to which he was afterwards called, first as a Regent, and afterwards as reigning sovereign. During the whole course of his government no man ever approached him without having evidence of his dignity, his condescension, his affability, and his fitness for the exalted station which he occupied. But these advantages, which shewed so conspicuously the polish of manner which he possessed, were not only observed by persons immediately around him, for I appeal to many of your Lordships who have transacted the business of the country which required an interview with the sovereign, whether his Majesty did not upon every occasion display a degree of knowledge and talent not to be expected of an individual holding his high station, and a profound acquaintance with public business even in its most minute details. But this is not all, he was a most munificent patron of the arts in this country and the whole world. He possessed a larger collection of the eminent productions of his own country's artists, than any individual, and it is as an individual, of him I here speak. The taste and judgment he displayed in these collections have never been excelled by any sovereign.

I would also beg to call to your Lordships' recollection the situation in which he found England and Europe in the year 1810, when he became Regent, and the situation in which he has left Europe and this country. If your Lordships look upon the great and stirring events of his reign, under what circumstances it commenced and terminated, I think you will agree with me in the sentiment, that we have reason to feel proud of such a sovereign.

June 29th, 1830

Principle of advances of Money for Public Works.

A noble Lord has cited an opinion of mine with respect to the advance of money for public works; to the principle laid down in the letter to which he alludes, I still adhere,—that no money should be advanced as a grant, for works of that description, even though they may be very useful; but, my Lords, I repeat, that there is a great distinction between on advance of money and a loan. The application of the proprietors of the Thames Tunnel, was for an advance of money, and not a loan; the parties, there, were not in a condition to pay the interest even of the money to be advanced, and therefore the application was refused, but my Lords, in the present case the money is advanced on the security of the tolls payable on a canal; yet even on that ground it would not be advanced, unless it were shown that the work will be of advantage not only to the province, but to the empire at large.

July 2nd, 1830

Declaration against Parliamentary Reform.

I now come to another point touched upon in his Majesty's speech, from which, as well as the allusions to it to-night, I have experienced considerable pain; I allude to the state of the public mind in Kent. Upon this point I cannot help agreeing in what fell from the noble Marquis, (Camden) the Lord Lieutenant of that county, who spoke early in the evening, namely,—that it is not to be exactly attributed to the distress prevailing there. It certainly does appear, from all I have heard, that the outrages are carried on by two different sets of people; one of which attack machinery, which they think interferes with their labour; and the other of which are engaged in burning and destroying property. What the immediate cause of these disturbances is, the government know no more than the magistrates and gentlemen of the county. We shall do all in our power in concert with these magistrates, and the Lord Lieutenant, to discover it; and, in the mean time, we shall afford them aid to put the law in force in order to prevent them.

This brings me to the recommendation which the noble Earl (Grey) has made, not only to put down these disturbances, but to put the country in a state to meet and overcome the dangers which are likely to result from the late transactions in France, namely,—the adoption of something in the nature of parliamentary reform. The noble Earl has stated that he is not prepared, himself, to come forward with any measure of the kind; and I will tell him that neither is the government. Nay, I will go farther, and say, that I have not heard of any measure, up to this moment, which could in any degree satisfy my mind, or by which the state of the representation could be improved or placed on a footing more satisfactory to the people of this country than it now is.

I will not now enter upon the discussion of this subject, as I dare say we shall have plenty of opportunities for doing so; but I will say, that I am thoroughly convinced that England possesses, at this moment, a legislature which answers all the good purposes of a legislature, in a higher degree than any scheme of government that ever has been found to answer in any country in the world;—that it possesses the confidence of the country—that it deservedly possesses that confidence—and that its decisions have justly the greatest weight and influence with the people. Nay, my Lords, I will go yet farther and say, that if, at this moment, I had to form a legislature for any country, particularly for one like this, in possession of great property of various descriptions, although, perhaps, I should not form one precisely such as we have, I would endeavour to produce something which would give the same results—namely, a representation of the people, containing a large body of the property of the country, and in which the great landed proprietors have a preponderating influence.

In conclusion I beg to state, that not only is the government not prepared to bring forward any measure of this description, but that as far as I am concerned, whilst I have the honour to hold the situation I now do amongst his Majesty's councillors, I shall always feel it my duty to oppose any such measures when brought forward by others.

November 2, 1830.

Irish Absenteeism deprecated.

I can assure your Lordships that there is not any man, either there or here, who is more aware of the poverty of Ireland, and the dangers to the empire from the state of the lower orders, than he who has now the honour of addressing you. But I would have noble Lords to observe that it is not by coming here to talk of the poverty of that country that we can remove it. If noble Lords will endeavour to tranquilize the country, and persuade those who have the means to buy estates and settle there; by holding out to them a picture of industry and tranquility with its other advantages, they will soon find the country change its aspect, and complaints of the dangers arising from its poverty will no longer be heard. The influence of the presence and fortunes of the proprietors of land in Ireland spent in that country, would do more to serve it than any legislative enactment parliament have it in their power to pass.

November 2, 1830.

Repeal averted by Emancipation.

The repeal of the union is opposed by the noble Duke opposite (the Duke of Leinster) and all his friends in Ireland: it is opposed by all the proprietors in Ireland, by the great majority of the Roman Catholics, by nearly all the Protestants of Ireland, and with one exception by the unanimous voice of the other House of Parliament.

Such is the present state of this question, but how would it have stood had not that other to which he alluded been carried two years ago? And how did that one then stand? Why, the noble Duke and all his friends, and a large proportion of the Irish people, were anxious that that question should be carried. Such, also, do we know to a certainty was the desire of the majority of the other House of Parliament, whilst at the same time there was in this House a minority in its favour, daily acquiring greater strength; and at present, I presume, no one will deny that a large body of the best informed people of this country were also decidedly for conceding this point. We do not now stand on worse ground on the question of the repeal of the union than we should have done had not the Catholic question been carried. I do not see the advantage, therefore, of repeating reproaches against me for having given way on that occasion from fear. I gave way because I conceived the interests of the country would be best answered by doing so; I gave way on the grounds of policy and expediency, and upon those grounds I am at this moment ready to justify what I did. The noble Lord must forgive me for saying that the state of irritation which has continued to exist in Ireland since that question was carried must not be attributed to the King's Ministers: they have done every thing in their power to conciliate, and heal the divisions which distracted that country for so many years previously to the settlement of that question. It is not my duty, any more than my inclination, to cast imputation on any man; but this I will say, that if the King's Ministers had been supported as strongly as they have been opposed in their endeavours to heal those divisions, Ireland would have been in a very different state from what it now is.

November 2, 1830.

Magistrates should be appointed by Lords Lieutenant.

Lords Lieutenant of counties are generally chosen in consequence of their possessing large properties, and from their weight and consideration in the counties over which they preside. They must, therefore, be the most highly interested in selecting proper persons, and a proper number of persons, whom they know will do their duty well as magistrates.

In choosing magistrates, in my opinion, it is essentially necessary that local knowledge should operate. Before any man should venture to recommend another to be appointed to the commission, he should have knowledge of his character, and of other circumstances, which can only be discerned by local knowledge.

Nov. 29, 1830.

The Agrarian Outrages of 1830.

It appears to me that the outrages which have taken place in the country are of two descriptions—the first is that open description of outrage, which there is no doubt, may be got the better of by the operation of the ordinary process of law; the second is that description of crime—the destruction of property by fire,—of the perpetrators of which Government have not hitherto been able to discover any trace whatever. I do not know what information the Noble Earl may have received on the subject within the last week, but up to that period we had discovered no traces whatever of these incendiaries.

It is supposed by some noble Lords, that the perpetrators of the second description of crime—the destruction of property by fire—are foreigners, and that they are following the example set in another country. I believe, however, there is no evidence whatever that foreigners have been engaged in the perpetration of those crimes. It is certain that they have been effected by a conspiracy of some kind or other; but whether the conspirators are foreigners or Englishmen, I believe that no man can at this moment possibly say. As to foreigners being in gaols, I can only say, that with reference to one county—the county of Hants—in which outrages of the most flagrant kind have occurred, there is not one foreigner among the persons with whom Winchester gaol is filled.

Nov. 29, 1830.

Our Portuguese Relations affected by the State of Ireland.

In reference to Ireland, it is of great importance that we should be on good terms with Portugal. Unfortunately, the great measure which I had the honour to prepare three years ago, has not answered so as to produce—I will not say all the advantages I expected from it, as I was never sanguine in my expectations, but the amount of advantage which some of your Lordships and part of the public expected. To use a vulgar expression, a new hare has started, and we must probably look to a length of time ere the agitation excited in Ireland by the new question shall have subsided. Now, I want to know, whether Portugal will not be as important to us during the agitation of that question as it has been previously? Will not our reception in the Tagus, and friendly occupation of it, be as important to England now, as it has been heretofore? I do not now wish to discuss the claims of Don Miguel and Donna Maria—this is not the occasion for it—I only mean to convey my decided opinion, that the friendship of Portugal is necessary to this country. If we deprive Portugal of the advantages of this wine trade for a revenue of 100,000 l., putting political economy and commerce out of the question, we shall make the greatest political blunder that has been seen for a long time past.

Feb. 21, 1831.

How is the Government to be carried on after the Reform Bill?

With respect to another subject (Reform) which must occasion discussion, I quite agree in the determination which has been adopted of postponing all discussions upon it till a future period; but when that period shall arrive, I hope that his Majesty's ministers, who, upon their own responsibility, have brought the question under discussion, will be so kind as to explain to the House in what manner, and by what influence, they propose that the Government of this country—the Monarchical Government of this country—shall be carried on, according to the principles and practice established at the Revolution.

March 3, 1831.

The Downfall of the Constitution predicted as the Consequence of the Reform Bill.

It is far from my wish to impute to the noble Earl (Grey) or his colleagues any desire to introduce revolutionary measures into Parliament; but, I must say this, that having looked at the measure which has been brought into the other House of Parliament under their auspices, I cannot but consider that it alters every interest existing in the country,—that in consequence of its operation, no interest will remain on the footing on which it now stands, and that this alteration must lead to a total alteration of men—of men intrusted with the confidence of Parliament. I am of opinion that this alteration must have a serious effect on the public interests,—an effect which, I confess, I cannot look at without the most serious apprehension. I do not charge the noble Earl and his colleagues with a desire to overturn the institutions of the country, but I cannot look at the alterations proposed by the bill without seeing that those alterations must be followed by a total change of men, and likewise by a total change of the whole system of Government. Why, I ask—for what reason—is all this to be done? I will not now enter into the question of what is the opinion of the other House of Parliament—but I will say again, as I have said before, in the presence of your Lordships, that I see no reason whatever for altering the constitution of Parliament.

It is my opinion that parliament has well served the country, and that it deserves the thanks of the country for a variety of measures which it has proposed, particularly of late years. I see no reason for the measure now proposed, except that stated by the noble Earl—namely, his desire to gratify certain individuals in the country. It is possible that a large number, nay, even a majority of individuals, in this country may be desirous of this change, but I see no reason, excepting that, for this measure being introduced or adopted.

Whilst I thus declare my sentiments, I beg your Lordships to believe that I feel no interest in this question, excepting that which I have in common with every individual in the country. I possess no influence or interest of the description which will be betrayed by the measure now proposed. I am an individual who has served his Majesty for now, I am sorry to say, nearly half a century; I have been in his Majesty's service for forty-five years—for thirty eventful years of that period I have served his Majesty in situations of trust and confidence, in the command of his armies, in embassies, and in his councils; and the experience which I have acquired in the situations in which I have served his Majesty, enables me, and imposes upon me the duty, to say, that I cannot look at this measure without the most serious apprehensions, that from the period of its adoption, we shall date the downfall of the constitution.

March 24, 1831.

Under the Reformed System, how is the King's Government to be carried on?

I have, myself, examined the bill, with reference to its effects on the county of Southampton. In that county there are several towns—Winchester, Christchurch, Portsmouth, Southampton, and the borough of Lymington. Several boroughs in that county are struck out of the representation by the bill, and there are, besides, a vast number of considerable towns left unrepresented, but the voters of these places are to come into the county constituency. According to the old system, the voters of the towns had votes for the county; now, copyholders and 50l. householders are to vote for the county. In the towns, these two classes are, for the most part, shopkeepers.

I am convinced that there are no less than 4000 or 5000 such inhabitants of towns in Hampshire, who will have votes for the county, as well as the freeholders. Now, of whom does this class of electors consist? As I before stated, they are shopkeepers—respectable shopkeepers—in the towns. I beg to ask, are they fit persons to be the only electors to return county members to a Parliament, which Parliament is to govern the affairs of this great nation, consisting of 100,000,000 of subjects, and so many various relations, foreign, domestic, colonial, commercial, and manufacturing? Men of the description I have mentioned, with their prejudices and peculiar interests, however respectable as a body, cannot be fit to be the only electors of members of the House of Commons. But, I beg to say that, however respectable this, or any other class of electors may be, there is a strong reason against any uniformity of system in the representation of the country. I have heard already of the establishment, in this town, of a committee formed for the purpose of recommending candidates for the representation to the different towns throughout the country. I confess, I do not believe that this committee has been established more than a few days; but I beg to say that, taking into consideration the means of combinations, and the facilities of communications in the country, such a body is dangerous. I know that such committees, in other countries, have been found to be effectual in putting down the Government. And I ask whether you should allow such a uniform system of election—it matters not in whose hands it is placed—that a committee, sitting in London, shall have the power to dictate what members shall be returned for Leeds, or for Manchester, for instance? I wish to know what security noble Lords have for their seats in this House, if such a committee as this should exist at the first general election of a reformed Parliament? But, my Lords, these are not all the objections which I entertain to this measure; I have others, founded upon facts, which I know to have existed in other countries. I was in France when the law of election was passed, in the year 1817; and this circumstance deserves your Lordships' attention, because the situation of the two countries is not dissimilar. At that period there were, in each department 300 persons, who, paying the highest amount of taxes, were chosen to manage the representation. The King and Government altered this, and gave the power of choosing representatives to persons paying taxes to the amount of 300 francs. Two years afterwards, they were obliged to alter the law again, and form two classes of electors. Since then, there have been two general elections, one more unfavourable than the other to the Government; and the matter ended in the formation of a Parliament, the spirit of which rendered it impossible for a Government to act.

My Lords, I do not mean here to justify the Government of Charles X.; and I trust the noble and learned Lord (Lord Brougham) will allow me, on this occasion, to declare that I never wrote to Prince Polignac in my life (much as I have been accused of encouraging the proceedings of that person), and I have never written to Charles X. from the time that monarch lost his son, and his grandson was born. In fact, I have never corresponded with any French minister without the knowledge of my colleagues. The noble and learned Lord on the woolsack may rely on it, that I had no more knowledge of Prince Polignac's proceedings, than the noble and learned Lord himself; or, most probably, still less. I am not the apologist of Prince Polignac; but, I say, that things had been brought to that state in France, that it was impossible but there should be a revolution.

When I see a similar mode of election established in this country—when I see the adoption of a uniform system of election—when I see the election placed in the hands of shopkeepers in boroughs all over the country—I think that we incur considerable danger, and put the country in such a situation as that no minister can be certain that any one measure which he brings forward will succeed, or that he will he enabled to carry on the Government. The circumstances of France and England are, in many particulars, alike, and we ought to take warning by the dangers of the neighbouring country.

I wish the House to advert to what the business of the King's Government in Parliament is. It is the duty of that Government to manage everything. I heard the noble and learned Lord on the Woolsack, in a speech of admirable eloquence and knowledge, propose a new judicial system at the commencement of the Session; but I tell him, that it is impossible for the Government ultimately to decide on that question; and that if a Parliament be constructed on the new plan, it will be too strong for Government on that question. So, also, in matters affecting commerce and manufactures, Government would depend entirely upon Parliament.

I want to hear how Government is to carry any measure, on the appointment of a new Parliament? There is a great question now before the House of Commons on the subject of tithes. How is any Government to meet that question? A Government may submit to the will of a majority opposed to its own view on other questions, but on the question of tithes and the Church, the duty of any Government is clearly pointed out—the King's Coronation Oath, and the Acts of Union with Scotland and Ireland, guaranteeing the integrity of the Church Establishment, and the protection of the estates and prosperity of the Church. But I want to know how Government is to maintain the safety of the Established Church, after placing Parliament on the footing proposed. I really do not wish to carry this argument farther than it will go; but, looking round, and considering the operation of the proposed measure in towns, as well as in counties, and forming the best judgment I can on affairs so complicated, I must infer, from every thing I see, that the Constitution of the country cannot be carried on as hitherto, if this plan be adopted. In such an event, you would alter your whole system of Government. I do not say the Crown cannot last. You may still permit the King's interference in the management of the army, the navy, and the ordnance; and the rest of the Government may he carried on by the House of Commons. Things may go on under such a system; but this will not be the British Constitution. It will not be the same England, which has been, for so many centuries, prosperous and glorious under our present Constitution.

March 28, 1831.

The Unreformed House a complete Legislative Body.

As to the present House of Commons, I maintain that it is as complete a legislative body as can be required; and that the House of Commons, since the peace particularly, has shown itself to be the most efficient legislative body that ever existed in any country in the world, not excepting this. I say, that it has rendered more services than any Legislature ever did in the same period—I say, it has continued those great services up to the present moment, and that those services have only been interrupted by the introduction of this discussion upon the Reform Bill.

March 28, 1831.

Reasons why the Duke resigned Office in November, 1830.

It is quite true, that when the late Government brought forward the Catholic question, they were supported by many noble Lords who were usually opposed to the Government; but it is not correct that the disfranchisement of the forty-shilling freeholders was made a *sine qua non* to ensure the support of the noble Lords to the Relief Bill. I certainly had the misfortune, on that occasion, to lose the support and regard of a great number of friends, both here and in the other House of Parliament—a misfortune I have never ceased to lament; yet I have the consolation of knowing, that in what I then did, I did no more than what my duty required of me; and I was not justified in relinquishing that measure by any intimidation, or by any imaginary circumstance of danger—which I had no right to apprehend. But I own that things were going on in Ireland which induced me to think they might lead to a civil war, in the event of our continuing to refuse the settlement of the question; and I am satisfied that I should have been wanting in duty, both as a man and a Minister, if I had hesitated to give up those opinions which I had previously entertained with regard to that measure. I afterwards had some difference with a noble Earl opposite (Earl Grey), but notwithstanding I felt called upon to retain the position I held in the Government as long as I enjoyed the approbation of my Sovereign, and the confidence of the Legislature.

Then came the Revolution in France, followed by that of Belgium; and like the former revolutions of Naples and of Spain, they naturally excited a strong sensation here; that excitement, increased by speeches made in various parts of the country, created a strong desire for Parliamentary Reform. But I did not think then, any more than I think now, that that desire was irresistible. If Parliament should see reason to decide that the proposed alteration in the Constitution is not necessary, and ought not to be made, I am confident the country will acquiesce in that decision. I believe that the wish for reform is strong and growing; but if the people see that the subject is fairly discussed, and honestly determined here, I am sure they will submit without a murmur. Already the sensation produced by the French and Belgian Revolutions has subsided; the natives of the country have seen the deplorable results by which those commotions have been followed, and are wisely warned by the sufferings of their neighbours.

Upon the defeat on the Civil List, finding I had the misfortune no longer to enjoy the confidence of the House of Commons, I thought proper to resign the situation which I held in his Majesty's service. Upon that occasion, the question of Parliamentary Reform had no more to do, as far as I was concerned, with the resignation which I tendered to his Majesty on the day following the defeat on the Civil List, than anything else in the world. I admit I resigned next morning, because I did not wish to expose his Majesty and the country to the consequences that might result from the Government going out on the success of the question of Parliamentary Reform. This is the truth; but, to say I resigned on account of Parliamentary Reform, is wrong; I resigned upon the ground before stated; and I resigned at that particular moment on the Tuesday, because I did not choose to expose his Majesty and the country to the consequences that might ensue from the occurrence of the case just mentioned. This is the real fact of the story. But the noble and learned Lord has said, that the late Ministry gave up the principle of Parliamentary Reform by their resignation; no such thing— we resigned because we did not possess the confidence of the House of Commons, and we thought that the same majority which defeated us on Monday on the Civil List, might defeat us Tuesday on Reform; and then we should have sacrificed (as the noble Lord says), the principle of Parliamentary Reform in the Commons. We did not think it worth while to make any farther struggle in order to retain office a day or two longer.

March 28, 1831.

The Civil List principle, on what arranged.

My Lords, the principle on which I and my colleagues drew up the Civil List, was always directed to enable the Sovereign, so far as was practicable, to defray all the expenses necessary to be incurred in supporting the dignity, splendour, and comforts of the Crown, without mixing them up with the other expenses of the Government. For this purpose, it was formerly the practice to grant a considerable sum for those various, but necessary expenses. Certainly, the Crown enjoyed great advantage in supporting its dignity, influence, and efficiency, as long as the system of supporting itself on its hereditary revenues remained in practice. That system, my Lords, was departed from at the commencement of the reign of Geo. III.; and a further departure from it has since taken place, into which I shall, with your Lordships' permission, examine presently, and compare that departure with those proposed by the late Government. From the accounts I have seen of the hereditary revenues enjoyed by Geo. II., I have reason to believe that were they now enjoyed by our Sovereign, and employed in defraying the civil expenses of the Government, and sustaining the dignity and splendour of the Crown, they would amount to a sum larger than would be necessary to meet those expenses, notwithstanding the increase which has been made in them by the increased salaries of the judges, the increased number of the public officers, and the vast increase of the royal family of England. I say, my Lords, that these hereditary revenues would be more than adequate to defray all these charges. I believe that these revenues, independent of droits and West Indian duties, amount, at the present moment, to 850,000 l. a-year; and these revenues, my Lords, I consider as much the King's property, as I hold the possessions of your Lordships to be yours. I make this statement, because it is important that your Lordships should recollect it, and the public should know that notwithstanding the magnitude of the expenses of the Sovereign, the Sovereign has as much right to the sum which I have mentioned, as any of your Lordships to your own estates. The system of giving the Sovereign the amount of certain taxes to defray the expenses of the civil government, was first departed from at the commencement of the reign of Geo. III., when a fixed sum was appointed, instead of that mode of payment, for its support. In process of time the expenses of the civil government increased, and the Civil List became a debt. The consequence was, that in the year 1815, an inquiry was instituted into the circumstances which had caused this increase of charges upon the Civil List, up to the period of the Regency. What was the course then adopted by Parliament? Why, it was to bring certain charges—as, for instance, the charges for ambassadors and ministers abroad—under the annual vote of Parliament; and the immediate object was to avoid thereby the fixing of any fresh debt, for which no estimate could be previously made, upon the Civil List. In 1820 it was determined that nothing whatever should be brought before Parliament, in connexion with the Civil List, that was a casual expense, or for which a regular vote could not be submitted.

The original system, I have already stated, had been departed from in the reign of George III., and the late Government in presenting their civil list made a still further departure from it, and upon this principle;—wherever a part of a salary was to be paid out of the civil list, and part out of the consolidated fund, it was resolved to pay all out of the consolidated fund. The course was adopted with regard to the salaries of the Judges, the Lord Chancellor, and the Speaker of the House of Commons, and also of various other offices, some of which have been since abolished. This was thought a less objectionable mode than that of subjecting those salaries to an annual discussion in the Committee of the House of Commons. We wished my Lords to place those salaries upon the consolidated fund, in order to prevent the possibility of the country being left without a proper and efficient administration of public affairs. We did not wish to leave the Government to the chance of being impeded by a small majority, in the House of Commons, which, according to other proposed plans, might diminish the salaries of public officers at pleasure. If my Lord we look to the period of the Revolution we shall find that there were long discussions respecting the right of the crown to its hereditary revenues, which ended in a concession of the principle that these revenues did belong to the crown. At that time nobody ever dreamed of separating the expenses of the crown from those of the civil government, and of making a separate provision for the support of the state and dignity of the crown, which should be subject to the controul of parliament. The plan of separation, my Lords, is one of modern invention altogether, and I totally dissent from it. Because, let us look to the situation in which the crown is placed under the operation of such a system, and we must observe that it will place the crown in a situation such as it ought not to be reduced to; namely that it will render it liable to be deprived of the assistance—

say of a public officer, whose salary may be lost by a single vote in a committee of supply.

April, 19th, 1831.

The Expenses of Ministers ruinous, unless they have large Private fortunes.

With respect to the reduction in the salaries of the great officers of state, I have only to observe, that even under the existing rate of salaries, unless a First Lord of the Treasury, (and the remark will apply to the other state officers) possesses a large private fortune, he must be ruined in consequence of the heavy expences entailed on him by his situation, and the inadequacy of the sum allowed by the public for the maintenance of those expenses. In proof of this, I may instance the case of three prime ministers—Mr. Pitt, Mr. Percival, and Mr. Canning,—all of whom were almost ruined by their being in office. I took upon myself to propose a provision for the family of Mr. Canning in consequence.

April, 19th. 1831.

The Roman Catholic Relief Bill settled the question of the Repeal of the Union.

It is not my intention at present to enter into the question, as to the expediency of granting the Roman Catholic claims; for I hope that question is for ever set at rest. The former government of this country derived some advantage from the settlement of that question; and I believe that this advantage will at least be admitted to have flowed from it,—that now there is no question either in this or the other House of Parliament, or among the public, respecting the necessity or expediency of repealing the Union. When I introduced the Catholic Relief Bill, I stated that political power already existed in the hands of the Roman Catholics, and that was a statement, generally admitted by noble Lords on both sides of the House. What the Bill effected was to give the capacity of enjoying political power to the higher classes of the Roman Catholics, and to take it out of the hands of those of the lower classes who did not exercise it themselves for their own purposes, and according to the suggestion of their own sentiments, but at the dictation of a body among the Catholic people, who, it will be admitted by everybody, ought not to possess any political power whatever,—I mean the Roman Catholic priesthood.

April, 21st. 1831.

If the Reform Bill be passed, it will be impossible to preserve inviolate the Union with Ireland.

My opinion is, that your Lordships will find it difficult, indeed, after having passed the Bill under discussion of the other House of Parliament, to maintain inviolate that Union which now exists between the two countries. I mean to say, that in the event of that bill passing, it would be impossible to maintain that article of the Union which recognises the Church of England as a branch of that Union, and which guarantees its safety. I beg to call to your Lordships'

recollection, that his Majesty is sworn to maintain that Union inviolate; and that, in adopting the Reform measure, the Parliament do actually expose his Majesty to the risk of consenting to a bill calculated to break down the Church Establishment in Ireland. This is the impression I have always entertained—and it is an impression which I cannot remove from my mind; and, I must confess, that when I heard the other night the noble and learned Lord on the Woolsack (Lord Brougham) assert that the Reform Bill had put down agitation in Ireland, on the subject of a Repeal of the Union, I was much surprised.
April 22, 1831.

Importance of Portugal to England.
There is no country in Europe whose alliance is so important to England as Portugal; there is no country, the preservation of whose independence is so important to us, as that of Portugal.
July 26, 1831.

A preventive Police checks Crime.
In all foreign countries there exists a preventive police,—but there is no such thing in England,—which preventive police has the effect of checking crime in a very great degree. We have nothing of the sort in England, neither can there be, according to the principles of our law and constitution. Such being the case, your Lordships must use great caution in drawing comparisons between convictions in this and foreign countries; if that is not done, the most erroneous conclusions will be arrived at.
September 6, 1831.

A War of Opinions the worst of Wars.
The truth is, that the government of Portugal has, for the last ten months, been looked upon with inimical feelings and with passion by the King's servants; and this measure[13] is not brought forward with any view to revenue, but for the purpose of opposing and embarrassing the existing Government of that country. The noble Lords opposite do not like the situation of the Government of Portugal; it is not to their mind; and they are anxious, either by revolutionary measures, or any other, to overthrow it. Let them, however, look well at the responsibility they are incurring. Let them consider the frightful consequences in which their planning may involve this country, and the whole of Europe. If their designs even met with a temporary success, they would inevitably lead to a war of opinion, to a war of religion—the worst of wars, and the most deplorable consequences for all Europe would ensue.
September 30, 1831.

[Footnote 13: The Wine Duties Bill; for regulating the tariff as regards Portugal.]

The Duke's Declaration against all Reform.

But, my Lords, if I wanted an example of the value of the House of Commons, I should find it in the opinion of the noble Earl (Grey) the last time, I believe, the last time that he spoke of the House of Commons. In the month of February, 1817, the noble Lord said, "constituted as it now was, he, in his conscience, believed that the House of Commons was, of all other institutions, in all the other countries of the world, the institution best calculated for the general protection of the subject. Supported by the people, in temperate and firm claims for redress, it was not only able, but certain to remedy every wrong. It was capable of acting as the most efficient control upon the executive, by diminishing the means of consumption, and reducing the pressure of a severe and grinding taxation." That was the opinion of the noble Earl himself, in 1817; and what, I would ask, has the Parliament done, subsequently, to deserve the disapprobation of the noble Earl? What had it done between 1817 and the moment when I pronounced that approbation of Parliament, of which my noble friend (Earl Winchelsea) and the noble Earl (Grey) have so much disapproved? When the noble Earl quoted what I said not quite a twelvemonth ago, he might, I think, quote it correctly. What I said was, that Parliament had done its duty by the country, and enjoyed its confidence. I said, that if I had to create a constitution of Parliament, I could not create that which now existed, because I did not believe the art of one man could invent such a system; but I said, that I would do my endeavour to establish one like it, in which property in land should be preponderant. That was what I said; and I afterwards had the satisfaction to hear the noble Marquis (Lansdowne) deliver a similar opinion. He stated that, in any system of representation which he could support, property and learning must be preponderant. I said that I should consider it my duty to resist the adopting of any plan of reform that should be brought forward. I spoke as a minister of the Crown; I meant to resist reform. The noble Lords say, that this statement of mine caused great enmity to me, and created that spirit of reform which has since pervaded the whole country. I beg the noble Earl's pardon; but the spirit of reform in this country was the consequence of the French revolution. It is true, that ever since the American war, a desire for Parliamentary Reform has been manifested, particularly when any disturbance or insurrection has occurred in any of the neighbouring foreign countries—above all, since the French revolution; and when there has been any extraordinary distress or difficulty in the country. At the same time, I believe that, from year to year, the manifestations of such a desire have been less frequent. I have, indeed, the authority of those most friendly to reform for saying that the manifestations of the desire for reform were less frequent, till the period of the revolution of July, 1830, than they had formerly been for a number of years.

October 4, 1831.
Electoral Pledges Unconstitutional.

It is on the ground of the dissolution, and of the Speech from the Throne,[14] that I charge the noble Lords with having excited the spirit which existed in the country at the period of the last general election; and with having been the cause of the unconstitutional practice, hitherto unknown, of electing delegates for a particular purpose to Parliament—delegates to obey the daily instructions of their constituents, and to be cashiered if they should disobey them, whatever may be their own opinion; instead of being, as they have been hitherto, independent members of Parliament, to deliberate with their colleagues upon matters of common concern, and to decide according to the best of their judgment, after such deliberation and debate. This is an evil of which the country will long feel the consequences, whatever may be the result of these discussions.

[Footnote 14: The Whig ministry dissolved the Parliament in April, 1831. A new Parliament met in June; and, on the 21st of that month, the King made the speech alluded to. In the interval there had been great excitement in the country.]

My Lords, this measure, thus delegated by the people, and thus brought forward by the Government in Parliament, for the decision of members thus delegated to give it the force of a law, alters every thing; and requires, as the noble Secretary of State (Lord Melbourne) says, new powers, in order to render it practicable to carry on the Government at all.

October 4, 1831.

A Democratic Assembly of the worst description will be elected under the Reform Bill.

Throughout the whole of the empire, persons of the lowest condition of life, liable to, and even existing under, the most pernicious influences, are to have votes; or, in other words, are to exercise political power. Persons in those stations of life do exercise political power already; but, in a few places, in large masses; preponderating over the influence of other classes of society. What must we expect when these lower classes will preponderate everywhere? We know what sort of representatives are returned by the places I have described. What are we to expect, when the whole will be of the same description?

We hear, sometimes, of radical reform; and we know that the term applies to universal suffrage, vote by ballot, annual parliaments, and their consequences. But, I declare, that looking at these changes pervading every part of the representation, root and branch, destroying or changing everything that has existed, even to the relative numbers of the representatives from the three kingdoms fixed by treaty, I should call this a radical reform, rather than reform of any other description.

I cannot but consider that the House of Commons returned by it will be a democratical assembly of the worst description; that radical reform, vote by ballot, and all the evil consequences to be expected from the deliberations of such an assembly, must follow from this establishment. I entreat your Lordships to pause before you agree to establish such a system in your country.
October 4, 1831.

The popular Will no ground for conceding Reform.
But we are told that the people wish for this measure; and when we express our sense of the danger which attends it, on account of the democratical power which it tends to establish, an endeavour is made to calm our apprehensions, by the assurance that the people are attached to the Government of King, Lords, and Commons.

If we are to rely upon that feeling of the people—if we are to adopt this measure because it is the pleasure of the people, and because they are attached to the Government of King, Lords, and Commons, why do we not, at once, adopt the measure which we know the people prefer—I mean radical reform; that is to say, universal suffrage, vote by ballot, and annual parliaments? If we are to make a change, there can be no reason for not going the full length that the people wish, if we can be sure that the measure will not injure the Government—that to which they are attached—of King, Lords, and Commons.
October 4, 1831.
Necessity of the Influence of Property in the House of Commons.
But before we go further, it is desirable that we should examine what is the Government of King, Lords, and Commons, as established in this kingdom. In this Government the King is at the head of everything. All the power is in his hands. He is the head of the Church, the head of the law. Justice is administered in his name. He is the protector of the peace of the country, the head of its political negociations, and of its armed force—not a shilling of public money can be expended without his order and signature. But, notwithstanding these immense powers, the King can do nothing that is contrary to law, or to the engagements of himself or his predecessors.

Every act of the Government, or of the King, is liable to be brought under discussion in, and is in fact controlled by, the House of Commons; and for this reason alone, it is important that we should consider of what description of men the House of Commons is likely to be composed, when we are discussing a question of Parliamentary Reform, in order that we may be quite certain that they will exercise their high function with wisdom and discretion.

It was on these grounds, that I, some time ago, called upon the noble Earl (Grey) to state by what influence he intended to carry on the King's Government in Parliament, according to the principles fixed at the period of the

Revolution, and in practice from that period to this, when this Reform Bill should be passed. The noble Lord answered immediately—not by means of corruption. I am aware of that, my Lords. I am convinced that the noble Lord is incapable of resorting to such means, as I hope he believes that I am incapable of resorting to them. I did not consider this any answer to my question, which I repeated in a subsequent discussion, on the motion of my noble friend, the noble Baron behind me (Lord Wharncliffe). The noble Earl said, that the Government had nothing to do with such questions; that Parliament was to decide for itself; and that there was no necessity for the interference of Government.

I beg your Lordships to consider what are the questions which in every week, and on every day, are brought under the discussion of the House of Commons—questions affecting the honour, the interests, the rights, the property, of every individual in the country, which the King is bound by his oath to protect, and in the protection of which, all are equally interested. They are questions regarding the proceedings of Courts of Justice, regarding the use of the public force, and hundreds of others, which occur daily, in which every individual is interested. I put legislation out of the question; but can the King from that Throne give to his subjects the necessary protection for their rights and property? No, my Lords. It is only by the influence of property over the election of Members of the House of Commons, and by the influence of the Crown and of this House, and of the property of the country upon its proceedings, that the great powers of such a body as the House of Commons can be exercised with discretion and safety. The King could not perform the duties of his high station, nor the House of Lords, if the House of Commons were formed on the principle and plan proposed by this bill.

October 4, 1831.

The Sacrifice of the Established Church will follow the Reform Bill.
There is one institution which would become peculiarly liable to attack in such a House of Commons, to which I wish to draw the attention of the Right Reverend Bench, and that is, the Establishment of the Church of England in Ireland. This Church is the object of a fundamental Article of the Treaty of Union between the two countries, and is secured by Acts of both Parliaments; and the King is, besides, sworn to maintain its right and possessions: can any man believe that, when the representatives for Ireland come to be elected in the manner proposed by the bill, the Church of England in Ireland can be maintained?

I have already shown that these representatives must be elected under the influence of the Roman Catholic hierarchy. Who are those who now show the greatest hostility to the Church, its rights, and possessions?—the Members for populous places. The reason is, that the deprivation of the Church of their property is one of the popular objects of the day. The object of the bill is, and its effects will be, to increase the number of this description of Members in Parliament, and to render the influence of this party predominant and irresistible.

I believe that the noble Earl (Grey) has already found the Members returned by Ireland, under this influence, very inconvenient to himself, upon more than one occasion; and it appears, that the right honourable Gentleman who conducts the affairs of Ireland in the House of Commons, was under the necessity, very lately, of giving up a measure which he thought important for the benefit and peace of Ireland, because the Members from Ireland, of this party, were opposed to it. How can the noble Lord suppose, that the Church of England can be protected, or even the Union itself preserved in a Reformed Parliament? There is no man, who considers what the Government of King, Lords, and Commons is, and the details of the manner in which it is carried on, who must not see, that Government will become impracticable, when the three branches shall be separate—each independent of the other, and uncontrolled in its action by any of the existing influences.

October 4, 1831.

Danger of a Democratic House of Commons.

A noble earl (the Earl of Winchelsea) who has spoken on this side of the House, has made an observation to your Lordships, which well deserves your attention. The noble earl has told you, that if you increase but a little the democratic power in the state, the step can never be withdrawn. Your Lordships must continue in the same course till you have passed through the miseries of a revolution, and thence to a military despotism, and the evils which attend that system of government. It is not denied, that this bill must increase beyond measure the democratic power of the state—that it must constitute in the House of Commons a fierce democracy: what must be the consequences, your Lordships will judge.

I will not detain your Lordships by adverting to the merits of the system of government which has existed up to the present moment, upon which my opinion is by no means altered. No man denies that we have enjoyed great advantages; that we have enjoyed a larger share of happiness, comfort, and prosperity, for a long course of years, than were ever enjoyed by any nation; that we have more riches, the largest fortunes, personal as well as real, more manufactures and commerce, than all the nations of Europe taken together; the richest, most extensive, most peopled, and most prosperous foreign colonies and possessions, that any nation ever possessed. There is not an important position in the world, whether for the purpose of navigation, commerce, or military defence, that does not belong to us.

If this democratic assembly should once be established in England, does any one believe that we should continue to enjoy these vast advantages? But a democracy has never been established in any part of the world, that it has not immediately declared war against property—against the payment of the public debt—and against all the principles of conservation, which are secured by, and are, in fact, the principal objects of the British constitution, as it now exists. Property, and its possessors, will become the common enemy. I do not urge this argument as one in which your Lordships are peculiarly interested: it is not you alone, nor even other proprietors, who are interested in the protection of property; the whole people, middling classes as well as the lower orders, are interested in this subject. Look at the anxiety prevailing in every part of London, in respect to the great revolution to be made by this bill. My noble friend, the noble baron (Lord Wharncliffe) has been ridiculed for adverting to the opinions of tradesmen in Bond-street and St. James's-street. Those in Bond-street consist of more than 200 respectable persons, who are well able to form an opinion of the effect of this bill upon the resources of themselves, the middling classes, and the poor, as they supply the luxuries of persons in easier circumstances, residing in that quarter of the town. Anything which can effect the resources of their customers, must be interesting to them, and they do feel that this bill must affect property, private expenditure, and the resources of themselves, and of those whom they employ. A noble lord on the other side, who adverted to this topic, greatly underrated the wealth of these tradesmen. I know of one, residing in Bond-street, who employs at all times from 2,000 to 4,000 workmen, whose trade depends, as well as the employment of this body of people, upon the expenditure of his customers: is he not interested in upholding the public faith, and the system of property now established in England? Are not the people, of all classes and descriptions, down to the lowest, interested in the maintenance of our extensive manufactures and commerce, in the conservation of our enormous dominions abroad, and the continued respect of all nations?

If I am right in thinking that this fierce democracy will be established in the House of Commons, does any man believe that that harmony can continue between the king and his government and the House of Commons, so necessary to insure to both general respect, and to the king's government the strength which is necessary to enable his Majesty to protect and keep in order his foreign dominions, and to insure the obedience of their inhabitants? We shall lose these colonies and foreign possessions, and with them our authority and influence abroad.

There is no instance of any country having maintained its strength or its influence in its foreign possessions, or the respect of foreign nations, during the existence of internal troubles and disturbance; and there is no case of the existence, without such troubles, of a Government consisting of King, Lords, and Commons, independently of each other, and the members of the latter depending solely upon the popular choice, and being delegates of the people. We have had an example in England of a House of Commons which was independent of the influence of the Crown; and of this House, turning the Spiritual Lords out of it, murdering their Sovereign, and voting the House of Lords useless. I will read your Lordships the account given by a man, who was knowing in his time (Oliver Cromwell), of what this House became.

"The parliament, which had so vigorously withstood the encroachments of the royal power, became themselves too desirous of absolute authority; and not only engrossed the legislative, but usurped the executive power."

"All causes, civil and criminal, all questions of property, were determined by committees, who, being themselves the legislature, were accountable to no law, and for that reason their decrees were arbitrary, and their proceedings violent. Oppression was without redress, unjust sentence without appeal; there was no prospect of ease or intermission. The parliament had determined never to dissolve themselves."

"At length the army interfered. They soon perceived that, unless they made one regulation more, and crushed this many-headed monster, they had hitherto ventured their lives to little purpose, and had, instead of assuring their own and their country's liberty, only changed one kind of slavery for another."

This is the account of the state of a house of Commons acting independently of all influence; and of the state to which it brought the country.
October 4, 1831.

Contempt of intimidation by popular meetings.

I do not deny that I always felt strongly the attempts that were made to intimidate your Lordships by public meetings. For all such meetings, I feel the greatest contempt; and I am perfectly satisfied that the house is superior to any intimidation founded on the proceedings of any such assemblages. I feel no concern for all those threats, whether proceeding from Birmingham or elsewhere. I have always thought, and I think still, that the law is too strong to be overborne by such proceedings. I know further, that there does exist throughout this country a strong feeling of attachment to the government of the country, as by law established. I know that the people look up to the laws as the best means of protection, and those laws they will not violate in any manner to endanger the government of the country, or any of its established institutions. I am afraid of none of these, but I will tell your Lordships what I am afraid of, I am afraid of revolution, and of revolutionary measures, brought in and proposed by his Majesty's government. I assert, and I believe that history will bear me out in the assertion, that there has been no revolution in this country, or any great change, which has not been brought about by the parliament, and generally by the government introducing measures, and carrying them through by the influence of the Crown. I would therefore entreat your Lordships to do all you can to defeat this measure—use every means of resistance which the just exercises of your privileges will warrant; and trust to the good sense of the country to submit to the legal and just decision you come to.
October 5, 1831.

Comparison of the Finance Administration of the Wellington with that of the Grey government.

I believe we find ourselves in this singular situation: we have an increased expenditure, (increased within this year,) and have, at the same time, a reduction of taxation, and no overplus whatever (or one not amounting to more than 10,000 l.) of revenue. I say we are in that peculiar situation, because I put out of the question those occasions on which ministers of the crown have thought it their duty to propose and effect loans, to carry on the public service of the country. Even in these cases, those who have made such propositions have thought it their duty to provide a surplus over revenue, in order to meet the unforeseen casualties in the amount of revenue, which every man knows must occur in so large a revenue as this country has the happiness to boast of. This principle of having a surplus revenue over the expenditure, has been considered advantageous with a view to the diminution of the national debt. I am aware that this is a part of the subject on which a difference of opinion exists. I am aware that many great authorities are of opinion that no surplus is necessary for the express purpose of reducing the national debt, and I perfectly agree with them that it is not desirable that a surplus should be created by borrowing, and thus creating new liabilities for the purpose of getting rid of the old. But I cannot look to what has taken place of late years, even in my own time, when I filled the situation of first Lord of his Majesty's Treasury,—cannot look to what took place then without seeing the advantage of having an overplus of income over expenditure, such as would tend to the gradual diminution of the public debt.

I am considerably within the truth when I state, that since the peace the interest of the public debt has been decreased by an amount more than sufficient to pay the interest of 100,000,000 l. of stock; and your Lordships will therefore see that some surplus of revenue, in order to lead to a diminution of the public debt, is highly desirable. I think it is a principle of the financial policy of this country that there should be such a surplus, and that it should be so applied. Besides, much of the revenue of this country depends on the seasons, and almost all on consumption; and the amount of consumption depends upon taste and fashion; and the change of taste and fashion, and other circumstances over which no man can have control, and which are liable to variations, may tend to a variation in the amount of the revenue, which nothing can provide against except a surplus revenue. It is on this principle that the government to which I had the honour to belong proceeded.

We should not think that an individual provided for his expenses who should leave a part of them to be paid within a future period, neither can we think all the expenditure of the country is provided for, leaving a part to be paid for in the next year. The sum expended for the service of the year is the sum to be paid, whether within the year or at any other period, for this sum provision ought to be made within the year, or debt is incurred. It is a new principle introduced into the financial system of this country; it is a principle which at any other time than the present, would never have been listened to, much less tolerated by parliament for a moment.

October 17, 1831.

King Leopold must be independent of Foreign Powers.
I entertain the highest respect for Prince Leopold, and I trust that that Prince will take upon himself the character of an independent sovereign, and I know that that illustrious person possesses all the talents and disposition calculated to form a great and excellent sovereign; but I must say, that in order to be so, he must be not only independent of this country, and of the Germanic states, but above all he must be independent of France.

January 26, 1832.
The Grey policy tends to War, Foreign and Domestic.
I say that the foreign policy of his Majesty's ministers is more likely to produce war abroad than any other system; and in the same manner their domestic policy is of all others, the best calculated to produce war at home.

January 26, 1832.

Irish Agitation deprecated.
My Lords, the main cause of the present excitement is the encouragement given in Ireland to agitators to disturb the country. I can tell the noble Earl, (Grey), that so long as encouragement is given to agitators, you may double and treble the regular army in Ireland,—you may heap measures of severity upon measures of severity, but you will not succeed in putting down agitation upon this question, or upon any of the others which may follow it.

February 27th, 1832.

Tithes the most sacred kind of property.
A noble Lord, the other night, in discussing the question of tithes, observed that the people of Ireland are ready to pay that for which they receive value, to pay their rent, and to pay all the taxes on the land, and that they wished not to deprive any man of his property. I say then my Lords, is any property held so sacred by our laws as tithes? In the first place, the King is sworn—his Majesty was sworn a few months ago—to protect the property and rights of the clergy, above all classes of men. I desire also, to bring to your Lordships' recollection, that in two recent Acts of parliament, in which we conferred notable advantages on the Dissenters from the Church of England, we endeavoured as far as we might by oaths, to secure the property of the church. If any principle, indeed, can secure property to any portion of his Majesty's subjects, the property of the church ought to be safe. It is a principle of the constitution that tithes, above all other property, should be secured to the owner.

February 27th, 1832.

The Grey Government charged with encouraging Political Reform.

My Lords, I never have made, and I never will make, a charge which I am not ready to repeat, and able to substantiate, and I will forthwith prove that which the noble Earl calls upon me to explain. In doing this I beg leave to remind your Lordships, that some months ago I suggested to the noble Earl, (Grey) that an Act of Parliament, which had been passed for the purpose of suppressing illegal associations in Ireland, was about to expire, and I asked him, if he intended to propose a renewal of that act. The noble Earl replied that he did; but my Lords, you will recollect that parliament was dissolved without any further notice of the act, and of course it expired. The result of this was, that the noble Earl stated in the House, when it met again, that the noble Marquis at the head of the Irish Administration felt that he could carry on the government of that country without any additional powers; and the consequences of the noble Earl having declined to apply to the legislature for any authority beyond the existing laws were, that agitation began again, and that meeting after meeting has been held, from that time to the present moment. This is not all, my Lords; the great agitator, the prime mover of the whole machinery, escaped the execution of the sentence of the law in consequence of the expiration of the Act of Parliament to which I have referred. Well my Lords, what has since taken place. This very person, the great agitator, whom the government had prosecuted to conviction, was considered to be a person worthy of the honours which the crown could bestow, and he received the highest favour which any gentleman of the Bar ever received from the hands of the noble Earl and his government; he received a patent of precedence, which placed him next the Attorney General, and above a gentleman who was once Attorney General, but was still a member of the same Bar. If this was not a premium given to that gentleman to continue his course of disturbing the country, I do not know what else could be so considered. I feel that no more effectual mode could be found to encourage agitation than to reward the promoter of it. But it is not alone in this respect that his Majesty's Government has encouraged agitation. What was the meaning, I ask, of the friends of government taking the course they have taken out of doors, with reference to the Reform Bill? What was the meaning of the letter of the noble Lord in another house, addressed to the Political Union of Birmingham, in which that noble Lord designated the sentiments of noble Peers on this side of the House as the "whisper of a faction?"—What was the meaning of two friends of government collecting a mob in Hyde Park, and the Regent's Park, on one of the days on which the House of Lords was discussing the Reform Bill? What was the meaning of those individuals directing the line of march of the assembled multitude upon St. James's, and publishing their orders in the papers devoted to government? And what was the meaning of the publications in the government newspapers, libelling and maligning all those who opposed the Bill? What was the meaning of all these deeds being allowed by government, and why did they tolerate and abet them, unless they calculated upon some advantages to themselves in encouraging such agitation? I don't accuse the noble Earl of instigating those mobs—I do not mean to say, that he was delighted at seeing my house assailed, or any other work of destruction committed; but I say some of his colleagues, and some of the friends of government, have encouraged and incited the people to works of violence. I must say, I have long felt on this subject very strongly. I feel that the country is in a most dangerous state. I find the country is in a most dangerous state, on account of government not taking the proper measures to put a stop to confusion and agitation; and on the contrary, in place of putting a stop to such scenes, allowing some Lords of his Majesty's household, to encourage and instigate the people to lawless acts.

February 27th, 1832.

[Earl Grey had risen and denied that the Government had encouraged agitation upon which the Duke made the previous short but energetic speech.]

Mr. O'Connell ought not to have had a Patent of Precedence.

It has been urged, that professional honours should not be withheld from a gentleman who is entitled to them, on account of political offences. I beg to set the noble Lord right on that point. The offences of which Mr. O'Connell was convicted, were not political or professional, but legal offences. They were pronounced such by the law of the country; and it was to an individual who had been convicted of such offences, that his Majesty's Government thought it right to give a patent of precedence in Ireland.

February 27, 1832.

Opinion of the "National" System of Education in Ireland.

I agree in opinion with the noble and learned Lord (Plunkett), who has declared that opinion with so much eloquence, that any system of education, to succeed, must be founded on religion; and that it cannot stand on any other foundation. The noble and learned Lord has truly said, that this is to be desired, not simply from the advantages to be derived from religious instruction, but for the promotion of those habits of obedience and discipline which it is necessary to instil into the mind of youth. I admit that the system proposed by Ministers is founded on, and justified by, the reports of the commissioners and of committees of the other House of Parliament; but the doubt I entertain is this—whether the system laid down in the reports, and in the letter of the Right Honourable Secretary for Ireland, is a system which would inculcate those habits of discipline and obedience which are required by the noble and learned Lord, and which would alone satisfy my own mind, that in adopting it we should be doing that which we ought to do: this is my apprehension. What I feel is this—that there is much doubt whether the new system of education in Ireland will apply to the education of nearly 500,000 persons, in the same advantageous way as is now the case with the existing Societies—the London Hibernian Society, the Sunday School Society, and the Kildare Place Society. What I would say is, that there is already going on a system of religious education, extending its operation to nearer 500,000 than 400,000 persons—a system of real religious education, founded on the Scriptures, which can be interfered with by nobody—neither by priest nor by any other man—and which is so directed by this Kildare Place Society, as not to give offence to anybody; and now, when the Government is about to establish another system, (which I have admitted they are justified by the reports in doing), I doubt much whether it will not be attended with less advantage than that which already exists.

I am, myself, by no means satisfied that the system which is to be substituted is as good as that which it is proposed to abrogate. If the system is to be changed, I consider that it would be better, perhaps, to have separate schools for the Protestants and Roman Catholics. Although I allow that this would be attended with many inconveniences, still I am inclined to think it would be better than the scheme proposed.

I really cannot see the difference between public and private education; or why causes of dispute should arise between two classes of persons, if educated by favour of public grants, rather than between the same classes if educated by private means. All classes of persons who are educated together, here, by their private means, agree quite well together, as Englishmen; and I do not see why they should not in like manner agree, if they happen to be educated by public grants.

February 28, 1832.

Character of the Irish Agitation.

The present state of things in Ireland is to be attributed to the system of agitation, established by persons who will never be quiet as long as the noble Lord at the head of the Government shall permit them to proceed. It is not, I repeat, to be attributed to the practices or conduct of the clergy, or to the Tithe Corporation Act, or even to the want of enforcing that Act, but to that system of agitation, combined in the most artful manner, and carried on with a perseverance unequalled on any other occasion; and the noble Lords may rely upon it, that the state of things which now prevails in Ireland[15] will continue to exist even after this measure shall have been adopted, if that system of agitation is not put an end to.

[Footnote 15: Resistance to the payment of tithe.]

March 8, 1832.

Protection, not Free Trade, the Principle of our Commercial Law.

Nothing can be more absurd, than to assert that there is free trade in this country; there is no such thing—there can be no such thing. Our manufactures

and our produce have been at all times protected. We have always given protection to the productions of our own soil, and encouragement to our domestic labours; and we have, therefore, rather discouraged, than otherwise, the rivalry of other countries. That has been our system; and I should be sorry to see any measure adopted by this House, opposed to that system under which this country has so many years thriven and prospered. We have always proceeded on the principle of protecting our manufactures and our produce—the produce of our labour and our soil; of protecting them against importation, and extending our home consumption; and on that universal system of protection it is absurd to talk of free trade.
March 9, 1832.

The Lord Chancellor's Patronage. Its Private Disposal Defended.
My noble and learned friend (the Earl of Eldon) has been attacked for having, in the exercise of the patronage of his office, not overlooked the interests of his own family. To be sure he did not, and he ought not to have done so; if he had, he would only have been departing from the practice of all his predecessors. Let me remind your Lordships, that for at least a century and a half back, the Lord Chancellor and Judges have invariably dispensed the patronage attached to their offices in favour of their own immediate relations; so that my noble and learned friend, in providing for his own family as well as he could, was only acting according to the uniform and acknowledged practice of all his predecessors. The fact is, that the office of Lord Chancellor would be very inadequately remunerated, unless the individual filling it procured the means of providing for his family; and I believe it will be found out ere long, what with this inadequate remuneration, and what with stripping off so much of the Chancellor's patronage, and what with the surrendering up so much of his bankruptcy fees,—that the remuneration will be so inadequate to the labour and change of habits, and expense consequent upon the assumption of the office,—that few eminent gentlemen at the bar will, in future, be disposed to accept of it.

For the reason by which I justified my noble and learned friend, I will say that the noble and learned lord opposite, (Lord Plunkett) was justified in the exercise of his official patronage. That noble and learned lord has a large family, and was perfectly right in placing them in those situations to which their abilities and pretensions were adequate. The only blame in such a case would be if he placed them in situations to which their abilities were not equal. I will therefore say that the learned lord was perfectly justified in the course he has pursued; and I will say more, that his high office and his great intellectual influence, fully entitled him to expect that the government, of which he was a member, should give his family a preference in filling up any situations to which, as I have stated, their abilities were equal. I agree with the noble Earl at the head of his Majesty's government, in hoping that this will be the last we shall hear of this senseless outcry against public men for this mode of disposing of the patronage of office. The time of the house is but ill spent with such discussions; indeed, I am sure that nothing can tend more to injure its character in public estimation, than these investigations of the family affairs of men in high stations; at all events, they tend more to lower the house than benefit the public, and the sooner we put an end to them the better.

March 12, 1832.

Peace with France desirable, but difficult to maintain.

There does exist in the minds of the people of France, a sentiment, which their government at the present day are but too prone to flatter. I allude to that morbid desire of extended conquest, which, at least for the last forty years, has so much influenced the character and proceedings of that people.

There is no man who would be more ready than I should in taking every step calculated to promote a good understanding between that country and this. I consider quite as much as the noble Earl (Grey) opposite can possibly do, that every measure tending to that end is a measure of necessity—is a measure of such urgency and importance, that I consider it second only to the honour and interests of this country,—those I take to be the very first objects to which a British Minister should direct his attention, regardless of every consideration which might interfere with them. Well then, admitting as fully as any noble Lord can desire, that it must be at all times a leading object with this country to preserve peaceful relations with France, I will tell the noble Earl opposite, that if he would remain at peace with France, peace must be preserved by this country in union with the other powers of Europe, and not by this country singly. I tell him that the affair at Ancona is but a trifling warning of that which will soon follow, unless a constant system of precaution be kept up. I tell him that if that affair be passed over without notice, new attempts will be made, every one of them more and more dishonourable and disadvantageous to this country. When I am told that we should not utter remonstrances against the French government lightly, nor too readily impute a disposition to disturb the amicable relations at present subsisting between the two countries, I answer that no one more earnestly desires peace than I do. There is no one entertains a higher estimate than I do of the resources—the immensity of the resources—possessed by that country both in peace and in war—no man living estimates more highly than I do the wisdom of her statesmen and the skill of her generals—no man is more ready than myself to concede to the French people the possession of a large amount of talent and of virtue, of physical and of moral resources, and of all that renders a state respectable or formidable in the eyes of other nations. But in proportion as we admit these facts, we are bound to watch closely that nothing be done or said derogatory from British honour or injurious to British interests.

March 16, 1832.

Opinion of the Reform Bill, 1832.

I beg your Lordships to recollect that this is the point which the House will have to consider:—the question is not whether alterations have been made in this part or that part, or in many parts of the bill which your Lordships objected to last session, but the question you will have to consider is this—Whether this bill, if passed and accompanied, let it be recollected, with the other bills at present in the other House of Parliament, will afford to the country a prospect of having a government under which the country can go on—under which it will be practicable that this or any other can be governed—or which, in the words of the noble Earl who addressed your Lordships first this evening employed last session—if practicable, would not be pernicious. That is the question which your Lordships will have to consider, when you come to the second reading of the bill. The principle of this measure is not reform, but the disfranchisement of some places and the enfranchisement of others, and also the granting of votes to large bodies of persons on a new qualification. The total alteration of the representation of this country, coupled with an alteration of the representation of Scotland, amounting there to a complete revolution, and the overthrow in Ireland of all the measures which were adopted in that country three years ago— these, and not reform, are what your Lordships must consider as the principles of the bill. I entertain the same opinion as the noble earl near me as to the necessity of reform. My opinion on this point is now as it was originally. But how comes the question now before your Lordships? it has been altered considerably, and is no longer what it was before.

The noble Earl has thrown out some imputations with respect to party motives—if the noble Earl meant them to apply to me he is much mistaken, I have no party views to serve. I believe there is scarcely an individual in this house, or in the country, who has so little to do with borough interests or county interests, or any sort of Parliamentary interests as I have. I have the same interest in the country as any other individual, that is to say, I wish to see the representation established on such a basis as will give the country a prospect of a practicable system of government.

If the bill should go into committee, I will lend my best assistance to render it as consistent with the true interests of the country as it can be made, keeping in view always this great point—that on the nature of the representative system depend the character and form of government.

April 10, 1832.

The House of Commons that carried Reform was an Assembly of Delegates.

The noble Baron, (Lord Wharncliffe) in a memorable speech delivered to this house in the month of March, 1831, previously to the last general election, stated to this house, in the strongest terms, that the result of that election must be to secure the return to the House of Commons of delegates of the people; not members of the House of Commons to consider de Adrias Regni, but to decide upon a measure of parliamentary reform proposed to them in a moment of excitement, and the result would be, to place this house in the situation in which it was placed last year, and in which it stands on the present occasion.

My Lords, is all to be lost, because the noble Lords opposite have taken this course? Is this House to be destroyed? Or is it to lend its aid to destroy the constitution, because Ministers persevere in this course? Would it not be more wise to call upon his Majesty to place things as they were, previous to this unfortunate and ill-advised revolution of parliament; to advise his Majesty to remove his ministers from his confidence, in order that things might be placed in the same situation in which they stood before, and that this house and the country might have an opportunity, if possible, of having a fair discussion on the measure of reform. What! my Lords, is it to be said that the country is to be tied down to be governed by a system which no man can say is practicable? and can any body deny that the House of Commons, which consents to such a proposition, is a delegated House of Commons? All the arguments regarding the decisions of the House of Commons must come to the same end. There would, no doubt, be ten decisions of the same kind, if it were left to the same house, because the house is pledged and returned for the purpose. But the country is not to be abandoned on this account.[16]

[Footnote 16: This and the other succeeding passages on the subject of Reform, were delivered on the second reading of the final reform bill, after the Earl of Harrowby and other Tory peers had resolved on giving way to the House of Common and the Crown.]

April 10, 1832.

Means by which the Reform Fever was excited and kept up.

There can be no doubt whatsoever that there was no opinion existing in the country, in the year 1829, and the beginning of 1830, in favour of parliamentary reform. I believe this is a fact which was fully admitted in the discussions of the House of Commons at that time. Then my Lords, came the French Revolution, which occurred at the period of the commencement of the elections of 1830, followed by the insurrection in Belgium; and there can be no doubt that these events occasioned a very great excitement at the elections of members of parliament. There were many declarations in favour of parliamentary reform; and all that passed on the subject of parliamentary reform on that occasion, was calculated to influence, and did very considerably influence, the opinions of that parliament upon that question. The noble Lords opposite then came into power, and I will say, my Lords, that they met a parliament ready to pass a measure of moderate parliamentary reform. But the noble Lords opposite thought proper, instead of carrying such a measure, to dissolve that parliament, and a new parliament was called under a degree of excitement in the public mind such as had never before been witnessed. The excitement has continued, to a certain degree, ever since, and it has been kept up by the strong opinion put forward and entertained, that it is the King who wishes for parliamentary reform in the manner proposed by this bill. Now, my Lords, I say it is no such thing; for my part, I do not believe one word of any such assertion. My opinion is, that the King follows the advice of his servants; but I believe that it is the idea thus engendered which renders it difficult that there should not be some reform. It is not, however, to be supposed that the King takes any interest in the subject. I entertain no doubt that the cause of the great excitement upon this subject is, that it is the King's opinion that the bill ought to be carried. The noble Earl would find the country cool upon the subject if the King's mind were altered. He would not be able to pass this bill; and indeed, I am sure, from experience, that if ministers, on any great constitutional question, were not convinced that the King would go through with them, it would be impossible for any set of ministers to carry any such measure.

April 10, 1832.

The best part of the Public do not wish the Reform Bill.

The opinion of the gentlemen of the country,—I speak from my own knowledge with respect to the southern counties, and from sure report as to other counties generally,—but I do say that the opinion of the gentlemen, of the landed property, and of the learning of the country, is against this bill. The bill is, on the other hand, supported by the noble Lords opposite, and by their adherents, certainly not a numerous class; it is also supported by all the dissenters from the church of England, and by all who wish it should pass, as a means of their obtaining votes, but I will repeat, that it is, in fact, opposed to the sentiments of all the real English gentlemen, of the yeomanry, and of the middle classes throughout the country. Yes, my Lords, I will say, that there is a change of opinion, and that the best part of the public are not desirous for the bill, but are, on the contrary, apprehensive of its effects. But the noble Lords will say;—"We hear none of this." No my Lords; and why do we hear none of this? Because there is scarcely a gentleman in the country who can believe that, if he were to attend a public meeting for the purpose of expressing his sentiments on this question, he would be secure or protected from the attacks of the mob.

April 10, 1832

No Compromise.

My Lords, I must now advert to what has fallen from another noble Earl (Harrowby), who opposed the bill strongly last year, but who last night came to a different conclusion, and asked if there was no hope of effecting a compromise? and he particularly called upon me to come to such a compromise. My Lords, these noble Lords have been trying a compromise for the last six months; if they have made no progress in effecting a compromise, what encouragement can they hold out to me and others to follow them upon this occasion. We know the evils of this bill; we know that it will consign the country to evils from which it cannot recover. Agree to a compromise! Why, he has not been enabled to advance one single step from last October up to the present moment. He, and his noble Friends who act with him, have remained perfectly stationary. If this be the case, I hope that those who intend to act with my noble Friends, will understand that there is no more chance of compromise on the present than on the last occasion; and that if they agree to the second reading, they agree to a bill with which the country cannot be governed. I beg then that the noble Lords will look to the responsibility they take upon themselves, in giving support to this bill. The Government are now decidedly responsible for that bill—they are responsible for the election of the House of Commons, that passed it—they are responsible for the excitement which caused these events—and they are, moreover, responsible for any evil consequences which may occur, if this House reject it. But when noble Lords change their sentiments, and are followed by many who voted against it last time, I beg them to recollect, that they will partake of a large portion of this responsibility, and that the country will look to them as responsible for whatever may occur.[17]

[Footnote 17: The bill was soon after carried by a species of compromise, Peers staying away from the division.]

April 10, 1832.

Revolutions may be effected by Laws as well as by Violence.

The noble earl (Grey) yesterday challenged me with saying that this bill is revolutionary. What I have always said is, that it has a revolutionary tendency; and I think it has a tendency so strong in that way that it must lead to revolution. The noble earl has said there is no violence; but, my Lords, revolutions may be effected by laws as well as by violence. I know there is no violence. Why, my Lords, there can be no violence,—the King's Government and the House of Commons are leagued with those who call out for change,—and there can be no occasion for resorting to violence. But, my Lords, this is not the only objection. One of the great and leading objections in my mind to this measure is, that it is one which goes to destroy that most invaluable principle of our existing constitution, the principle of prescription, which sanctions the descent and secures the possession of all kinds of property in this country.

April 10, 1832.

The Demagogue will drive the Gentleman from the Representation.

The noble Earl has told us, that men possessing property in these boroughs will continue to possess their just influence in them—that they will have political influence in the elections—that it will continue, and that it ought to continue.

But I would appeal to your Lordships, whether your own experience, in matters of this description, confirms the correctness of this statement? It is true that, in some of these boroughs, noblemen possessing large properties in the neighbourhood will still possess a great and paramount influence; and, indeed, in some places, in consequence of the effect of the double franchise, the influence of the great proprietors in the vicinity may be raised greatly beyond what it is at present. But in those towns in general, it will be the demagogue, and not the nobleman or gentleman of property, who will possess the influence over the elections there. The latter cannot command such an influence, unless through the means of a constant expenditure which it would be impossible for any one to support. The demagogue will obtain his influence by other means, and will ultimately drive the gentleman out of the field. I beg your Lordships to observe what will be the effect of such a state of things in the constitution of the House of Commons; and I beg to ask whether, with such men the representatives of those boroughs, it will be possible to carry on anything like a government or a steady system of policy, through the means of this assembly.

April 10, 1832.

Prophetic Contrast of the New with the Old System.

I know that according to the constitution of this country, a member of the House of Commons when he goes there is a member for all parts of England, and not a representative for the particular town or place for which he is elected; he is in fact looked upon as a member for all the Commons of England. This was hitherto the meaning which was attached to the character of a Member of the Commons House of Parliament. But the case will be widely different should this Bill be passed, and should Members of Parliament be subjected to a system of instruction on the part of their constituents. That system, however, already exists in parts of England, and more especially in the Metropolis, and in the Borough of Southwark. Your Lordships will remember that an honourable and gallant officer, formerly connected with the noble Lords opposite, was obliged to retire from the representation of Southwark, last summer, because he happened to differ with his constituents; and also that a worthy Alderman was in a similar manner reprimanded by his constituents in the city of London, for a similar offence. What then, I would ask your Lordships, is to be expected hereafter, should the system laid down in this Bill be established in this country? Why every member of the House of Commons would become the mere delegate of his constituents, instead of representing the people at large. It has been observed that such representatives would in every case merely consult the wishes of their respective constituents, instead of looking to the advancement of the interests of all classes. I have before me a letter written by a gentleman to some of his constituents in this neighbourhood, in which he desires not only that the electors shall direct the votes of their representatives, and point out the course which they should pursue in parliament, but goes much further. The letter, which is directed to the parishioners of St. Georges in the East, says, "there ought to be an union formed in every parish between the middle classes and the operatives,—first for the protection of person and property; and secondly, to be ready to express the opinion of the parish on any public measure, and in case the minister or the House of Commons are lukewarm in the cause of the people." The extract which I have just read is taken from a letter written by a great advocate of the Reform Bill, not for the sake of the Reform Bill itself, but because it would lead to something further. This letter affords a proof of the kind of system which will be put into operation with respect to the members of the House of Commons, should this Bill be passed. Let your Lordships, then, for a moment, compare the system this Bill would establish, with the system of representation which has so long existed in this country, and under which this country has been raised to such an eminence of glory, and power, and prosperity.

We have, under the existing system, the county representation, and the representation in cities and boroughs. The county representation consists principally of freeholders, and the members for counties represent not only the lower classes, but the middle and higher orders. The representatives for the great maritime towns, and for the larger description of towns in the interior of the country, represent likewise the lower and middle classes. The representatives for the pot wallopping boroughs, for the scot-and-lot boroughs, and for the single borough of Preston, where the franchise is vested in the inhabitants at large, represent the lowest orders of the people; and in this manner this borough representation represents all classes and descriptions of persons, who have any thing to do with the business transacted in the House of Commons. Instead of this system, which has raised this country to its present elevation, we are called upon to establish by this Bill a system of elections which will be confined to one single class of the community; and as the county representations will be no check upon this class of persons, the voters in the counties being mostly of the same description, and as the united representation of Scotland, and of Ireland, will be a check upon them, such a system will tend at once to a complete democracy. This, then, is the system which we are called upon to establish in the place of that which at present exists, and under which all classes and interests of the country are represented in Parliament, and it is under such a system as this that it is pretended the general business of the state can be carried on, and the government maintain sufficient power to preserve existing institutions.

April 10, 1832.

Popular tendency of the Old System of Representation.

I would call the attention of your Lordships to the changes which have taken place in the government of the country during the last twenty years,—to go no further back,—and to the improvements which have taken place in what is called the popular sense. A noble friend of mine, last night, truly stated that the influence of the Crown was decreasing from the period of the revolution up to the year 1782; and that it has been still further diminishing from that period up to the present time, till at last there are not more than fifty persons in the

House of Commons holding public offices. In that period, and more especially in latter years, the influence of the crown in this respect has been greatly diminished. First of all, there has been a large reduction of all such kinds of offices; and in the next place, in consequence of the different constitution and regulations of the customs and excise, and other public departments; and thus the influence formerly possessed by the Crown has gradually passed away.

With the influence of the Crown, then, thus diminished, if a Bill of this description should pass, to make such an extensive change in the constitution of this House, it would be impossible to carry on the government of the country. But there has also been another most remarkable alteration with respect to the constitution of Parliament within the last four years. In the year 1828, the Test Act was repealed; and this I beg your Lordships to recollect, that the effect of the repealing this Act was immediately to bring into operation a large body of electors, who must of course have had considerable influence in subsequent elections. Again, in the following year, the disabilities of the Roman Catholics were removed, which made another important difference in the constitution of Parliament. Has sufficient time been given to those measures to ascertain their effect? Is it not reasonable, is it not right, that we should try the effect of those measures on the constitution, before we proceed further, before we adopt a measure which will effect such extraordinary changes as this proposed Reform Bill? There can be no doubt but that those measures to which I have alluded, must have had considerable effect in the elections which have since taken place, and more especially when any measure of Parliamentary Reform has been adopted, of the same extensive character as that contemplated in the Bill.
April 10, 1832.

Gradual Reform Recommended.
There can be no doubt that there is a general desire in the country,— I do not deny the existence of it, for it is stated in all the addresses and all the petitions on the subject;—that there is a general desire in the country that some Reform in Parliament should be taken into consideration, to do away with the abuses in the system of elections of Members of the House of Commons. Without enquiring into the cause, if the fact be as I have stated, which I believe no one will dispute, it is the duty of Parliament to proceed steadily and gradually in making amendments in the representation. We should consider maturely every step that we took,—we should not proceed all at once to do every thing, we should go on gradually and deliberately; and thus in process of time, we might arrive even at the measure which has been recommended by the noble Earl at the head of his Majesty's government; but this must be in process of time. After a considerable length of time had elapsed, and after we had maturely considered every step that we had taken, it would be only after we had done all

that, that we could adopt a measure to the extent of that recommended by the noble Earl. This we must do, if we desire to maintain the venerable monarchy under which the country has flourished for so long a time. The effect of this measure, if carried now, will be to establish such a government as exists elsewhere, (in France) which the noble Earl has described as a government which no man could think fit for the administration of affairs in this country.

April 10,1839.

Effect of Agitation on Business.

I believe that as soon as this Bill was proposed, and as soon as the excitement which it occasioned was apparent, all expenditure of all descriptions ceased,—men ceased to lay out money in great enterprises—and those who expended their incomes to the full amount, began to consider whether it was not expedient to make provision for a future day, for a period of trouble and difficulty, which might be anticipated from these changes. It is to these circumstances that I am induced to attribute the want of commerce and trade in the country. If your Lordships look to the situation of our neighbours it will appear that the same causes have produced precisely the same effects, and that these causes have proceeded further amongst them, than they have with us, because they have existed for a longer period of time. Among them popular delirium has been carried nearly to its full extent; among us it has only begun. I particularly complain of the system of agitation which now prevails in England, for this reason, that it falls upon the poorest and lowest classes of the community. The expenditure of the rich gives comfort and ease to the middle classes, but it gives subsistence to the poor; and it is for want of this subsistence and comfort for the lower classes, that agitation has been carried to such an extent.

April 10, 1832.

Military Force will be required to Govern the Country if the Reform Bill is carried.

The noble Viscount, one of his Majesty's Secretaries of State, who spoke yesterday upon the subject, admitted that he did not expect that the Reform measure would relieve any of the distresses of the country. It certainly does appear most extraordinary, that a Minister, particularly a Secretary of State, should say of a measure, which he is supporting himself, and which he knows must have such extensive consequences as the measure now proposed, that he does not believe that it will tend to relieve any of the existing distresses of the country. But I say not only that it will not relieve any of the distresses of the country, but, on the contrary, that it will deeply aggravate them. But let us go a little further, and see whether this system is good; and whether the system of cheap government, which it is to introduce, is likely to produce good to the country. And here, again, I would wish to call the attention of your Lordships to what is passing in another country. If your Lordships will take the trouble of examining what has passed in France in the course of the last two years, you will see that, during that period, that country has expended 50,000,000 l. sterling beyond its usual expenditure. Its ordinary Budget, notwithstanding every description of saving that could be made from the Civil List, and in other establishments, which have been cut down as low as possible—still its ordinary Budget exceeds the Budget of the former reign—the extravagant reign of the Bourbons—to the amount of 10,000,000 l. sterling; and, including those laws for two years, there is the extraordinary expenditure of 50,000,000 l. in that space of time. To say, then, that popular excitement tends to cheap government, is monstrous and absurd, and it is impossible for any man who regards these facts to arrive at that conclusion. We are called upon to adopt a system which is to lead to these results. I ask, then, whether such a system can be more effectual in this country, than that under which we have so long prospered? I ask, whether the Civil Government will have more power—whether it is possible that the Government can be carried on with a smaller proportion of the army? I beg your Lordships to observe the transactions which have occurred at Paris within the last two years, and you will see that, while Louis XVIII, and Charles X. were able to maintain the peace and tranquillity of the capital with a gendarmerie of from 500 to 1000 men,—since the period of the revolution of July, 1830, the Government has not had less than 60,000 once a month put into requisition to maintain the peace of the city. I say once a month, upon an average, not to exaggerate the facts; being convinced that upon not less than twenty-four occasions the army has been under arms.

If the system now proposed to your Lordships is adopted, will any man tell me that it will be possible for any Government to be carried on, as the Government of this country has hitherto been, by a civil power, aided by a small military force? In the course of this last summer, events of a fearful character occurred, nearly at the same time, in this country and in France. I allude to the disturbances at Bristol and at Lyons. The riots at Bristol were put down by ninety men, as soon as an officer was found who would employ the force entrusted to him. But what happened at Lyons—were the disturbances there so easily quelled? The events at Lyons—a larger town, I admit, but not much larger than Bristol—required 40,000 troops to be brought against the town, under the command of a Marshal of France, the present Minister-at-War, and a Prince of the Blood, before tranquillity could be restored. I entreat, then, your Lordships to consider well, first of all, the causes of this difference,—to see that it is the sovereignty of the people that you are called upon to establish in this country,—and whether it is possible to carry on the civil Government of England, as it has hitherto been, under such a Government as you would establish, if you pass this Bill.

April 10, 1832.

Fiscal Regulations for the Extinction of Slavery not defensible.

I can hardly bring myself to believe that any Government can think of forcing the Colonies to adopt Orders in Council, by holding out, at once, promises and threats; by saying that those Colonies which adopted them should not pay taxes, and that those which did not adopt them should continue to pay them. Did any man ever before hear of taxes being imposed, for any purpose whatever, excepting to supply the necessities of the State? If taxes be necessary for the purposes of the State, in the name of God let them be paid; but, if they be not necessary, they ought not to be imposed at all, nor allowed to continue. Parliament is not justified in imposing taxes for a specific purpose of punishment.

April 17, 1832.

West India Property not to be Sacrificed to the Fancies of Abolitionists.

It is really desirable that this question should be well understood in this country. West Indian property is as much entitled to protection as any other property which exists in Great Britain. Petitions are sent up from all parts of England, praying for the immediate abolition of slavery; and the execution of that measure is urged as a duty incumbent upon us. Those persons who take a part in these proceedings, forget the enormous amount of property belonging to his Majesty's subjects which is involved in the question; and it is necessary to bring back their attention to the consequences which will result, not only to the colonists, but to the public, from the annihilation of that property, by the prosecution of any of their fancies respecting the abolition of slavery. In truth, it is absolutely impossible to derive any advantage from that property except through the medium of slavery; and through slavery alone can the individuals interested in the occupation of that property be sustained in life.

April 17, 1832.

Speech explaining the Negociations, in May, 1832, for the formation of a Tory Government on the principle of Moderate Reform.

My Lords, I have the honour to present to your Lordships a petition from the inhabitant householders of Cambridge against the Reform Bill; and, as this is the first time I have had occasion to address your Lordships since I have been charged by his Majesty with a most important commission, I conceive that your Lordships, or, at least, some of you, may be desirous that I should avail myself of this, or some other early opportunity, to explain the nature and termination of the transactions in which I have been engaged; and I confess, my Lords, that having been exposed to extreme misrepresentation, and having been vilified in the most extraordinary manner, in respect of these transactions, by persons in another place, who, with the exception of their conduct in this instance, have some claim to be considered respectable, I am anxious to take the first opportunity of stating to your Lordships, and the country, the nature of the transactions in which I have been engaged, and the grounds on which I have proceeded. Your Lordships will recollect, that in the course of the last week—I think it was on Wednesday—his Majesty's ministers informed your Lordships that they had offered certain advice to his Majesty in reference to the important subject of the Reform Bill; and, as his Majesty had not thought proper to follow that advice, they had considered it their duty to tender their resignations to his Majesty, and which resignations his Majesty was pleased to accept. His Majesty was graciously pleased, on that day on which he was so left entirely alone by his ministers, to send for a noble friend of mine—a noble and learned Lord (Eldon), who had held a high place, as well in the service as in the confidence of his Majesty, to inquire whether, in his opinion, there were any means, and if so, what means, of forming a Government for his Majesty on the principle of carrying into execution an extensive reform in the representation of the people. Thus it appears that when his Majesty had the misfortune of disagreeing with his servants, respecting the advice which had been tendered to him, he happened to have had so little communication with other men, and was so little acquainted with their opinions on public affairs, that he felt it necessary to send for my noble and learned friend, who was out of the immediate line of politics, in order to obtain his assistance, and to seek for information at his hands. My noble and learned friend came to me, and informed me of the difficulty of his Majesty's situation, and I considered it my duty to inquire from others what their opinions were, because, I confess to your Lordships, I was equally unprepared with his Majesty for the consideration of such a question.

Upon inquiry, I found that a large number of friends of mine were not unwilling to give confidence and support to a government formed upon such a principle, and with the positive view of resistance to that advice which was tendered to his Majesty. Under these circumstances I waited on his Majesty on Saturday, and submitted to him my advice. That advice was not to re-appoint his late ministry, nor was it to appoint myself. I did not look to any objects of ambition. I advised him to seek the assistance of other persons well qualified to fill the high situations in the state, expressing myself willing to give his Majesty every assistance, whether in office or out of office, to enable his Majesty to form an administration to resist the advice which had been so given to him. My Lords, these were the first steps of the transaction; and if ever there was an instance in which the Sovereign acted more honestly by his former servants—if ever there was an instance in which public men kept themselves most completely apart from all intrigues, and from all indirect influence—using only those direct and honourable means of opposition, of which no man has reason to be other than proud, this is that instance. And when I came to give my advice to his Majesty, instead of advising him with a view to objects of personal ambition, as I have been accused of doing upon high authority,—I gave that advice which I thought would best lead to another arrangement, and I stated that I was ready to serve his Majesty in any or in no capacity, so as best to assist him in carrying on a government to resist the advice which had been given him by his late ministers. And here, my Lords, I beg your Lordships to examine a little what was the nature of the advice which was tendered by his Majesty's ministers to his

Majesty, which his Majesty thought proper not to follow, and which I considered it my bounden duty to enable his Majesty to resist. I do not ask any man to seek any further explanation of this advice, than that which was given by the ministers themselves. It was neither more nor less than this. The Government, feeling some difficulty in carrying the Reform Bill through this House, were induced to advise his Majesty to do—what?—to create a sufficient number of peers to enable them to carry their measure, to force it through this House of Parliament. Now, my Lords, before I go further, let me beg you to consider what is the nature of that proposition? Ministers found, in the course of last session, that there was a large majority in this House against the principle of the bill. Now, my Lords, what is the ordinary course for a minister, under such circumstances, to pursue? My Lords, it is to alter the measure, to endeavour to make it more palatable to that branch of the legislature which was opposed to it. Such is the usual course; but, in this case, the minister says "no. I will next session bring in a bill as efficient as that which has been rejected." And what did he do? My Lords, I have no hesitation in saying that, notwithstanding the opposition of this House, he brought in a measure stronger and worse than any of the measures before introduced; and this measure he wishes to force upon the House by a large creation of peers. How many peers, it is not necessary to state—it has not even been stated, by the noble Lords opposite: it is enough to say, a sufficient number to force the Reform Bill through the House. It is only necessary for me to state the proposition. If this be a legal and constitutional course of conduct—if such projects can be carried into execution by a minister of the crown with impunity—there is no doubt that the constitution of this House and of this country is at an end. I ask, my Lords, is there any body blind enough not to see that if a minister can, with impunity, advise his Sovereign to such an unconstitutional exercise of his prerogative as to thereby decide all questions in this House, there is absolutely an end put to the power and objects of deliberation in this House—an end to all means of decision; I say, then, my Lords, thinking as I do, it was my duty to counsel his Majesty to resist the following of this advice; and, my Lords, my opinion is that the threat of carrying this measure of creation into execution, if it should have the effect of inducing noble Lords to absent themselves from the House, or to adopt any particular line of conduct, is just as bad as its execution; for, my Lords, it does by violence force a decision on this House—and on a subject, my Lords, on which this House is not disposed to give such a decision. It is true, my Lords, men may be led to adopt such a course, by reflecting, that if they do not adopt it, some 50 or 100 peers will be introduced, and thus deliberation and decision in this House be rendered impracticable; or men may be led to adopt it with the view of saving the Sovereign from the indignity of having so gross an alternative imposed upon him. But I say, my Lords, that the effect of any body of men agreeing publicly to such a course, will be to make themselves parties to this very proceeding, of which I say, we have so much reason to complain. The only course of proceeding at this eventful crisis, worthy of the men with whom I have the honour to be connected, was to advise his Majesty—was to counsel his

Majesty—to resist the advice which had been given him, if he could find means of carrying on the government of the country without acceding to it. But this part of the transaction, my Lords, requires particular explanation upon my part—his Majesty insisted that some "extensive measure of reform" (I use his own words) "in the representation of the people" should be carried. I always was of opinion, and am still of opinion, that the measure of reform is unnecessary, and will prove most injurious to the country. But on the last occasion when I addressed your Lordships,—in the committee on Monday se'nnight,—I stated my intention to endeavour to amend the bill in committee, and to do it honestly and fairly. Still, however, I thought that, amend it as we might in committee, it was not a measure which would enable the country to have a government capable of encountering the critical circumstances and serious difficulties to which every man must expect this country to be exposed. This was, my Lords,—this is, my opinion. I do not think that, under the influence of this measure, it is possible that any government can expect to overcome the dangers to which this country must be exposed. But my Lords, this was not the question before me; I was called on to assist my Sovereign in resisting a measure which would lead to the immediate overthrow of one branch of the legislature—a measure which would enable the ministry to carry through this house the whole bill unmodified, unimproved, and unmitigated. I had then, my Lords, only the choice of adopting such part of that bill as this house might please to send down to the House of Commons, suffering the government hereafter to depend upon the operation of that part of the bill rather than upon the whole bill, or else of suffering the whole bill to be carried, and the House of Lords to be destroyed. My Lords, my opinion is not altered; no part of the bill is safe; but undoubtedly, a part of the bill is better, that is to say, less injurious, than the whole bill; and, certainly, it must at least be admitted that it is better than the destruction of the constitution of the country by the destruction of the independence of this house. Under these circumstances, my Lords, I gave my consent to assist his Majesty in forming a new government. I know many may be of opinion that I should have acted a more prudent part if I had looked to anterior circumstances, and if I had regarded the opinions and pledges I had given, and if, placing my attention exclusively upon the desire of acting a consistent part in public life, I had pursued a different course, and refused my assistance to his Majesty, I should have done better and more wisely.

I do not mean to detract from the merits of those who thought proper to pursue a course contrary to mine upon the occasion. I am grieved that it should have been my misfortune to differ with some right honourable friends of mine, with whom I have been for many years in habits of cordial union, co-operation, and friendship, and from whom I hope this momentary separation will not dissever me. Nay, my lords, their position was different from mine. I was situated in a position very different from that in which they felt themselves to stand. They regretted that they could not take the same course with me; but for myself, my Lords, I cannot help feeling that, if I had been capable of refusing my assistance to his Majesty—if I had been capable of saying to his Majesty, "I cannot assist you in this affair, because I have, in my place in parliament, expressed strong opinions against a measure to which your Majesty is friendly," I do not think I could have shewn my face in the streets for shame of having done it—for shame of having abandoned my Sovereign under such distressing circumstances. I have, indeed, the misfortune of differing from many noble Lords, but I cannot regret the steps I have taken. If I have made a mistake, I regret it; but I am not aware that I have made any mistake. It was impossible that I could shrink from his Majesty in the distressing circumstances under which he was placed. I will not detain your Lordships longer with a detail of the circumstances which led to the dilemma in which we are now placed. But, my Lords, if you will only look back to the commencement of those transactions— if you look to the speech which his Majesty made from the throne to this and the other house of Parliament, in June 1831,—if you recollect that his Majesty stated, in very strong terms, that that important question should receive the earliest and most attentive consideration, saying, "—Having had recourse to that measure for the purpose of ascertaining the sense of my people on the expediency of a reform in the representation, I have now to recommend that important question to your earliest and most attentive consideration, confident that, in any measure which you may propose for its adjustment, you will carefully adhere to the acknowledged principles of the constitution, by which the prerogatives of the Crown, the authority of both Houses of Parliament, and the rights and liberties of the people, are equally secured."

Now, my Lords, I ask, could it be believed, at the time his Majesty made this speech, that the rights of this house—the power of deliberating and deciding independently upon such a question as this—would be destroyed by a creation of Peers, and by a creation to an extent which could not be much less than one hundred? If any man at the time foretold this, it would have been said he was dreaming of things that were impossible. But to this state, my Lords, have we been brought by this measure. When I first heard of this bill being proposed to be carried by a creation of Peers, I said it was absolutely impossible. I could not believe that any minister of England would be led by any considerations whatsoever to recommend such a measure to his Majesty. The first time, indeed, I heard the matter mentioned with any degree of authority, was when a Right Rev. Prelate thought proper to write upon the subject to some people in a town in the county of Sussex. I could appeal to those sitting near me if this be not the fact—if I did not uniformly declare that the thing was impossible—that the very idea of it ought not to be mentioned. That it should never be imagined that any minister could be found who would recommend such an unconstitutional—such a ruinous—such an unjust exercise of the prerogative of the crown; for, my Lords, I do maintain that the just exercise of the prerogative of the Crown does by no means go to the extent of enabling his Majesty to create a body of Peers with the view to carry any particular measure. Under the circumstances, then, I think your Lordships will not think it unnatural, when I consider his Majesty's situation, that I should endeavour to assist his Majesty to avoid the adoption of such a recommendation. But, my Lords, when I found that in consequence of

the discussions on Monday in another place,—which by the way proved so clearly what the sentiments of the leading men then were, that Peers should not be created for such a purpose:—when I found from these discussions that it was impossible to form a government from that house, of such a nature as would secure the confidence of the country, I felt it my duty to inform his Majesty that I could not fulfil the commission with which he was pleased to honour me, and his Majesty informed me that he would renew his communications with his former ministry.
May 17, 1832.

The state of Ireland under Lord Grey, a Conspiracy against Law and Government.
    The noble Lords at the head of the Irish government have a most particular objection to these extraordinary measures, adopted to enable the government to afford protection to the lives and property of his Majesty's subjects. If I do not mistake—and I am sure that I am in the recollection of many noble Lords present—I myself reminded the noble Earl that the association act would terminate at the end of the session of Parliament of 1831; and the answer of the noble Earl was, that it was intended to bring in a bill to continue that act. My Lords, Parliament was dissolved unfortunately, and the association act was not only not continued, but the convictions which had already taken place under it were not carried into execution.
    It might naturally be supposed that, when the Lord Lieutenant found that he could not give protection to his Majesty's subjects even when he had the association act, it would, at least, have been continued. No such thing. When Parliament reassembled, the question was again put by one of the noble Lords near me, whether it was intended to propose a renewal of that act; and the answer was, that the noble Lord at the head of the Irish government thought that he would tranquillize the country without having recourse to extraordinary measures. From that day to this there has been no security to property—no security for person; there has been no enjoyment of peace or tranquillity in Ireland. That is the state in which it has continued from that time to the present. Now, my noble friend stated most truly that this is the result of a conspiracy; I say the same; and before I sit down, I will prove that it is a conspiracy, and nothing but a conspiracy, which tends to deprive a large class of his Majesty's subjects of their property,—which renders their lives insecure,—a conspiracy which tends to the overthrow of all government, if they do not adopt some measure to put it down. On this ground alone I address your Lordships; I wish to warn the people and the government of the real nature of that which exists in that part of the United Kingdom. We have heard of an attempt, which was lately made by a clergyman, to avail himself of a sale under a distress, for the purpose of obtaining payment of a part of what was his due. A body of troops were assembled, by direction of the magistrates, for the purpose of protecting the sale. It appears, from an account of a nature usually tolerably accurate, that, on

the first day appointed for the sale, an assemblage of 20,000 people collected together; on the second day the number was 50,000; and on the third it amounted to 100,000. I will take an unit from each of these numbers, and even then I defy any man to shew me how that body could have been assembled but by a conspiracy. Who led them there? My Lords, the Priests. I have seen a letter from an officer who commanded one of the bodies of troops employed on the occasion, in which such is stated to be the fact.

When, my Lords, I know that that conspiracy exists, and that it goes to prevent a large proportion of his Majesty's subjects from enjoying their property—when I know that the same conspiracy may be applied to any other description of property—to any man's life, to his house, to his honour, or to anything else that is most dear to man, I do say, it becomes the noble Earl at the head of his Majesty's Government to adopt some measures, in order to do that which Government can do, to get the better of that conspiracy. It must not be said that, under the British Constitution, there is no power to prevent such a conspiracy: I say, there is a power, and that power resides in Parliament, which can give the Government, under this best of all Constitutions, the means which shall at the same time protect the property and the liberty of every individual in the state. Yes, my Lords, Parliament possesses the power to bestow on the Government the means of putting down this conspiracy—a conspiracy not against the Government itself, but against those whom the Government is bound in honour to protect. I take this question of tithes to be one of the most serious questions that can be brought under the consideration of Parliament. I do not object to the noble Earl's measure—indeed, I really do not know what that measure is—but what I say is, that the noble Earl is bound, and the King is bound by his oath, to protect the property of the Church—yes, his Majesty is sworn especially to protect that property. But it is not the property of the Church alone—what do you say of the lay impropriator? Is a man to be robbed and ruined, because he possesses property in tithe?

There is no public grievance in Ireland. Tithes are no public grievance. Tithes are private property, which a deep laid conspiracy is attempting to destroy. The noble Lord knows that he cannot get the better of it. I tell the noble Lord that he will be, at last, obliged to come to Parliament for a measure to enable him to put down the conspirators. I recollect the famous affair at Manchester; and remember perfectly well to have heard a most able and eloquent speech made by the noble and learned Lord in another place, upon the subject of collecting large numbers of persons together; and I well remember his able and eloquent justification of the magistrates for the part they assumed upon that occasion. I want to know why the magistrates at Carlow and at Cork did not obtain the same support when pursuing a similar course? I know I shall be told in answer to this, that I am a person very desirous of spilling blood. My Lords, I am not recommending the spilling of blood; I want to save human life by Legislative means. I do not want to have recourse to arms against crowds and mobs of people; but what I want is, that the real conspirators should be got the better of, and not that the mere instruments and victims of their wicked work should be punished. But if the course pursued at Manchester against the collection of large bodies of armed people was correct—if the attack was rightly made upon those armed people—I want to know why the same was not done at Cork and at Carlow, where the troops stood in the midst of the people three days, who at last were suffered to carry off the distress, without the clergyman being able to satisfy his claim?

The noble Lord has said, that Ireland is in a state of great tranquillity. Now, I certainly must say, that as far as I have heard, I cannot believe in the existence of that tranquillity. It may be perfectly true, by moving a large body of troops from the country into a particular district, together with a great number of police and magistrates, that, for a moment, tranquillity may be restored to that district; but there is no gentleman in the country feels himself in a state of security. There is, however, one test, to which I wish to bring the noble Secretary of State. I want to know this—has he, in any one case, carried into execution the provisions of the Tithe Act? Is there a single instance of any tithe having been collected by Government under that Act? If the clergy are to be paid out of the Consolidated Fund, and that Act is not to be enforced, I must say that the noble Lord may make what boast he pleases as to the state of Ireland; but there is no man who will believe one word about the tranquillity of Ireland, until the noble Lord can produce evidence of the collection of some tithes under that Act.

What I want to see is, the affording of some security to property—some protection to life; and that some assurance should be given to the peace of the country being established and preserved.

July 3, 1832.

Necessity of conciliating the Protestants of Ireland.

I come now, my Lords, to that part of the subject which is certainly very painful to me, because I conceive it to be that in which I may say the Government has been much to blame; and that is, their treatment of the Protestant Church of Ireland. My opinion is, that in the treatment of that Church they have certainly thrown the Protestants of Ireland entirely aside. There is no doubt whatever that the Protestants, who, like other classes of men, were more or less divided amongst themselves, are now nearly unanimous in their opinions upon the subject of the Government. They are nearly all of them, at the present moment, opposed to the Government—irritated by a strong sense of the injury done to them, and the insecurity of their situation, which is certainly most painful to everybody who wishes well to the union between the two countries.

July 3, 1832.

The Church should Educate the People.

We have the Established Church—we have the Established clergy; and the whole law of the country is, that the clergy of the Established Church should have the charge of the education of the people, particularly of Ireland. But, under the proposed system, the schoolmaster is simply to teach the obligations which are due to society from every individual, and the pupil is not to refer to divine authority for those obligations—he is not without permission to refer to that alone which can render those obligations binding.

July 3, 1832.

The Duke of Wellington's Government opposed to the Appointment of Otho as King of Greece.

The late government were no parties to the selection of Prince Otho; on the contrary, he was a person to whose appointment they had objected, as appears on the face of the protocols; and the objection exists at the present moment, though not to such an extent as it did, a year and a half having elapsed since it was first made. I object to the arrangement now, because the interests of this country have been essentially altered in the Mediterranean. His Majesty has now essential duties to perform in the Adriatic. When I see France remaining in possession of Algiers, notwithstanding the provisions of the treaty, and when I observe what has been done by her at Ancona, I must say the interests of this country have been grossly neglected in that quarter. July 18, 1832

The giving the Town-franchise to the Catholics, will lead to the Destruction of the Protestant Church.

The reason assigned for getting rid of the freemen is, because they would support the Protestant interest in towns. Now, I have no hesitation whatever in stating, that the interest connected with the Church and the Protestant institutions of the country must give way it the franchise is transferred into the hands of the Roman Catholic population. It is easy to say that there ought to be no difference between Roman Catholics and Protestants. I wish to God it could be so; but the circumstances of Ireland are such as to render it necessary, that a counterpoise should be given to counteract the influence which the Roman Catholics will acquire by the bill. I wish to carry the principles of 1829 into effect, and that can not be done if both parties are placed upon an equal footing. I think it most unfair to give the Catholic population of towns the power of returning Roman Catholic Members of Parliament; and I shall, therefore, seeing that the rights of freemen are to be abolished, object to the 40s. freeholders being retained.

July 20, 1832

The Albocracy.

In this country (India), as in all others, there are certain established qualifications for justices of the peace and for jurymen, and no disqualification, in any part of the world, is equal to that of colour. The white man has an influence which the black man has not. This distinction prevails most in those countries in which a liberal system of Government has been established, as in the United States of America, and the various states existing in the southern portion of that continent. Indeed, a term has been invented to designate it in Columbia, in which express laws have been made for the support and maintenance of the "Albocracy."
August 14, 1832.

Effect of the Savings of the Grey Government.
I give the noble Earl at the head of his Majesty's Government full credit for the diminution in the expenses of the country which has been effected by the Government, but I cannot help thinking that such diminutions will prove to be generally detrimental to the country, inasmuch as they are effected merely for the purpose of meeting a deficiency in the revenue for the moment. But the fact is, that many of these reductions are applicable to the army, to the navy, to the militia, and other most essential services of the country, which, although not estimated for this year, must be provided for at a future period. For instance, one branch of these savings is that for training the militia; the saving, under this head, is 190,000 l.; but it is quite clear that this sum must again be expended when the militia shall be trained in future years. Another saving is that of freight, transport, and provisions of soldiers from one part of the world to another. Now, it is very true, that during the present year this reduction may be made, because it does not happen that the change of regiments in the West India colonies and India takes place; but such will not be the case in another year, and the expenditure of 45,000 l. on that head, which does not appear in these estimates, must again occur.

Another item of reduction is in the purchase of timber for the navy service, which amounts to the very considerable sum of 400,000 l. It is evident that the magazines of this country must be kept up, and all that is really done by this apparent saving, is to throw the burden, to this extent, on future years. With a view to a secure and adequate supply, and to the proper seasoning of stores, and with a view to the probability that it may become necessary for his Majesty's service to make some great exertion, it is impossible that less than double the amount of the estimate of the present year under this head, can permanently suffice. Now, it is impossible to look upon these savings in any other light than as temporary, and I will go so far as to say that it would have been a much better principle of economy to spend this money than to save it, if the distressed state of the finances had not absolutely required the reduction of the expenditure. But I cannot help taking another view of the subject. It is necessary for the country, and essential to the character of the Government, that they should look beyond a mere balance of income and expenditure, with a view to be prepared for unforeseen emergencies which may arise. Can any body say, that the Government is now left in the situation in which it ought to be left with respect to finances? This is the last session of the present Parliament. A reformed Parliament will meet next session, and it is impossible for any man to say what will be the conduct of that Parliament with respect to finance. But this is not the only ground on which it is desirable that the finances of the country should be in a more satisfactory state.

I say, my Lords, that I regard these financial difficulties with the greater apprehension, when I remember that occasions may arise, and are in fact, likely to arise, in which it may be necessary for his Majesty to call forth all the resources of the country. When I look to the state of Ireland, when I turn my attention to our foreign relations, and above all, when I call to mind the present condition of the Peninsula, I find it impossible to shut my eyes to the alarming truth, that events are on the eve of occurring, which may call forth to the utmost, every exertion which Englishmen are capable of making, and may demand, as I have said before, all the resources of the empire.

August 15, 1832.
Policy of the Wellington Administration towards Portugal.

The noble Earl (Grey) has stated, that the late government was the cause of the usurpation of Don Miguel. Now that is a mistake in point of time; for it will be found that Don Miguel was brought to Portugal, when the noble Viscount opposite, (Viscount Goderich) was at the head of the government. It is true that I was in office when Don Miguel landed in Portugal, and when he usurped the government over which he was placed as Regent. The noble Earl has stated, that at that time the British army was there, and might have prevented the usurpation. I deny the fact; the British Army had been withdrawn before the usurpation. It is true that, before the army was withdrawn, Miguel had dissolved the Chambers, and had given indications that it was not his intention to carry into effect the constitution of the country; but he had given no indication of a resolution to usurp the Sovereign power; and that usurpation was occasioned by a decree of the Cortes, acquired for that purpose. In point of fact the army was withdrawn; and even if it had not been withdrawn, what was its force? Why it only amounted to 5,000 men, which would not have been enough to effect anything. I deny therefore, that the government has been the cause of the usurpation. When Don Miguel did usurp the sovereign authority, the late government did all they could; they ceased their diplomatic relations with Portugal, and then brought away the minister from thence.

Then the noble Earl says, that the state of things just mentioned existed when he came into office; and that the late government was willing to recognize Don Miguel, provided he would grant a general amnesty. The noble Earl has omitted to state all. It would have been fair, had the noble Earl stated what had previously occurred. The first thing we did was to advise a reconciliation between the two branches of the House of Braganza, and we referred the question to Brazil. The Emperor of Brazil was perfectly ready to go to war if we would make war for him, but he would not go to war himself, because, in fact he had no resources of his own to do so. What then became our duty? Our duty was to place Portugal in the society of nations as soon as we could, and to endeavour to induce Don Miguel to do that which would have the effect of attaining that object. For that purpose, we called on Don Miguel to reconcile the country to him, by some act of grace towards those who had been connected with the former government of the country. But it is not true that we desired to impose any condition with respect to that act of grace. The principle on which we invariably acted was to make an act of amnesty be given without any condition whatever, because it was our wish not to interfere in any manner whatever with the government of Portugal; and it would have been interfering, had we made any condition which we might have been afterwards called upon to enforce. We would not make ourselves responsible for that amnesty. We urged him repeatedly to grant it, and if he had done so, he would most undoubtedly have been recognized; and we fully expected, when that paragraph was inserted in the King's Speech, that he would have given the amnesty, and have enabled us to recognize him. I have no hesitation in saying, that I was exceedingly anxious at that time to recognize this Prince, not because I disputed the claim or right of the other branch of the House of Braganza, nor because I ventured to decide upon that right, but I wanted to do that which was done by the government of this country in a similar case with respect to France,—I wanted to recognize the authority of the king *de facto*, in order to enable him to carry on the government of the country with advantage, not only to himself, and his country, but also to Europe. If I had remained in office much longer, I would have done it in order to remove from that country, and from Europe, the inconveniences which have resulted from the existing state of things in Portugal. It was not done before, because the amnesty was not given.

Much has been said about the cruelty of this Prince, and the hatred borne towards him by the people of Portugal; but I think there has been some extraordinary exaggeration upon that subject. The noble Earl states that we left things in this state when he left office. It is perfectly true; but we have, over and over again, pressed upon the noble Earl the necessity of taking Portugal out of the state in which it was placed, and of recognizing that government, with a view to prevent that state of affairs which has since come to puss. The Emperor of Brazil has no power to enter into a war in favor of his daughter, nor can she be put in possession of Portugal, except by revolutionary means,—namely, by employing bands of adventurers, collected in various quarters, and paid by God knows whom.

August 15, 1832.

The Civil War in Portugal fomented by Earl Grey's Government.

I believe if there be any country in the world in which it is both the duty and interest of England to prevent the existence of hostilities, that country is

Portugal. We are bound by treaties to defend her, as she is, in case of need, to defend England. It is affirmed that we are under engagements to preserve a strict neutrality towards the two Princes now opposed to each other in Portugal; but we are bound in honour and good policy to protect that country, in which his Majesty's subjects have such interests invested, and with which they carry on such extensive commerce: yet the present government have hazarded all these interests by permitting this war to be carried on there by a foreign power. The king, in his speech, calls it, indeed, a "civil war." My Lords, it is a revolutionary war—a war carried on by means furnished in this town, and for the advance of which the inducement is the hope of plunder. It is carried on by persons who have no interest in the war excepting plunder. Yet this is the war which his Majesty has been advised by his servants to call, upon the assembling of his parliament, "a civil war between the two branches of the house of Braganza in Portugal." The king is made, by his Ministers, to declare that he is anxiously desirous to put an end to this war. "I shall not fail to avail myself of any opportunity that may be afforded me to assist in restoring peace to a country with which the interests of my dominions are so intimately connected." Now, I know something of war, and I know something of war in that country; and I will tell noble Lords how they can put an end to it at once. Let them put forth a proclamation recalling his Majesty's subjects from the service of both parties engaged in the contest,—let them, at the same time, carry into execution the law of the country; let them, when the commissioners of the customs, in the execution of their exclusive duty, seize vessels carrying out troops, ammunition and officers, who, I am able to prove, are at this moment serving in those armies, leave the adjudication of such seizures to the proper tribunals; and let not the King's ministers interfere, and let them employ the British fleet in the Levant, and other places, to which the attention of his Majesty's government ought to be directed, instead of being employed in watching the shores of the Douro and the Tagus—let them do all this, and they will soon find that peace will be restored to Portugal without any further sacrifice. But I am sorry to say these are not the measures adopted by his Majesty's government, nor is the law carried into execution by that government. My Lords, I engage to prove, that though the commissioners of the customs did, in the autumn of 1831, detain certain vessels in the Thames, having on board the very troops, ammunition, and arms which have been since employed in this war; and although these commissioners are, by the act of parliament, the persons appointed to carry it into execution,—they were ordered, by a superior power, not to interfere.

February 5, 1833.

Don Miguel de facto King of Portugal.

Don Miguel having been appointed Sovereign by the Cortes, it was not the business of the British government to offer any opposition to their choice; and as long as we continued in office, we were seeking for the means of recognizing

Don Miguel as Sovereign, *de facto*, of Portugal. In point of fact, I have no doubt, if we had remained in office a fortnight longer, we should have effected that recognition; for it was never intended to make the proposed amnesty an indispensable condition of that step. Our object in recognizing him, was to prevent those disasters which I apprehended must arise from the conflict of extreme opinions in the Peninsula.

February 5, 1833.

The Catholic Oath is a Principle.

His Majesty has sworn to maintain the established Church of England in Ireland; and secondly, that in the very last arrangements made to remove the disabilities, as well of the Dissenters from the church of England as of the Roman Catholics of Ireland, words were inserted in the oaths to be taken by them, for the security of the Protestant establishment. I consider those oaths as principles; and that we ought not to run counter to them in any manner whatever.

February 5, 1833.

The Protestants of Ireland are the friends of order in Ireland, and they are the natural friends and connections of England. I entreat you never to lose sight of this important truth.

February 5, 1833.

The Game Laws increase Poaching.

Since the passing of the Game Act, poaching has enormously increased. It is consistent with my own knowledge, also, that as regards my own estate, until this law passed, there was little or no poaching upon it, but that evil has greatly increased since that period. In fact, not long since, I lost a servant in an affray with poachers, and I at once determined to give up preserving game; but I was induced to relinquish my intention in consequence of learning that the keeper, whom I was about to discharge, could not get employment in any other part of the country. This, alone, is the reason why I still preserve my game. I am thoroughly convinced that, in the neighbourhood in which I reside, poaching has increased threefold since the passing of the present Act. I think that result is entirely owing to the circumstance that the person who is in possession of the game is entitled to carry it away and sell it, and cannot be questioned as to the manner in which it came into his possession.

May 31, 1833.

Importance of Portugal to England.

If there be any nation in the world for which more than another this country feels—and justly feels—an interest, it is Portugal. The alliance between this country and Portugal is among the most ancient to be found in the history of nations; it is an alliance repeatedly recognised by all Europe; it is one from which this country has derived advantage almost from a period beyond memory; and for the preservation of which, in better times than these, and in order to rescue that country out of the hands of her enemies, she has expended her best blood and treasure.

June 3, 1833.

The Emancipation Act of 1833 a Premature Measure.

In the discussions on the abolition of the slave trade, it was more than once declared by the advocates of that measure, that they had no intention of following it up by an attempt at the abolition of slavery; but, on the contrary, those who contended most strenuously for the abolition of the slave trade, declared that it was not intended that it should be followed up by the abolition of slavery in the colonies, but that their intention was, by means of the abolition of the slave trade, to ameliorate the condition of the slaves, and improve the state of society in the colonies. But I will not believe, from all that I have heard and read, that even the most earnest advocates of the abolition of the slave trade intended, immediately, to follow up the amelioration of the condition of the slave, by the total abolition of slavery. That men should look forward to the abolition of slavery in the colonies as consequent on the improvement in the state of society, and the state of slavery, is probable; and there is no doubt that a great improvement has resulted from the abolition of the slave trade, coupled with the measure, but that the one step should be considered as an immediate consequence of the other, I altogether deny; and I appeal with confidence to the discussions which formerly took place.

In all countries, where it is proposed to make large bodies of slaves free, the first thing that is described as necessary to be considered is, whether the country is in a condition to bear the change; the second, whether the slave whom it is proposed to constitute a freeman, will work for hire? These are points with respect to which it has always been considered necessary to have full and convincing proof before emancipation should be granted. The noble Earl tells us that, in this instance, there is no proof to the contrary. I think that there is proof to the contrary. We have heard of the adoption of a measure of this nature within the province of Colombia. But supposing it to be true, that 100,000 liberated negroes have shewn a disposition to labour, or have actually laboured for hire in Colombia, still I contend that that circumstance affords no proof whatever that the same results would follow from the liberation 700,000 or

800,000 negroes in the British possessions. But I by no means concur with the noble Earl as to the sufficiency of the case of Colombia, as a case in point. I have the authority of a very intelligent person, who was resident in Colombia at the time that the transaction took place, and who, in writing upon the subject, states positively that the experiment was a most dangerous one; and that although the liberated negroes laboured for awhile, yet that a few years afterwards, they could not be got to work at all. This is further proved by the fact, that in the course of four or five years it was found necessary to introduce a measure for the promotion of agriculture, which measure, it was admitted, was called for, in consequence of the great difficulty that was found in getting the free negroes to work.

June 23, 1833.
Difficulty of preventing free labour in the Colonies anticipated.

Look at our own colonies in tropical climates, and see whether you can find any disposition in the free negro to work in the low grounds. If you look at Surinam, or any other of the tropical climates, where free negroes are to be found, you will find a total absence of any disposition, on their part, to work for hire, or for any other consideration whatever. But says the noble Earl, "the negroes work in Africa;" of that fact, begging the noble Earl's pardon, I do not think he can produce any proof; but even supposing that he could, I contend that the fact does not bear upon this question—the question here is not whether the negro, in a state of freedom, will work in Africa, but whether, being made free, he will voluntarily labour in the low grounds in our possessions within the tropics? I say, that there is no proof of such labour on the part of negroes, in any part of the world. In one quarter of the globe, in which I have some knowledge, I am certainly aware that men do labour very hard for hire in low grounds within the tropics; but those men are in a condition but little removed from absolute slavery, because they are the lowest in a state of society, which from them upwards is divided into the strictest castes. But in our West India possessions the case is very different; there, this difficulty from the moment of their first discovery, to the present hour, has always existed; a difficulty arising from the circumstance, that in those tropical climates, a man instead of working for hire, works only for food,—and having obtained that food, which he can procure by very little exertion, he thinks of nothing save the luxury of reposing in listless idleness beneath the shade. That is the great difficulty which surrounds this question.

June 25, 1833.

Depressing the West India Colonies will lead to the Introduction of Foreign Slave Grown Sugar.

Supposing that the growth of the sugar should, from the causes I have mentioned, fail in the West Indies, where are we to get sugar? We must get it no doubt from the colonies of other countries, where it is produced by the labour of slaves. What then, will those who are so anxious for the abolition of slavery say, if, in consequence of this measure, the slave trade should be revived, with all the added horrors of its being carried on in a contraband manner; and if, instead of decreasing the amount of slavery in the world, we should increase it, in Cuba, and in the other foreign West India possessions, over which we have no control, and into which it would be impossible for us to introduce any measure, regulating or ameliorating the condition of the slave.

At this moment we consume more of sugar, even excluding Ireland, than all the rest of Europe put together; and I leave it to your Lordships to consider whether it would be possible, under any circumstances whatever, that this country could go on without a supply of that article. How can that supply be furnished, supposing that the production in our colonies should fail, except by the produce of slave labour from the colonies of other countries?

June 25, 1833.

East India Company; Eulogium on its Administration.

Having been so long a servant of the East India Company, whose interests you are discussing, having served for so many years of my life in that country, having had such opportunities of personally watching the operation of the government of that country, and having had reason to believe, both from what I saw at that time, and from what I have seen since, that the Government of India was at that time, one of the best and most purely administered governments that ever existed, and one which has provided most effectually for the happiness of the people over which it is placed, it is impossible that I should be present when a question of this description is discussed, without asking your Lordships' attention for a very short time whilst I deliver my opinion upon the plan which his Majesty's ministers have brought forward. I will not follow the noble Marquis who opened the debate, into the consideration of whether a chartered company be the best, or not, calculated to carry on the government or the trade of an empire like India, that is not the question to which I wish now to apply myself. But whenever I hear of such discussions as this, I recall to my memory what I have seen in that country—I recall to my memory the history of that country for the last fifty or sixty years. I remember its days of misfortune, and its days of glory, and call to mind the situation in which it now stands. I remember that the government have conducted the affairs of—I will not pretend to say how many millions of people,—they have been calculated at 70,000,000, 80,000,000, 90,000,000, and 100,000,000—but certainly of an immense population, a population returning an annual revenue of 20,000,000 l. sterling, and that notwithstanding all the wars in which the empire has been engaged its debt at this moment amounts only to 40,000,000 l., being no more than the amount of two years revenue. I do not say that such a debt is desirable; but at the same time I contend that it is a delusion on the people of this country to tell them that that is a body unfit for government, and unfit for trade, which has administered the affairs of India with so much success for so many years, and which is at length to be put down,—for I can use no other term,—upon the ground that it is an institution calculated for the purposes neither of government nor trade.

My Lords, there is a great difference between the East India Company governing India, and carrying on their trade with China as a joint-stock company, and carrying on the same trade as monopolists. It was my opinion, and the opinion of those who acted with me, that we ought, in the first instance, at all events, to have endeavoured to have prevailed upon them to continue trading with China as a joint-stock company. If at this moment, they had chosen to have continued to trade as a joint stock company, I would have allowed them; I would have adopted measures for the purpose of inducing them to do so, and to carry on the government of India. It is perfectly true, my Lords, that the people of this country were, and are, desirous of participating in the trade to China; but I am not aware that they ever expressed a desire to see the company deprived of any branch of that trade. But then, my Lords, the noble Lord asks, "how would you secure to them their dividends?" Why, my Lords, their dividends, supposing the trade had turned out so ill as the noble Lord expects it would have done, would have been secured to them, as they must be at present, by saving all unnecessary expense in India—those dividends would have been secured to them, as they still will be, and as under all circumstances they must be, by bringing down the whole expences of the Government of the country. But we had another resource—we might have relieved the East India Company, trading to China no longer as a monopolist, but as a joint stock company, from a part of the burden of the provisions of the Commutation Act. I cannot help thinking, if that course had been adopted—or even supposing, according to the calculations of my noble Friend behind me, we had been obliged to abandon that course, by desiring the East India Company to withdraw from trading with China—that they still would have been in possession of their capital, which might have been disposed of for their advantage, and they might have been continued in the Government of India. I entreat your Lordships to observe, that such an arrangement would have been attended with this advantage, that they would not have had to draw their dividends from India. One of the greatest inconveniences attending this arrangement is, in my opinion, the increased sum which must be annually brought home by remittance to this country from India, to such an amount that the inconvenience is very great, so great, that I very much doubt whether the process can be carried on; and it must be most prejudicial to the commerce of the country.

June 5, 1833.

Reform un fait accompli.

Now that the Reform Bill has become the law of the land, I have considered it my duty not only to submit to it, but to endeavour to carry its provisions into execution by every means in my power.

July 19, 1833.

Repudiation of the Holy Alliance.

I have passed part of my life in the foreign service of my country; but I most sincerely protest, that I never did join with any holy alliance against the liberties of Europe.

July 19, 1833.

Expediency and Principle.

If the world were governed by principles, nothing would be more easy than to conduct even the greatest affairs; but, in all circumstances, the duty of a wise man is to choose the lesser of any two difficulties which beset him.

July 19, 1833.

Protestantism to be supported.

It is our duty, in every case, to do all we can to promote the Protestant religion. It is our duty to do so, not only on account of the political relations between the religion of the Church of England and the Government, but because we believe it to be the purest doctrine, and the best system of religion, that can be offered to a people.

July 19, 1833.

Importance of preserving the authority of the East India Company.

The noble Lord who spoke last, quoted the opinion of Sir John Malcolm. My Lords, I wish the noble Lords opposite had taken the advice of Sir John Malcolm, upon the subject of forming an independent body in London, representing the interests, and carrying on the concerns, of India. My Lords, it is persons of this description who interpose an efficient check upon the Government. I say, therefore, that it is much to be lamented, that instead of placing that body in the state of independence in which they were heretofore placed, they are to be reduced to a situation in which they will lose a very considerable portion of their power and influence. It is of the utmost importance that the greatest possible care should be taken to preserve the authority of the company in relation to their servants. Depend upon it, my

Lords, that on the basis of their authority depends the good government of India.
July 5, 1833.

After Emancipation, the Protestants of Ireland ought to have been conciliated.
The noble and learned Lord (Plunkett) said, that many of the evils that afflicted Ireland, and for which the Church Temporalities Bill was intended as a remedy, were occasioned by the delay of the measure of Emancipation, after the year 1825. Why, I ask, by its delay after the year 1825? I beg to know from that noble and learned Lord how long the system of agitation existed in Ireland both before and after the year 1825? Why, my Lords, it has existed ever since the commencement of the discussion of the Roman Catholic Question—that is to say, ever since the days of the restrictive regency. From that period to the present moment, there has been nothing but agitation, except during parts of the years 1829 and 1830. Agitation commenced in Ireland upon the conclusion of events in Paris, and in Brussels. Those events occasioned such agitations and discussions as obliged the noble Duke, who was then at the head of the Government in Ireland, to carry into execution the Proclamation Act. Then came a change in the administration, and the noble Earl assumed the reigns of power. He immediately chose for the Lord Lieutenant (Lord Wellesley) a nobleman for whom I entertain great respect but who certainly was nearly the last person who ought to have been selected for that office. After the Roman Catholic Question was settled, what ought the government to have done? Most certainly they ought to have done everything in their power to conciliate—whom? The Protestants of Ireland. Everything had already been granted to the Roman Catholics which they could possibly require; and the object of the government ought to have been to conciliate the Protestants. But, instead of that, the noble Earl sends over to that country, as Lord Lieutenant, the noble Marquis, who was the very last person that ought to have been appointed; because, when holding that situation previously, and on receiving information that his Majesty's government entertained views favourable to the emancipation of the Catholics, he did, immediately, before his departure for Ireland, issue a sort of proclamation to the people that agitation should be continued for the purpose of obtaining the desired boon.
July 19, 1833.

Irish Agitation Characterized.
Now, my Lords, in order to enable your Lordships to understand what this "agitation" is, I beg leave just to describe it to your Lordships. It is, first of all, founded upon a conspiracy of priests and demagogues to obtain their purpose—whether justifiable or not, is not the question—by force and menace, and by the use of terror and of mobs, wherever that terror and those mobs can be used to

produce an effect upon his Majesty's Government favourable to their views. This agitation they have maintained by orations, harangues, and seditious speeches at public meetings—by publications through a licentious press—by exaggerations—by forgeries—and by all other means which it is in the power of that description of persons to use, in order to excite the multitude; and then, when they are excited, to make them appear in large bodies to terrify and overawe the people. If, my Lords, any person ventures to oppose himself to these proceedings, he is either immediately murdered or his house is destroyed, his cattle or other property carried off, and combinations are formed to prevent resistance, or the discovery of the guilty. In short, all measures are adopted which go to, and which are intended to, destroy the Constitution of this country. This, my Lords, is what is called the system of "agitation."

July 19, 1833.

What constitutes a Blockade.

To constitute an effective blockade, it is unnecessary to say that the port in question must be actually blockaded; and, further, that notice must have been given of such a blockade. No capture could be made without previously warning off vessels. There are various modes of notice; but the most authoritative manner of giving notice is through the Government of the power to be so warned. It should never be forgotten, however, that there should be certain means in existence to enforce the blockade at the time of notice.

July 19, 1833.

Objection to the reduction of the Number of Irish Bishops.

I object to the proposed reduction of the number of Bishops in Ireland, and I totally dissent from the argument upon which the propriety or expediency of that reduction is founded. I am willing to admit that if we were now, for the first time, establishing the Protestant Church in Ireland. I might be inclined to think that twenty-two Bishops were more than was necessary to the supervision of some 1000 clergymen; but when I take into account, besides the fact that the higher number has been in existence for centuries—when I consider the importance of the Protestant Church in Ireland in relation to the political ties of the two countries—when I consider, as a Right Reverend Prelate has remarked in the course of the debate, that wherever a Protestant Bishop is removed, there a Catholic Prelate will remain, who, doubtless, will possess himself of the palace, and perhaps the church property, of the reduced Protestant See; and when, above all, I consider the peculiar circumstances of Ireland, so different from those of this country, and which may make the episcopal superintendence of thirty or forty benefices in the former country a matter of more trouble and anxiety than the 600 or 1000 benefices which an English Prelate may control, I cannot but object to the proposed reduction. Besides, there is another circumstance which is worthy of attention in the discussion of this subject, and that is, that the Bishops of England have the assistance of their Deans and Archdeacons, which their Irish brethren have not. The twenty-two Bishops of Ireland have personally to perform all the duties which the Bishops of this country perform through their Deans and Archdeacons.

July 19, 1835

The Jews' Right to Citizenship denied.
The noble and learned Lord (Brougham), and the most reverend Prelate (Whately), have both stated that they cannot understand the distinct principle upon which the opponents of this measure rest their opposition to the admission of the Jews to seats in the legislature. Now I beg the noble and learned Lord, and the most reverend Prelate, to recollect that this is a Christian country and a Christian legislature, and that the effect of this measure would be to remove that peculiar character. Your Lordships have been called upon to follow the example of foreign countries, with respect to the Jews; but I think that, before we proceed to legislate on such a subject as this, it is indispensable that the necessity for the introduction of the measure should be shown. I ask, what case has been made out to shew a necessity for passing this measure? When your Lordships passed the bills for the removal of the Roman Catholic disabilities, and for the repeal of the Test and Corporation Acts, the reason assigned was, that it was unnecessary to keep up the restriction on the classes of Christians affected by those acts. But there is a material difference between the cases of the dissenters and Roman Catholics, and the Jews—the former enjoyed all the benefits and advantages of the constitution before the restrictions were imposed. Was that the case with the Jews? Were the Jews ever in the enjoyment of the blessings of the English constitution? Certainly not. The Jews were formerly considered as alien enemies, and they were not allowed to live in this country,—I think from the time of Edward I. to the period of the Commonwealth. It cannot, therefore, be said that the question of the Jews can be put on the same ground as the claims of any class of Christians in the country.
August 1, 1843.

The Jews have no Right to Civil Equality.
The noble and learned Lord on the Woolsack (Lord Brougham) has referred to a certain Act of Parliament which passed, giving certain privileges to the Jews, and which he said, was in the very form of words proposed in this bill. It is true that this Act conferred benefits on the Jews, but then it must be recollected that it was confined in its operation to certain of the colonies; in the first instance to Canada, and subsequently to Jamaica and Barbadoes, and others of the West Indian colonies. But then, was there not a very good reason for this? European

inhabitants were much required in the colonies at the time the act passed; and this was to give encouragement to the Jews to go thither and settle. No such necessity exists now, with regard to this country,—we do not wish Jews to come and settle here. Not one word has been said to shew that any necessity exists for passing this measure. The noble Lord, who addressed your Lordships early in the debate, adverted to the state of the Jews in France, I entirely agree with the illustrious Duke near me, and the right reverend Prelate, that this country is not bound to follow the example of foreign nations in legislating for any portion of the community. But it ought not to escape attention, that Buonaparte, in legislating for the Jews, did not go the full length of this bill; and before he did anything for them, he ordered a strict inquiry into their case to be made. I ask, are your Lordships prepared to assent to this bill, without any inquiry being instituted as to its necessity, or without any reason being assigned? This bill is not the result of inquiry, but it has been introduced on a very different principle,—namely, because it suits the liberal opinions of the day.

The noble and learned Lord on the Woolsack, has endeavoured to shew that, by retaining the words—"upon the true faith of a Christian," in the Statute Book, you encourage men who have no regard to the obligation of an oath, and thus maintain hypocrisy, while it operates as a restriction on conscientious persons. "You admit," says the noble and learned Lord, "men like Mr. Wilkes, Lord Shaftesbury, or Lord Bolingbroke, but you shut out conscientious men who will not take the oath." I am prepared to allow that there are some men whom no oath or affirmation can reach; but this is no reason why we should give up every test and oath. Are we on this account to throw aside every guard for the maintenance of Christianity in the country? The Right Reverend Prelate has stated very clearly and plainly the reason why we should not pass this bill—namely, that this is a Christian country, and has a Christian legislature, and that therefore, the Parliament, composed as it is, of Lords Spiritual and Temporal, and Commons, cannot advise the Sovereign, as the head of the Church, to sanction a law which will remove the peculiar character of the legislature, I say that we cannot advise the Sovereign on the throne to pass a law which will admit persons to all offices, and into the Parliament of the country, who, however respectable they may be, still are not Christians, and therefore ought not to be allowed to legislate for a Christian Church. The noble Marquis, for whom I entertain the highest respect, seemed surprised that I should smile when the noble Marquis spoke in somewhat extravagant terms of the distinctions which have been acquired by these persons in foreign countries. I must apologize to the noble Marquis for having smiled at that moment, but it certainly appeared to me that the noble Marquis was rather extravagant in his praise; and, I may be allowed to add, that I have never been so fortunate as to hear of those persons being in the stations which he described. The noble marquis stated that there were no less than fifteen officers of the Jewish religion at the battle of Waterloo; I have not the least doubt that there are many officers of that religion of great merit and distinction—but still I must again repeat they are not Christians; and, therefore, sitting as I do in a Christian legislature, I cannot advise the sovereign on the throne to sanction a law to admit them to seats in this house and the other house of parliament, and to all the rights and privileges enjoyed by Christians. The noble and learned lord on the woolsack said, that when the observation is mode that Christianity is part and parcel of the law of the land, it is meant that that Christianity is the Church of England. Now, I have always understood that it was the Christian dispensation, generally; and I believe that when Christianity is talked of as part and parcel of the law, it means the Christian dispensation, and not the doctrines of the Church of England.

August 1, 1833.

Defence of a Metallic Currency.
I always have maintained, and I always shall maintain, that the only proper basis of our money system is a solid gold circulation. Upon that basis I considered our monetary system fixed since the measure of 1819, followed up as that was by improvements in 1826: I really think the principle of those measures the best that can be applied to our circulation. Detailed payments being made in gold, the larger payments might be made in paper, and depend on credit; the true support of the credit of whatever paper might be in circulation being, that it was liable to be paid in gold on demand at any time, at the bank of England, or at the branch-banks of the bank of England; so that, if any man chose not to give credit to the bank of England, he had only to demand gold for his paper; or any creditor might, at once, demand from his debtor payment in solid coin. That however will, to a certain extent, not be the case under this bill. I am aware that, eventually, the holder of the paper can repair to the bank of England and demand gold as heretofore; and must, therefore give credit to somebody for the amount. That I consider a depreciation of the paper of the bank of England. It is a depreciation to which if I had been a bank director, I would never have consented; indeed, I cannot understand why the bank agreed to this proposition. I am persuaded that, ere long, great inconveniences will occur from the provision; and those inconveniences will be felt in a depreciation of bank paper. What is the object of the arrangement? It is either intended to give the bank a power of issuing paper which, under the existing system, it does not possess, or to facilitate credit generally throughout the country, and enable the country banks to undertake operations which they could not otherwise attempt. It is evident that the noble earl himself sees that the consequence will be to facilitate and increase the issues of the country banks. That will augment all transactions; and the result must be a great increase of prices, and the ruin of many individuals. Nothing of this kind would happen, if the present system were continued; namely, if the bank of England continued to issue the number of its notes which the necessity of the public might seem to require; and by the regularity of its proceedings give such a check to the issues of the country banks, as should be calculated to establish a sound and healthy circulation. Under the existing system, the bank would proceed so as to prevent the country banks

from giving credit, except in cases which justified the accommodation, and the circulation and commerce of the country would continue in a wholesome state.
August 23, 1833.

The Duke of Wellington's reasons for supporting the Poor Law Amendment Bill.
I concur with the noble and learned lord on the woolsack, and with the noble lord opposite, as to the necessity of this measure. I agree, first of all, in the existence of grievances consequent upon the existing administration of the poor-laws, but I do not concur in the opinion expressed by the noble and learned lord (the Lord Chancellor) in disapproving of the provisions of the statute of Elizabeth; but I do disapprove of a system of administration which differs in each and every of the 12,000 parishes in this country, and in each of which different and varied abuses have crept in. I maintain that it is impossible for parliament to frame any law that can by possibility remedy or apply to the abuses which prevail at the present moment—abuses which are as varied in their character as they are numerous. It is their general existence all over the country—it is their existence in a different shape in every parish of the kingdom—which renders the appointment of a central board absolutely necessary, with powers to control the whole of the parishes in the land, and to adopt such remedies as will secure a sure administration of these laws throughout the country. If my noble friend, who has spoken in opposition to this measure, had recently attended to parliamentary business more assiduously than he has done, he would have found that the subject has been submitted to the house by several noble lords, and has also been under the consideration of every administration that I have known; but no plan has ever been suggested, or scheme proposed, to remove and remedy the evils of the existing laws, which in my judgment at all equalled the present, and for it I must return the noble lord opposite, with whom it has originated, my sincere thanks. The present remedy for the evils of the existing laws is most unquestionably the best that has ever been devised; at the same time I must observe, that as the central board of commissioners must necessarily have very extraordinary and full powers, it will be necessary that they should keep such a record of their proceedings as shall render them liable to the actual control at all times of the government and parliament of the country. I doubt much whether the provisions of this bill give such a controul to the government as will afford a full knowledge to the parliament at all times of the course pursued by the commissioners; but in committee on the bill, I shall consider whether some alteration is not necessary, in order to make that control more active. There are several other clauses in the bill which require much alteration and modification. I entirely approve of the removal of the allowance system, which is one of the greatest evils arising from the existing poor-laws; but I am of opinion that it ought gradually and slowly to have been destroyed, and without a fixed day for its termination being specified in the bill. I would recommend that this clause should be left out, and that

power should be given to the commissioners to carry gradually such alterations in this respect into effect, as to them may seem meet.
July 81,1834.

Tests no Security to Religion.
The noble duke, amongst other matters, has adverted to the union between church and state, with respect to which he has made some observations which are undoubtedly worthy of consideration, but to which I do not intend, on this occasion, to offer any answer. I will, however, just observe, that I apprehend what is generally meant by dissevering the union of the church and state is, that there should be no established religion. To that proposition, I trust it is superfluous for me to say that I am a most decided opponent. It is, however, a subject which I cannot now pretend to discuss. It is my opinion, that to leave religion to rest upon the voluntary efforts of the people, is a notion which we are not at present in a situation competent to entertain. It is so very great a change, and so totally different from all that we know and observe, that we are absolutely precluded, from want of experience, from entering upon the consideration of the question. It is not a just criterion, by which to form a judgment, to refer to the experience of other nations—such as the existence of Christianity in Rome before it became the established religion of the empire, or the existence of religion in a country so distant and so unlike our own, in all its circumstances, as the United states of North America. That, my lords, is the opinion I entertain, and therefore I will no longer occupy your lordships by any further discussion on this subject. I belong to the church of England, and am a friend of that church, from feeling and from conviction. I do not say that I have examined all her doctrines, or that I am master of all the grounds upon which her rites and ceremonies stand—I do not say that I am able to discuss with my noble friend those one thousand questions, which Bishop Law said arose out of the thirty-nine articles, but I believe her doctrines to be scriptural, and I know her principles to be tolerant. But, my lords, I beg leave to say, that I adopt those doctrines upon another ground, which perhaps may expose me, with some in the present day, to censure. My lords, I espouse those doctrines because they are the mode of faith delivered down to me by my forefathers; and because they are the mode of faith which I find established in my country. I am not prepared to remove the basis upon which is founded (though it may be apart from) the structure of the religion of my country. I do not think that such is the wish of the majority of the dissenters; but, at all events, it seems to me a course calculated to lead only to a state of general scepticism and universal suspension of religion among the people. But while I say this for myself—while I claim to found my attachment to my religion upon principle, it is necessary that I should say precisely the same thing for that great body of men who may be called the dissenters of England. Their consent is rarely contemporaneous with the establishment of the church of England herself. The dissenters from the church

of England are those who thought that the Reformation did not proceed far enough. Their dissent did not show itself against the established church when in power and prosperity; but the dissenters from that church grew up first when the Roman Catholic religion was dominant in this country, and when both the members of the new church of England and the dissenters were alike suffering under persecution; therefore, it is a dissent founded on principle. Considering the weight which dissent has in this country, and considering the extent to which it prevails, many attempts have been, from time to time, made, as we all know, at a religious comprehension of all denominations of Christians in the body of the church. Such attempts have been made by some of the greatest prelates that the church has ever known. These attempts have all failed; but, surely in our days, it may be thought wise to attempt at least a general civil comprehension of all classes, by admitting them, if it be possible to do so, to those benefits which are to be derived from the public institutions of the country.

I will not go into the foundations of the universities. I am not for raising any quibble on that subject. I apprehend that they have grown up, as all other institutions have done, very much from a series of accidents, and the force of chances. One college has been founded by one individual, and one by another; but, however they have grown up, they have, in fact, become, and are now considered, as the national seminaries of education. I would reserve to them, in every respect, their corporate rights. I would respect them as places where the religion of the country is taught, and professed; but undoubtedly I would if possible, for the sake of general peace and union, and for the sake of bringing together those who are now divided, try, with the sanction and approbation of the universities themselves (and we know perfectly well that most of their distinguished members are of opinion that this can be done); I would, I say, try whether we could not open the gates of these universities to that great body of this country, who unfortunately dissent from the doctrines of the church of England. I would not do so, however, rashly, nor with any violence to honest prejudices, or to those well-intentioned feelings which some persons are found to cherish.

The noble duke has said that tests are no securities against the admission of atheists or schismatics, and that a man may take them who dissented from them, if he chose to stifle all his feelings of right and wrong. But, my lords, I beg leave to say that tests are no security against any man. It is impossible ever to have looked at the history of religion in any state, or at any period, and not to feel that the test laws have been the weakest ground upon which any faith could stand. Were tests any security for the heathen religion against the vital spirit of the heaven-descended energy of Christianity? Yet we are aware that every act of the life of a heathen was in itself a test. He could not sit to his meat, he could not retire to rest, he could not go through the most simple transactions of life, without some act of acknowledgment offered towards some heathen deity. Unless these observances were attended to by the Christians, they were subject to the most cruel punishments, and yet such means failed to preserve the dominant faith. In fact, it is well known that one of the most violent persecutions of the Christians, instituted by the Roman emperors, was followed, as it were, almost immediately by the establishment of Christianity as the dominant religion of the empire. Were tests any security to the Roman Catholic religion, against the growing light and energy of the Protestant faith? Tests of various kinds were adopted at the very moment the new doctrines showed themselves, but it was soon found that they were vain and fragile against the light and strength of the new doctrines. Were tests any security to these very universities themselves? I have not looked very deeply into this subject; I have no doubt that if I were to look closer into it, I should find more instances of the sort; but I find that about fourteen years after the establishment of King's College, in the university of Cambridge, a decree was sent down there by King Henry VI., admonishing the scholars, that is to say, in the language of the present day, the fellows of that college, against the damnable and pernicious errors (so it styled them), of John Wickliffe and Richard Peacock, and denouncing the pains of expulsion from college, and perjury, against those of them who should show any favour to those doctrines. Yet, in two years after this, this very king's college became what, at that time was called the most heretical, but which now, in our time, would be called the most Protestant college in the university; and we know that these doctrines thus fiercely denounced, and strongly guarded against by tests, about fifty or sixty years afterwards became, by law, the established religion of this country. It is upon her native strength—upon her own truth—it is upon her spiritual character, and upon the purity of her doctrines, that the Church of England rests. Let her not, then, look for support in such aids as these. It is by these means, and not by tests and proscriptions, that protestantism has been maintained; let her be assured of this.

August 1, 1834.

Cause of the dismissal of the Melbourne Administration in November, 1834.

I am not responsible for the dissolution of the late government. The late government was dissolved from the absolute impossibility of its going on any longer. When a noble earl (Spencer), whom I do not now see in his place, was removed from the House of Commons, by the necessity of taking his seat in this house, it was impossible for the late government to go on. I will just desire your lordships to recollect that it was stated by the noble earl (Grey), who so worthily filled the situation of prime minister for nearly four years, when his noble colleague (Lord Althorp), in the House of Commons, thought proper to resign, "that he had lost his right hand, and that it had thus become absolutely impossible for him to continue to carry on the government, or to serve the Crown with honour or advantage." Not only did the noble earl make this declaration of his inability to go on upon the retirement of his noble colleague from his majesty's councils, but the noble viscount opposite, himself, when he afterwards came to form his government, stated that the noble earl (Spencer), having consented to retain his office and position in the House of Commons, he was prepared to undertake to preside over his majesty's councils, and carry on the business of the country. But this was not all; for I happen to know that, when the noble viscount found that he was likely to be deprived of the services and assistance of that noble lord in the other house, he felt that his administration would be placed in circumstances of the greatest difficulty and embarrassment. Besides that, it was perfectly well known to his majesty, that the influence of that noble lord in the other house of parliament was the foundation on which the government to which he was attached, reposed; and, that that support being removed, it must fall. When, therefore, his majesty found that it was fairly put to him whether he would consent to arrangements for the late government proceeding as it best could, or whether he would consent to steps being taken for the formation of another administration, it was surely natural for his majesty to consider his own situation, and the situation in which the late government was lately placed by the death of the late Earl Spencer.

February 24, 1835.

Why the Duke of Wellington held so many offices, ad interim, *in November,* 1834.

I gave his majesty the best advice which, under the circumstances of the case, it appeared to me practicable to give. I advised his majesty to send for that right hon. gentleman (Sir R. Peel), a member of the House of Commons, who seemed to me to be the most fit and capable person to place at the head of the new administration, as first lord of the treasury. That right honourable gentleman was then in another part of the world, and some time must necessarily elapse before it would be possible that he could return to this country. It appeared to his majesty and to myself, however, to be essentially necessary that, in the meantime, the government should be taken possession of and administered. This step I considered to be absolutely necessary, and I also felt it to be absolutely necessary that, whoever might exercise the authority of government in the interval, should take no step that might embarrass or compromise the right honourable baronet on his return. It was only on that ground that I accepted, for the time, of the offices of first lord of the treasury, and secretary of state for the home department.

The noble viscount has made a little mistake in alleging that I was appointed to three departments at once. He makes it a matter of charge against me that I exercised the authority of the three secretaries of state; but the noble viscount knows very well that the secretary of state for the home department is competent, under certain circumstances, to do so. It was for the public service, and the public convenience, and no other reason whatever, that I, my lords, consented to hold, for a time, the situations of first lord of the treasury, and secretary of state for the home department. But I want to know whether this was, as the noble viscount insinuates, an unprecedented act? When Mr. Canning was secretary of state for the foreign department, he was appointed first lord of the treasury. The latter office Mr. Canning received on the 12th of April, and he did not resign the seals of the foreign department until the 30th of that month. During the whole of that period Mr. Canning discharged the duties both of secretary of state for foreign affairs, and first lord of the treasury. My lords, I am quite aware that there were at that period, two other secretaries of state, but the fact is as I have stated it, that Mr. Canning exercised at the same time; the functions both of first lord of the treasury, and secretary of state for the foreign department. The transaction in my case was, therefore, not unprecedented; and I must also say, that when the noble viscount thought proper to blame me, as he did, he was bound to show that my conduct, in that respect, had been attended with some evil or inconvenient result. Now, it does not appear that it has been attended with any such result. The fact is, that during the whole of the time that I held the two offices. I cautiously avoided taking any step which might be productive of subsequent embarrassment or inconvenience, and when my right honourable friend took possession of his office, I can undertake to say that he did not find himself compromised by any such act.

February 24, 1835.

Lord Londonderry's appointment to the Embassy at St. Petersburgh.

My lords, having learned that it would not be disagreeable to my noble friend to be employed in the public service, I did concur in the recommendation, or rather, my lords, I did recommend to my right honourable friend, Sir Robert Peel, that my noble friend should be appointed ambassador to the court of St. Petersburgh. I made this recommendation, founded as it was on my own personal knowledge of my noble friend for many years past,—on the many great and important military services he has performed, and on the fitness he has proved himself to possess for such an appointment in those various diplomatic employments he has filled during a long period of time; more particularly at the court of Vienna, where for a period of nine years, he performed most important services to the entire satisfaction of the ministers who employed him, up to the last moment of his employment. He returned from the discharge of that office, my lords, with the strongest testimony of the approbation of the then secretary of state for foreign affairs. I was aware, my lords, of the peculiar talents of my noble friend in certain respects, for this particular office, and of his consequent fitness for this very description of diplomatic employment, especially on account of his being a military officer of high rank in the service of this country, and of distinguished reputation in the Russian army. I knew the peculiar advantages that must attach to an individual conducting such an embassy on that account. Under these circumstances, I was justified, my lords, in recommending my noble friend, and I was glad to find that my right honourable friend concurred in that recommendation, and that his majesty was pleased to approve of it. I may also add, that the nomination of my noble friend having been communicated in the usual manner to the court of St.

Petersburgh, it was received with approbation at that court. For all these reasons, my lords, it was with the greatest regret I learned that this nomination,—for it had gone no further than nomination,—was not approved of in another place; for it is in consequence of that expression of disapproval that my noble friend, with that delicacy of feeling which belongs to his character, has declined the office.

March 16,1834.

Prerogative of the Crown in appointing Ambassadors.

There can be no doubt whatever that there is no branch of the prerogative of the crown greater, or more important, than that of sending ambassadors to foreign courts; nor is there any branch of that prerogative the unrestricted use of which ought to be kept more inviolate. But, my lords, the ministers of the crown are responsible for these nominations. They are also responsible for the instructions under which my noble friend, or any other noble lord so nominated, is bound to act. They are, moreover, responsible for the proper performance of these duties on the part of those whom they select—to the other house of parliament, and to the country at large. It is impossible, therefore, for me to believe that the House of Commons would in this case proceed so far as to interfere with that peculiar prerogative, and to say that an individual who has been already nominated by the crown should not fill the situation; inasmuch as, by so doing, the House of Commons would not only be taking upon itself the nomination of the officer, and the direction of the particular duties to be discharged by him—but would also be relieving the minister from the constitutional responsibility of the appointment. I do not think that sentiments of such a description, on a subject of this delicacy and importance, are very general; and I cannot bring myself to believe that a vote affirming such a violation of the royal prerogative would have passed the House of Commons.

March 15,1835.

I

The Roman Catholics interested in maintaining the Established Church.

The great bulk of the Roman Catholics are as much interested as the Protestants of the established church in maintaining the safety of the established church.

June 10, 1835.

Defence of the Thirty-nine Articles.

I conceive that there is no cause to complain of the subscription to the thirty-nine articles, as practised in Oxford. The explanation given by the most reverend prelate is entirely borne out by the statues of the university, and by the practice that prevails there; and this explanation agrees entirely with that given by a right reverend prelate, who was formerly head of one of the colleges at Oxford. It might, perhaps, be desirable that some other test should be adopted to prove that the individuals to be matriculated are members of the church of England; the most important point is, that Cambridge and Oxford should be filled only by members of the Church of England—upon that I consider the whole question to rest. The noble earl said, in the course of the discussion, that I advised your lordships not to consent to the bill introduced last session; because, if you did, you would have to carry to the foot of the throne a measure which would tend to subvert the union between church and state. My meaning in so doing was neither more nor less than this—that it was absolutely necessary that the universities, founded as they are, should educate their members in the religion of the church of England. Your lordships could not go to the king, and ask his consent to a bill which had for its object to establish in the university a system of education different from that of the church of England, without attacking the very foundation of the principle of the connexion between church and state. But the noble lord says, the church herself does not exact subscription to the thirty-nine articles from each individual. It is very true that the church of England does not require subscription from her members, nor would the university of Oxford require it, but as a proof that the person subscribing was a member of that church, or of the family of a member thereof.

The noble earl stated that individuals might obtain admittance to the universities both of Oxford and Cambridge, notwithstanding that they were dissenters; but there is a great deal of difference between casually admitting dissenters, and permitting them to enter into the universities as a matter of right. I see no objection to the admission of the few now admitted, who must submit to the regulations and discipline of the university, and of its several colleges; but I do object to the admission of dissenters into the universities by right; and my reason for making this exception is, that I am exceedingly desirous that the religion taught there should be the religion of the church of England; and I confess I should be very apprehensive that, if dissenters of all denominations were admitted by right, and they were not under the necessity of submitting to the rules and regulations of the several colleges, not only would the religion of the church of England not to be taught there, but no kind of religion whatever. I state this on the authority of a report which I have recently received of the proceedings of an institution in this country for the instruction of children of dissenting clergymen; from which it appears absolutely impossible, for any length of time, to adhere to any creed, or any tenet or doctrine in these seminaries, in which every doctrine is matter of dispute and controversy. I was rather surprised to hear the noble viscount opposite—a minister of the crown—express his preference for polemical disputations in the universities. I should have thought that he would have felt it to be his inclination, as well as duty, by all means to protect the universities from such disputes, and from a system fruitful in such controversies; and probably to end in a cessation of any system of religion or religious instruction whatever, on account of the different opinions of the members.

July 14,1835.

University Tests rendered necessary by Toleration.

The tests in our universities are the children of the Reformation, which the system of toleration wisely established in this country has rendered still more necessary, if we intend to preserve the standard of the religion of the church of England. If we open the door wide and say "We will have no established religion at all—every man shall follow the religion he chooses"—if, in a word, we have recourse to the voluntary system,—then we must make up our minds to take the consequences which must follow from the enactments of the bill and the polemical and other controversial agitations to which it must lead. But, supposing the object of the noble lord, to put an end to these tests, to be desirable, I can conceive no mode of effecting this object so objectionable as the interference by parliament with the privileges of the universities, secured to them by charter and repeatedly acknowledged and confirmed by parliament.

July 14 1835

Irish Clergy—their Depression by the Melbourne Government.

I do say that the Protestant people and clergy of Ireland have great reason to complain of the want of protection to their rights and properties manifested on the part of the government of this country; and this is the cause of those disputes and those circumstances which the noble lord opposite (Lord Melbourne) has complained of in the few words he has addressed to the house on the subject. Far be it from me to wish for the renewal of any dissensions in Ireland; and, God knows, I would go any length, and do any thing in my power to put them down in the extent to which they now exist; but we are mistaken if we suppose that they can be put down by oppressing one party, or allowing one party to oppress another, or by extinguishing—an extinction which for the last three or four years you have attempted and are now about to complete—that description of property in Ireland allotted to the payment of the clergy. This is the circumstance which occasions the present dissensions in Ireland, and which has induced the present discussion in this house. The noble lord opposite cannot lament the cause of such discussions more than I do; but if he be determined to do his duty, let him give the protection of his majesty's government to the Protestant clergy and people of Ireland, as he does not hesitate to do in the case of other classes in that country; and the evils which he so much deplores will soon cease to exist.

July 16, 1835.

A Power of Revising Railway Acts ought to be Reserved by the Legislature.
I certainly have a very strong feeling on the subject of all these railways to be traversed by the aid of steam. I sincerely wish that all these projects could prove successful; but, in proportion as they may be successful, in the same proportion is it desirable that there should not be a perpetual monopoly established in the country. Under these circumstances, I have a strong feeling that it is desirable to insert in all these bills some clause, to enable the government or the parliament to revise the enactments contained in them at some future specific period. I conceive that, by carrying these measures into execution, a very great injustice is often done to many landed proprietors in the country; and they are forced either to submit to great inconvenience, or to contend against that inconvenience by incurring a very large expense, both in this and the other house of parliament. If some measure of the description to which I allude be not adopted, and if these railroads are to become monopolies in the hands of present or of future proprietors, we shall hereafter be only able to get the better of such monopolies by forming fresh lines of road, to the farther detriment of the interests of the landed proprietors, and at a great increase of expense and inconvenience. These circumstances have most forcibly struck my mind. I have had the subject under consideration for some days; I have conversed with others respecting it; and it appears to me that some plan ought to be devised in order to bring these railroads under the supervision of parliament at some future period. I therefore am anxious that the further proceedings in all these bills[18] should be suspended for a short time, in order that I may propose some clause, or introduce some measure, to meet the object to which I have referred. I think it is a subject the consideration of which ought not to fall on any individual. It is, I conceive, a matter which the government should take into its especial consideration. I am, however, perfectly ready to share with the government the responsibility of proposing such a measure to the house.
[Footnote 18: Some railway bills before the Home of Lords.]
June 3,1836.

Moderation of the Opposition in the House of Lords towards the Melbourne Government.
From my own experience, I must take the liberty of observing, that I consider the conduct pursued by noble lords on this side of the house, throughout the present session, to have been marked with the utmost moderation. For myself, I think I am correct in stating, that since the address to the throne in answer to the king's speech, with the exception only of one occasion, when I requested the noble viscount to postpone the Corporations (Ireland) Bill till after the Easter holidays, I never entered the house till after Easter. Since that period, I have certainly taken part in the proceedings that have been going forward in the house, and I have felt it my duty to oppose some of the measures of government; but I think I shall be borne out when I say that I

have accompanied the vote which I have given with observations expressed in terms of great moderation. I have acted on all occasions to the best of my opinion, and in a way which I thought most calculated to be beneficial to the country. The noble viscount has been pleased to taunt us for not having addressed the king with a view to obtain his and his colleagues' removal from the situations which they hold. If the noble viscount would look at the manner in which they were appointed to office, if he would look at the whole history for the last twelve months I think he would find sufficient reason for our not having adopted that course of proceeding. The noble viscount knows very well upon what ground he stands, and knowing that, it would have been just as well in him if he had avoided his taunts against us for not having asked the king to remove him from office. I would take the liberty to recommend the noble viscount to consider himself not as the minister of a democratic body in another place, but as the minister of a sovereign in a limited monarchy, in a country, great in point of extent, great in its possessions, and in the various interests which it comprises; and that considering these circumstances, he should, in future, concert such measures as he has reason to think may pass with the approval and suit the general interests of all,—meet the good will of all,—and not of one particular party in one particular place only. If the noble viscount will but follow that course for some little time, he will find no difficulty in conducting the business of government in this house, but will find every facility afforded him in forwarding measures of the above description. I would beg the noble lord to recollect one fact, in regard to the church of England, whether in England or Ireland. Let him recollect that the avowed policy followed by this country during the last three hundred years, has been to retain inviolable the church establishment. We are called here to consult particularly for the good of the church; and if the noble viscount brings forward any measures relating to that subject, let him recollect that all measures of such a kind must be discussed by us with that particular object in view. This is not only the old feeling of this house of three hundred years' standing, but it is that on which we acted no longer than eight or nine years ago, when we had occasion to review the safeguards and general landmarks whereby the church establishment of this country was defended.

August 18, 1836.

The Quadruple Treaty. Effects of our Intervention in Spain.

It is well known to your lordships that I was one of those who objected to the treaty called the "Quadruple Treaty." It is perfectly true that I was afterwards instrumental in carrying it into effect; because it was my duty, in the situation in which I was placed at that time, to carry into effect those treaties which his majesty had entered into, whether I had originally approved of them or not. I cannot, therefore, now, disapprove of the due execution of the quadruple treaty by others; nor will I refuse my assent to the proposition that the measures which his majesty has adopted in execution of the treaty are satisfactory as far as we have any knowledge of them. If any measures should have been adopted, not already provided for in the treaty, it will be our duty to consider them calmly and dispassionately. Much discussion has taken place in other countries with respect to the course pursued by other members of this alliance, in the execution of this treaty. I must say, that so far as I am enabled to form a judgment of the treaty, (and I know nothing more than what appears on the face of the treaty itself) it seems to me that it has been fairly executed by all the parties who subscribed it. When I had the honour of serving his majesty in 1834, I was called upon to state whether the treaty in question would be carried into execution. I then stated what I understood was the meaning and scope of the treaty;—viz. that there should be no armed intervention in the internal affairs of Spain, which should tend to affect the independence of that country. That was my sense of the treaty at the time—it is my sense of the treaty at the present moment—it was so understood by the other parties to the treaty. It was the understanding of all parties that there should he no military intervention in the internal affairs of Spain. This was the understanding of the treaty, and in the month of November, 1834, this explanation was communicated and was satisfactory to the Spanish government.

I consider that the attempt by his majesty's government, aided even by the strongest power in Europe, to force upon Spain any form of government, must fail. Those who should make the attempt must take upon themselves not only the expenses of their own army in a most expensive contest, but those of the civil and military government of Spain; and they must hold their position in Spain, and defray their expenses till the new government should be settled and submitted to, and tranquillity established in the country. I should like to see how the Commons House of Parliament, or the Chamber of Deputies, would treat a proposition that should call upon them to agree to a vote of money for any such operation, for the purpose of forcibly imposing a liberal government on Spain, or on any other country. I contend my lords, that this scheme is absolutely impracticable. His majesty's ministers may rely on it, that they have undertaken that which they never can perform; and that the sooner they place themselves on the footing on which they ought strictly to stand with reference to the quadruple alliance, the sooner will the pacification of Spain, which we must all of us anxiously wish for, be accomplished. I feel, for one, the strongest objection to anything like interference with the internal affairs of the Peninsula. I object to it, not only on account of the vast expense it must inevitably entail upon this country, but still more so on account of the injury which it inflicts on the parties existing in that state. Of my own certain knowledge I can state, that the individuals composing these parties in Spain, have actually been ruined, their properties confiscated, their fortunes sacrificed, by the course which his majesty's government have pursued. Acting under the assurances of his majesty's government, individuals have adopted a certain line of conduct. They followed his majesty's government, as a party in the state. His majesty's government, thus acting, is obliged to move forward with the democratic movement The unfortunate persons I have alluded to have, in consequence, been abandoned, their fortunes sacrificed, and their prospects blighted for ever. Events like these, my lords, which affect the character as well as the influence of the country, inclined me to be more adverse to such interference than I should be on the mere score of expense. I do not mean to oppose the address, but in taking this course, I beg to be clearly understood as not holding myself bound to approve of the employment of any force beyond that stipulated for by the quadruple treaty, which treaty parliament has recognised.

January 30,1837.

The Poor Law Act has surpassed his expectation.

My lords, I supported the bill while it was in this house; and having given that support to the bill from being a witness to the evils, and being apprehensive of the consequences likely to have attended the former system, I conceive it to be my duty to come forward on this occasion, and to state that this bill has surpassed any expectation which I had formed of the benefits likely to result from it. The bill, my lords, may require amendment in certain parts, and it appears that his majesty's government have taken measures to ascertain what points in the bill so require amendment. I, for one, am ready to pay the greatest attention to the points which may be brought under the consideration of this house. But I must say that I approve of the measure as far as it has gone hitherto, and I have witnessed its operation. I do not talk of what I have seen generally, I talk of the details of the management of the bill, from having witnessed that management in different workhouses, in different parts of the country in which I have resided; and I must say that it has been practically beneficial, and particularly in cases such as these. First of all, it has put the workman and his employer upon a true and friendly footing of confidence. Then it has connected the man of property, the man of the highest rank in his country, with the lowest class, with the labouring class, by admitting such to the board of Guardians. I can mention some noble lords, who are ornaments to this house, and who constantly attend at the weekly meetings of the guardians, being elected guardians by the parishes in the neighbourhood in which they reside. No measure could be attended with better results, and being convinced that it will effect still greater benefits, sincerely thinking so, I should be ashamed if I did not step forward, and at once avow my sentiments respecting it. I avow at once that I supported the bill at the time his majesty's ministers proposed it—that I do not repent of what I did on that occasion in so supporting it—but, on the contrary, that I rejoice in the part I then took; and I now congratulate his majesty's ministers on its success.

April 7, 1837.

The Universities—their Education System the admiration of the World.

The working of all these colleges and of the system on which they are regulated, is for the benefit of the public; and in each and every college the object is to carry into execution the will of the founder, just as it would probably have been had he lived to this period. In every case the great object of the governing authorities is, to benefit the public by the education of the youth who resort to these institutions. The noble viscount (Melbourne) could not help admitting that these institutions have worked well, and that latterly a great improvement has taken place in the system of education pursued under their auspices. The noble viscount has also spoken of the great improvement in the system of education pursued in the new university of Durham, and in other new universities elsewhere. But, nevertheless, the noble viscount could not help admitting that the old universities of Oxford and Cambridge possess the merit of having established in England an excellent system of education, which is, in point of fact, the envy and admiration of the world.

April 11, 1837.

The Quadruple Treaty condemned.

My lords, I must confess that I did not approve of the original Quadruple Treaty. I considered it inconsistent with the ancient principle and the policy and practice adopted in this country with regard to Portugal, to avoid to interfere in the disputes between the two princes of the House of Braganza, which had been the policy of this country for many years. It sanctioned the introduction of Spanish troops into Portugal, which measure was inconsistent with our defensive relations with Portugal, and which had been objected to and prevented in that very contest between the rival princes of the House of Braganza. Yet it gave no fresh assistance to bring the contests in Portugal to a conclusion, excepting the promise to give the aid of this country by the employment of a naval force in co-operation with the Spanish and Portuguese troops, which aid was not necessary. Another objection which I entertained to the Quadruple Treaty was, that it mixed up France and this country in the offers and promises made to Don Carlos and Don Miguel, in the fifth and sixth articles of the treaty. These powers became, in fact, guarantees for the performance of these engagements, as well as for the performance of the engagements made under the same articles of the treaty to the subjects of Portugal and Spain. It is impossible to describe the inconvenience of such articles; they require the interference of government in hundreds of little questions. I have felt the inconvenience of those articles since their adoption; I stated my objections to them at the time, and I have seen no reason, since, to alter the opinions I then formed.

April 21, 1837.

Effects of the Additional Articles to the Quadruple Treaty.

By the first of the additional articles to the treaty, the King of the French obliged himself to take such measures in those parts of his dominions which adjoined to Spain, as might be calculated to prevent succours of men, arms, and warlike stores being sent from France into Spain; and the King of Great Britain engaged, under the second of the said additional articles, to furnish such arms and warlike stores as her majesty the Queen of Spain might require; and further to assist her majesty with a naval force if necessary. The Duke of Braganza was to give his best assistance to serve her majesty, that he might be called upon to render. So that those additional articles were essentially different from the terms and provisions of the original treaty, by which the removal of the two princes from Portugal was effected. I do not mean to say, that, in the preamble to that treaty, allusion is not made to the affairs both of Spain and Portugal, but there still is a remarkable difference between the words used in the treaty and the additional articles; and moat particularly in relation to the part to be taken by this country.

April 21, 1837.

The Legion and the Stock Exchange.—Impotency of our interference.

I contend, as I have before contended in this house, that his majesty's present ministers (Lord Melbourne's government) ought not to have departed from the position which the previous administration had established while they were in power. I will not pretend to say what would have been the result of their following out that course, but this I do say, that the course pursued by his lordship's government has not benefited the military or the financial affairs of Spain, or promoted the peace of that country or the general tranquillity of Europe, or attained any of the political advantages which the noble viscount boasts have been attained by his departure from that position which the previous government had occupied and left to their successors. But, my lords, it did unfortunately happen that certain parties in this country had been connected with the Spanish finances; and it was important to those parties that the red coats should make their appearance in Spain, and that the name of "Great Britain," and of the British legion, should be mixed up in the operations of the war. Money was raised in this country to defray the expense of the equipment of the "Legion," as it was called, of 10,000 or 12,000 men, and also of their pay, their food, and maintenance, for a certain number of months; and the noble lords, in order that this scheme might be carried into execution, gave their consent to the order in council for the suspension of the Foreign Enlistment Act. The corps gathered in this country, and went to Spain, in the spring of the year 1835, nearly two years ago. Their first operation upon their arrival at St. Sebastian, was a march over the very same ground to the very spot which was the scene of the late disaster. My lords, up to that moment, the Eliot convention, as it is most honourably and justly called, had been carried into execution. It was on that day departed from on both sides, and from that day to this, I firmly believe, from all I have seen and read,—and I have read much on the subject within the last few days—there has been no certainty in the execution of that convention. Not only has there been no certainty in the execution of that convention, but, notwithstanding the millions of money that Spain has expended,—notwithstanding the blood which has been shed and the number of lives that have been lost,—I will venture to say, that the military affairs of the

Queen of Spain are in a worse condition now than they were in the month of May, 1835.

The whole of the policy of the British government, therefore; all the operations of the British legion, backed by the British squadron; have effected nothing more nor less towards putting an end to the war, and giving peace to Spain and to Europe, than the removal of the blockade of St. Sebastian from one point to another, so as not to come within the liability of being affected by the 68-pounders of the British steamers, under the command of Lord John Hay.

April 21,1837.

Uselessness of the operations of the Legion, and Lord John Hay's Squadron, at St. Sebastian.

If the noble lord supposes that the safety of St. Sebastian had been more or less endangered by the blockade, I can assure him that he is much mistaken; for, from what I know of that fortified town, which is one of the first or second order in Europe, I can take upon myself to say that the Carlists might have been left in their original position without any danger whatever to the town, because they could not make an attack upon such a fortress. In the whole course of the war they have not, to my knowledge, taken by an attack any fortified post; or even any open town of any magnitude, prepared for its defence. They could not have distressed St. Sebastian for provisions, because its communication with the sea could not be prevented. I say, it could not be prevented, even if the whole British fleet were blockading it, instead of being there to relieve it. The amount of inconvenience felt in the town from the Carlist force being in the neighbourhood, was neither more nor less than the unpleasantness of ladies and gentlemen, residing there, being prevented taking their evening walks in the neighbourhood. This is the whole amount of the inconvenience from which the town was relieved. This was the whole amount of the service rendered.

April 21,1837.
Strictures on General Evans.

My lords, I will go a little further. I will say, that I firmly believe that the connexion between the legion and the fleet has been injurious to the military operations of the queen of Spain's generals. That is my decided opinion, founded upon my knowledge of the nature of the country, and of the position of both parties. My lords, there is one point to which I refer; that is, the want of communication between the Queen of Spain's generals, which can be relied upon. If corps of the size of those now employed are not actually joined, there must be a certain communication between them; for, without communication there can be no co-operation; and any attempt at co-operation would, in my opinion, in all probability, lead to disasters such as have recently taken place at Hernani. How are these troops situated? General Evans's troops are at St. Sebastian; General Saarsfield is at the other side of the Borunda, at Pampeluna; and Espartero, with his army, is at Bilboa. It is impossible that there can be any communication between these three, except by the French frontier, and by sea from Socoa, or by the Ebro. An arrangement is made for an attack, and a day named. What was the consequence? General Evans made an attack, but General Saarsfield, at Pampeluna, does not attack; there is a frost or snow, or rain, or some physical impediment which prevents a movement on the part of Saarsfield. General Evans cannot be informed in time, and the enemy has opportunity and leisure to throw his whole force upon General Evans; who, even if the troops had behaved well, would have been compelled to retire. The position, therefore, of the legion at St. Sebastian, in order to co-operate with the British squadron, that there might be something like British co-operation, was not an operation of war, it was one of stock-jobbing. My lords, it is a matter of much surprise to me, that General Evans, who, having acquired the confidence of his majesty's government, and that of the Queen of Spain, I presume must be an able man—it is, certainly, a surprising circumstance, that having had experience of the difficulties of carrying on communication in that country, and having met with a check in the month of January, 1836, for want of communication, he should not have felt the danger of his position, and should have omitted to put himself in communication to a certainty with corps in whose co-operation he was to act, instead of keeping himself at a distance, in order that he might carry on operations in concert with his majesty's fleet.

April 21, 1837.

Undisciplined state of the Legion.

The noble lord has stated that he will not recall the marines. I would beg to remind your lordships, and the noble viscount in particular, of this fact—that the marines are properly the garrisons of his majesty's ships, and that upon no pretence ought they to be moved from a fair and safe communication with the ships to which they belong. The noble lord states, that he is responsible, and that he will take upon himself the responsibility. I have commanded his majesty's armies, and have incurred as many risks, and faced more difficulties than, I hope, the noble lord will ever have to encounter. I have been engaged in hostilities of this description, where co-operation was carried on upon the coast; and though I certainly would do as much for the service, and I believe I may say, have done as much for the service, as the noble lord, yet I would not venture, and have never ventured, to put any corps whatever in co-operation with the Spaniards, or in any situation whatever in which the detached troops could not communicate with the corps from which they were detached; and, above all, upon the sea-coast, where the troops detached could not hold communication with the ships. The first order to each of these detachments was, to keep the communication with their ships. The loss of 400 or 500 marines may not materially involve the honour of this country, but the lives of the men ought not to be endangered, as they must be, if care be not taken that they should have a communication with a point of safety, without some very extraordinary cause.

We hear of the operations of the marines with the Austrians. But the Spanish troops, and particularly the British legion, are not the Austrians. I cannot consider this corps of General Evans to be in a state of discipline and subordination, such as a body of troops ought to be in, with which his majesty's marine forces ought to be connected. They have suffered very considerably; their losses have been great, and have affected their subordination, their good order and discipline, particularly in the presence of an enemy. A disaster or panic may occur among the best troops; but among such, order can be re-established. It does not appear that these are in the state in which they ought to be, to render it safe to co-operate with them. No efforts of their officers can, in such cases, have any effect upon them.

April 21, 1837.

Intervention, if at all, should be on a National Scale.

The noble viscount says that we are carrying on these operations with the object of maintaining the peace of Europe; and these objects are, more especially, put forth in a pamphlet which is attributed to a colleague of the noble viscount, who has applauded his opinions, if he has not gone further, and adopted them as his own. Is the noble lord desirous, in accordance with the policy so set forth, to press upon the nation the adoption of the system of a general combination of the powers of the west, upon principles offensive as well as defensive, against the powers of the north and east of Europe? If so momentous an affair and such a course are seriously contemplated, they should not be commenced by stealth, but in a manner worthy of the character of a great nation like Great Britain. It is not by allowing Spain to raise a legion here in the first instance, and afterwards by sending a few hundred marines, that any really important object can be accomplished. But if the noble lords are in earnest, a message should be sent to parliament, and the support of the country should be called for, to this new scheme of policy; and a commanding force should be sent, in order to carry it into execution. But I recommend the noble viscount well to consider the length of time which must elapse before these operations can be brought to a conclusion; the expense which must, in the first instance, be incurred; and the lengthened period which must elapse before the troops can be withdrawn, and the other expenses can be discontinued, which must be incurred if this scheme be undertaken. The noble lord must establish a government in Spain; he must have the assistance of a Spanish army; and he must pay, equip, and provide for, not only his majesty's troops, but every Spanish officer and soldier employed in the settlement of the government of the country. It may be said, that there are financial resources in Spain; but I am much mistaken, regarding the state of the Spanish military establishments and Spanish finances, if there are not non-effective establishments, such as pensions, retired allowances, expenses of garrisons, and others, which will consume the whole of the pecuniary resources of Spain, however well managed, even without including the interest of the existing debt. I think that, if this country should have this matter fairly brought under its view, it would not be thought advisable to enter upon the scheme proposed in this pamphlet. But we are told that France ought to act this part; and that we ought to give France our moral support. France act! At whose expense? France would have the same difficulties—nay, greater difficulties—than this country. Is it intended that we are to subsidise France? No such thing; we are to assist with our ships and marines on the coast, but it is France that is to carry on the operations in the interior, and pay this expense. Is it believed that Louis Philippe has lost his senses? If we cannot expect that France will pay all this expense, what is to become of the integrity of the Spanish dominions, and the independence of the Spanish government, after the operations shall he concluded?

April 21, 1837.

Necessity of Conciliating the Protestants of Ireland.

My anxious wish, my lords, has always been—and I have frankly stated it more than once in my place in this house—that the Protestants of Ireland should be on the best terms with the government of this country, and that the government should give them every protection and support in its power. My firm opinion is, that the safety of this country in connection with Ireland, the safety of the union, the permanence of the union, and, indeed, the honour of the empire, all depend, in a great measure, if not entirely, on the good understanding which may subsist between the government and the Protestants of Ireland. I am also certain that the prosperity of the Protestants in Ireland, and the safety of their persons, of their riches, and of everything dear to men, depend on their being on terms of good understanding with the government; but that things will not go on as they ought to go on, until government induces the Protestants of that country to return to that good understanding. That has been my opinion ever since the commencement of these unfortunate dissensions, seven years ago; and I should be sorry to say, this evening, one word which might be calculated to increase the irritation now existing between both these parties. The noble viscount (Melbourne) has admitted that the Protestants of Ireland have great reason to feel the awkwardness of their present position, and to entertain jealousy of the government; and I must own that the noble viscount, instead of aggravating that description of feeling which he admits the Protestants of Ireland ought to have, should use, as I conceive, every exertion in his power to conciliate them, and to make them feel that they may depend upon the government for the protection of their lives and property, and that they will not be sacrificed to those who are preaching up sedition against the institutions of their country, and insurrections against the persons and property of her people. These Protestants are in number not less than 2,000,000. I believe they hold, my lords, about nine-tenths of the property of Ireland; and I am sure that they are persons of the best education and of the best conduct in that country. I believe that the province in which they reside is as well cultivated and as well conducted in every respect as any portion of England; and the inhabitants of it deserve on every account all the protection which the government can afford them. Let us see, my lords, whether they have not reason to feel jealousy of the government in consequence of the transactions of the last few years. Look at the total destruction of the property of tithe—look at the treatment of their church—look at the various occurrences which have taken place, and see whether they have not reason to apprehend that there is a latent intention of putting down the Protestant livings in Ireland, and of substituting a voluntary system in place of their present church establishment. Do you suppose that men of their description do not calculate on the events which are likely to happen? Do you suppose that they do not read the history of past times? We have heard the noble viscount talking of the history of the year 1782, and of the year 1798, and of various other transactions. Let us look at the letters of Henry Lord Clarendon, formerly chief governor of Ireland; and, having looked at them, let any man ask himself whether the Protestants of Ireland have not a right to conceive that matters are advancing rapidly to the state described by that noble personage, and whether the same description of power is not now growing up which exercised so enormous an influence on the government of his day. I consider that the statements made by the different peers who have spoken to night from this (the conservative) side of the house ought to have, and I trust they will have, a powerful effect on the Protestant mind of this country. At the same time that these statements are brought forward, and the facts are made known to the public, showing that neither property nor life is secure in Ireland, his majesty comes down to parliament with a speech, in which he says, "Ireland is in a state of tranquillity;" and yet there is not one gentleman residing in Ireland who was not aware, when that speech was delivered, that a general association had been formed and was in existence in Dublin for the sole purpose of agitation—of that agitation which, as Lord Wellesley told the country, was the cause of disturbances as undoubtedly as any one circumstance ever was the cause of another. Do your lordships suppose that the Protestants of Ireland are not aware of that fact?

April 28, 1837.

Lord Normanby's Gaol Deliveries.

What was the next step of which the Protestants of Ireland complained? The lord lieutenant, they say, went into the country, from place to place, without having any communication either with the judges or with the magistrates;—and that is a fact on which I greatly rely—the lord lieutenant, they say, released at every county gaol which he visited a certain number of prisoners. I have said, that the Protestants of Ireland have a very peculiar interest in the impartial administration of the law, and in the tranquillity of the country, because they form the great body of its landed proprietors. They must look at such a transaction with jealousy; and if there had been no circumstances connected with such a transaction save those which have been stated this evening, it must, I think, be admitted, that if the conduct of the lord lieutenant was not without precedent (and I believe that no precedent can he found for it) it has yet been still of such rare occurrence that it ought never to be repeated. I do not mean to say that this power of enlarging prisoners has never been exercised, but I maintain that it had never previously been exercised in such a manner. I do not pretend to be acquainted with the technicalities of the law on this subject; but it occurs to me that several of the persons who have been released in this peculiar manner by the lord lieutenant, had surely been guilty of felony. I do not know exactly what the state of the law is, at present, upon this subject, but I apprehend that persons who have been found guilty of felony ought to have some document conveying their pardon, or in default of its production they become, I believe, liable to certain fines and forfeitures. But in the present case persons guilty of felony have been enlarged without any writing at all, at the simple order of the lord lieutenant, I must say, that a proceeding of this sort is highly irregular, and that it is such an exercise of power as a lord lieutenant in the ordinary discharge of his duty ought not to repeat; and further, that this was an exercise of power which was most likely to produce a very pernicious effect on the minds of the Protestants of Ireland.

April 28, 1837.

Objections to the Irish Corporations Bill of 1837.

I stated, on a former occasion, that these corporations existed in their present shape, and were brought to their present state, principally with a view to the support and protection of the religion of the Church of England established in Ireland. Whatever may be done with respect to these corporations for the future, in my opinion that object ought never to be lost sight of. It may be doubted, from what has lately occurred in this country, whether that opinion is so unanimously adopted as it was in former years; but I may venture to say, the support of the Church of England in Ireland is still the policy of this country—the policy which his majesty is sworn to maintain—the policy which this house is called, by writs of summons, to uphold—the policy which every member of this, or the other house of parliament, is sworn to uphold by the oaths which he has voluntarily taken. Under these circumstances, I think I may safely say that, according to the ancient constitution, according to the modern constitution, according to the uniform policy of this country for the last 300 years, the maintenance of the Church of England in Ireland forms a prominent and important point of legislative concern. Looking to this bill now under consideration, in relation principally to that policy, it goes undoubtedly to establish a very large number of corporations in Ireland, the mode of their formation being to give votes to the very lowest class of the population of the towns in which these corporations are to be formed. This is to be done, not upon evidence of their possessing property—not, as in England, upon residence, upon the payment of rates, or on the evidence of their possessing anything in the nature of property; but simply on the condition that the parties possess a 5l. or a 10l. qualification, made up of all kinds and descriptions of property put together, and this without any proof whatever, excepting the oath of the parties themselves, of their possessing even that qualification. It is well known to your lordships that a system of perjury prevails in all parts of Ireland, with a view to establish franchise of this description. I have recently seen accounts of enquiries before select committees in certain parliamentary elections which have taken place in that country, and it is impossible to glance at them without being impressed with the conviction that, if any description of franchise depend solely on the oaths of the holders, every species of enquiry will be nugatory; and it will be just as wise to establish at once a system of universal suffrage, as to establish a system of franchise in such a manner. These corporations, thus formed by persons holding a franchise of this description, acquired solely by their own swearing, and without any evidence whatever of their possessing any property except their own oaths, establish a system upon which no reliance can be placed, and on which no establishment whatever can safely depend. If your lordships want any proof of the danger to the church of Ireland by the establishment of corporations of this description, I will refer your lordships to the declarations, I would not say of those who are the declared enemies, but I must say, the strongest opponents of the church, and who are found, on every occasion, making the greatest possible exertions against the church in Ireland, These persons are heard declaring publicly and repeatedly, almost under the very view of the government—"Give us but this corporation bill, and all the rest must follow." If there be any doubt about it, I beg to say, I shall not be disposed to listen to the threats of any man; but when my own senses convince me that such must be the result, I mean danger to the establishment, I do say it is my duty to attend to warnings of the description to which I have adverted.

May 5, 1837.

Eulogium on King William the Fourth.

I have served his late majesty in the highest situations; I have been in his council as well as the noble viscount (Melbourne). I, indeed, did not serve him so long as the noble viscount, or even under any such prosperous circumstances as the noble viscount; but I have had opportunities of witnessing, under all these circumstances, the personal advantages of character so ably described by the noble viscount. It has fallen to my lot to serve his majesty at different periods, and in different capacities; and, while I had the happiness of doing so, upon all those occasions I have witnessed not only all the virtues ascribed to him by the noble viscount, but likewise a firmness, a discretion, a candour, a justice, and a spirit of conciliation towards others,—a respect for all. Probably there never was a sovereign who, in such circumstances and encompassed by so many difficulties, more successfully met them than he did upon every occasion on which he had to engage them. I was induced to serve his majesty, not only from my sense of duty—not alone from the feeling that the sovereign of this country has the right to command my services in any situation in which it might be considered that I might be of use—but from a feeling of gratitude to his majesty for favours, for personal distinctions, conferred upon me, notwithstanding that I had been unfortunately in the position of opposing myself to his majesty's views and intentions when he was employed in a high situation under government,[19] and in consequence of which he had to resign that great office which he must, beyond all others, have been most anxious to retain. Notwithstanding that, my lords, he employed me in his service; and he, as a sovereign, manifested towards me a kindness, condescension, and favour, which, so long as I live, I never can forget. I considered myself, then, not only bound by duty, and the sense I felt of gratitude to all the sovereigns of this country, under whom I had lived, but more especially towards his late majesty, to relieve him from every difficulty I could, under any circumstances.

[Footnote 19: William the Fourth, when Duke of Clarence, was under the necessity of resigning the office of Lord High Admiral, while the Duke of Wellington was premier.]

June 22, 1837.

Agrarian Disturbances in Ireland are earned by Political Agitation.
The noble earl opposite has stated, that the tranquillity mentioned in her majesty's speech from the throne, on opening the present parliament, was not intended to mean judicial or agrarian tranquillity, but political tranquillity. And what is the sort of political tranquillity existing in Ireland? I believe that a very few days before the speech in which the word tranquillity is used was delivered, the association which was assembled in the capital of Ireland, under the eyes of the noble earl opposite, was dissolved; but, at the same time, her majesty was given to understand, that she was not to have the choice of her ministers, but that they must be selected by the gentleman who was the founder and the head of that association. Now, to talk of tranquillity—political tranquillity—in any part of that country, looking at the situation in which it is placed, is vague and idle. The noble earl has said, that the agrarian disturbances in Ireland are not to be attributed to political agitation. Now, one of the greatest authorities that ever appeared in this or any other country—a noble relation of mine—stated, that "agrarian disturbances in Ireland were to be attributed to political agitation, and to nothing else, as much as effect was to be attributed to cause in any instance whatever." I say, then, that in Ireland they have agrarian disturbances because they have political agitations.

November 27, 1837.

Principle of Imprisonment for Debt.

One of the causes of debts being incurred in this country is, in a great degree, the power which creditors at present possess to arrest their debtors upon *mesne* process; and I still further believe that it is the facility which is thus given of obtaining credit, that has been the cause of the great mercantile prosperity of the country. The enormous transactions upon credit are such, that both individuals and the public generally, require further means of recovering debts than exist in other countries.

December 5, 1837.

The Case of Dr. Hampden.

The late king was advised to appoint that gentleman to be Regius Professor of Divinity in the university of Oxford. There can be no doubt that the general opinion of the university was, that that gentleman's theological tenets were not exactly orthodox, or consistent with the articles of the church of England,—an opinion which the publication of certain works by that gentleman has tended to establish.

Several persons in the university considered it their duty to petition his majesty, praying, if the appointment had not been completed, that he would not make it. I believe that another address was presented to his majesty, entreating his majesty not to sanction that appointment, which, however, was made, contrary to the views of the university at large; and a short time afterwards, Dr. Hampden thought right, in his inaugural lecture, to state that he then felt it his duty to explain the opinions which had been complained of. I do not pretend to be a judge either of those opinions or that explanation; but this I will venture to say, and I believe your lordships will concur in the opinion, that in proportion as Dr. Hampden found it necessary to give an explanation of his sentiments, in the same proportion were those justified who thought proper to disapprove of them. I believe it will be admitted that, if a clergyman who published certain opinions, not being orthodox, thought proper to come forward and explain those opinions, at least they who were opposed to such opinions had some justification, on their being repeated, for the course they had taken in disapproving of them. This is all I wish to say respecting the opinions and explanation of Dr. Hampden. His appointment having been made, notwithstanding the petition of a vast number of the clergy of Oxford, and the general opinion expressed there that it should not be made, a request was preferred to the heads of houses that they would propose some measure to the convocation which would have the effect of marking the disapprobation on the part of that body of the opinions and appointment of Dr. Hampden. The noble earl has alluded to the act of convocation excluding Dr. Hampden from being one of those to appoint the select preachers, and also from sitting at the board of heresy. I am not disposed to say anything against Dr. Hampden; but this I must say, that, considering the whole transaction, my opinion is, the convocation did as little upon that occasion as it was possible to do, consistently with the necessity which existed of taking some notice of that gentleman, his opinions and conduct. Since that period, I really believe that the university, and the bishops of the church of England, and all the persons who have any influence on this question, have done everything in their power to put it down, and prevent it becoming a subject of discussion, even in the university or elsewhere. For myself, I can say, I have invariably pursued that course, it being my object to prevent any discussion on the matter; and I never should have mentioned it, here or elsewhere, publicly, if the noble earl had not forced it upon me on the present occasion. I certainly lament the transaction, principally because I consider it is likely to produce a schism in the church; and I have been as anxious as any man can be in my situation, to prevent the university from proceeding on the subject in such a manner as may, by possibility, lead to that result.

The noble earl adverted to the conduct of a gentleman who is now vice-chancellor of the university, and who has, in his capacity of head of a house, prohibited the attendance of the students in divinity upon the lectures of the Regius Professor. I do not at all pretend to be competent to mark the difference between the private and public lectures of the Regius Professor; but I certainly do not approve of the course taken by that gentleman. In my opinion, the question is not one to be considered by the head of a house; for, in fact, no ordination can be conferred by him or the Regius Professor of Divinity. Ordination can only be conferred by the bishops of the church; and whether the students attend the lectures of the Regius Professor of Divinity, or those of the Margaret Professor, or of any other professor, I will say, it is the duty of the bishops of the church to consider who are the persons coming for ordination, and whether they are qualified or not, without taking into consideration the certificates of the Regius Professor of Divinity, the head of a house, or any other individual. It is, I contend, the duty of the bishops to examine into the subject themselves, without reference to the certificate of any individual whatever. I must observe, however, with regard to the course adopted by the vice-chancellor, that I am thoroughly convinced, not only from what that gentleman has stated to me, but from my knowledge of that gentleman's conduct, and his character for candour and fairness, that he had the very wisest motives in pursuing that course, from which he departed as soon as he found that the bishops of the church had determined upon observing a different line, conceiving that he was then relieved from all charge and responsibility in the situation which he held. Such is the history of that transaction; and I have only to say, with respect to that gentleman, and with respect to others of the university of Oxford, that it was their anxious wish and desire to avoid taking any step in reference to Dr. Hampden, lest it should, in any manner whatever, lead to what they would consider the greatest possible misfortune—a schism in the church.

December 21,1837.

A great country cannot wage a little war.

January 16, 1838.

Conduct of the Canadian Leaders.
I differ entirely from the noble and learned lord in thinking that the act of 1831 established the British constitution in Canada, for it is not consistent with the British constitution to leave the civil government of the country—and especially to leave the judges of the land—to be provided for by an annual vote of the parliament. I say, my lords, that the British constitution, for the last hundred and fifty years at least, has made a fixed and not uncertain provision for supporting the dignity of the crown, for meeting the expenses attendant on the administration of the civil government, and most particularly for the independence of the judges of the land. But is that the state of things in Lower Canada? No. I maintain that the act of 1831 did not establish the British constitution in the colonies of Upper and Lower Canada, but something quite distinct; for it gave to the people a popular representation, which, in my opinion, is the cause of all the disputes that have followed, and of the insurrection which has taken place. It gave individuals the power to create prejudices in the minds of the people, to weaken the loyalty of the Canadians, and to raise them in hostility against her majesty's crown and government. And what has been the object of these individuals in the course which they have pursued? They have supposed that, by creating dissatisfaction amongst the people, they could thereby throw off the authority of the crown; and, by gathering the people around them, overturn the government established in the colony. Such have been the objects of those individuals who have been seen running off to the neighbouring territories of the United States as soon as they found their own persons exposed to danger. This turned out to be the real state of the case; for the would-be leaders left the unfortunate people in a state of rebellion against her majesty's government, and ran off themselves, letting the unlucky inhabitants return to their houses as best they could; and forcing them to submit, with the best grace they might, to the mercy of her majesty's government.

January 18, 1838.
Evils of popular Rights.
I warned the noble lord against endangering the establishments of the country, by giving anything like an authority to a popular assembly to withhold the funds necessary for carrying on the civil government; for nothing is more needful to a country than to uphold the civil power, and the independence—as well pecuniary as political—of the judges of the land. And let noble lords learn, from the events in Canada, and other dominions in North America, what it is to hold forth what are called "popular rights," but which are not popular rights either here or elsewhere; and what occasion is thereby given to the perpetuation of a system of agitation which ends in insurrection and rebellion, and the coming to blows with her majesty's troops.

January 18,1838.

Importance of reducing the Canadian Rebels.

I confess, my lords, that I have a feeling for the honour of my country, and I cannot but believe that if, by any misfortune, we should fail in restoring peace in Lower Canada, at an early period of time, we shall receive a blow, with respect to our military character, to our reputation, and to our honour, of which it will require years to enable us to remove the effects.

January 18,1838.

An Elective Legislative Council in Canada deprecated.

My lords, there is one topic which has been adverted to by the noble and learned lord (Lord Brougham), upon which I think it necessary to say a word, although it is not alluded to in the address, and will more properly form a subject of the discussion on the bill which is to be brought in upon some future day—and that is the establishment in Lower Canada of an elective legislative council. The noble and learned lord, with all his knowledge of Lower Canada, has not, in my opinion, sufficiently adverted to the fact of the difference of the two races of inhabitants in that country. My lords, it may be easy to talk, here, of establishing an elective council, but if the noble and learned lord will look into the discussions which have taken place upon that subject, and to the opinions that have been delivered upon it by the different parties, in that colony, he will find that British inhabitants are to the full as much opposed to that arrangement as the French are in favour of it, he will find that in point of fact, they would be in a state of insurrection against that arrangement, in the same degree as the French are now supposed to be in a state of insurrection in favour of an elective legislative council. I will likewise beg the noble and learned lord, and I would entreat the noble viscount opposite, and every member of her majesty's government, to attend to this fact, that an elective legislative council is not the constitution of the British monarchy; that a legislative council appointed by the monarch is the constitution of this country; that this was so stated in the discussions upon the bill passed in the year 1791, by all the great authorities who discussed that measure, amongst others by Mr. Fox himself. That gentleman said, "that a legislative council, appointed by the monarch, is an essential part of the British constitution."

January 18, 1838.

Concessions to Democracy cannot be rescinded.

Your lordships ought also to recollect that, since the passing of the reform bill, the taxes required from householders paying 10l. of yearly rent have been greatly reduced, and I believe that the poor-rates have also been diminished. These reductions have afforded great relief to that particular class of persons, greater than has been given to any other portion of society; and I think that,

under the circumstances, the amount of qualification ought not to be further diminished, for, if it be, a worse description of electors will be the inevitable consequence. I perfectly recollect that a noble friend of mine, whom I do not now see in his place, warned your lordships, on a former occasion, of the danger of making any approach to democracy in a measure like this; and he told your lordships that, if once such a measure was adopted, you could never turn back from it. If it be found, when carried into operation, to act ever so injuriously—if its tendency be found to be ever so destructive to the peace and well-being of society—still you cannot fall back on the point from which you started; for, if once granted, the measure must be permanent.
March 8, 1838.

Short-sighted Conduct of the West Indian Colonists.
There is no man in this house, or in the country, who has been more anxious than myself, that the measure passed for the abolition of slavery should be entirely successful. I have, however, conceived from the first, that the only chance of its success would arise from the colonial legislatures acting with good faith, and carrying the measure, after it had passed the imperial parliament, into strict execution; for which measure they have received what they acknowledge, by their adhesion to the principle of the bill, a competent compensation. It appears, however, to be beyond doubt, that they have not carried the new system into execution as they ought to have done; and some two or three years ago, your lordships were under the necessity of consenting to a bill, rendered necessary in consequence of the legislature of Jamaica having refused, under not very creditable circumstances, to enact a law which it had positively promised to pass. Under these circumstances, considering that we are now approaching to within a couple of years of the period when a new state of society is to be established in all the British possessions where slavery has ever existed, I must say, I think parliament ought not to hesitate about adopting some measure of the description now proposed, for the purpose of carrying into full and complete execution the object which the imperial legislature had in view when the emancipation act was passed. It appears to me, that if the legislatures of the colonies had acted as sensible men ought to have done, in the circumstances in which they were placed four years ago, they would have had before them, and the British parliament would have had before it, a very different prospect from that which, I fear, exists at the present moment.
March 13, 1838.
Lord Melbourne's Government Inimical to the Church.
It appears that the policy of her majesty's government is—I will use the mildest term that can be employed—not to encourage the established church. I am afraid that it will appear from what passed in another place, in the last session of parliament, and even in this, that the church of England—the established church of England—is not to be encouraged by her majesty's

government. I am sure that those who recollect what has occurred in parliament, during the last few years, will admit that no great encouragement has been shown by ministers to the church of Ireland, that branch of the established church of England which is stationed in the latter country. I say therefore, my lords, that this is the policy of the government of this country; and, I must own, also, it is most sincerely to be lamented by every friend of the constitution, and of the peace, order, and happiness of the community.

March 30, 1838.

A Free Press in Malta deprecated.

Now, in regard to this matter of a free press in Malta, I crave your lordships' attention to the facts of the case for a moment, and I beg the house to bear them in mind. What is Malta? It is a fortress and a seaport—it is a great naval and military arsenal for our shipping and forces in the Mediterranean. We hold it by conquest. We hold it as an important post, as a great military and naval arsenal, and as nothing more. My lords, if these are the facts, we might as well think of planting a free press on the fore deck of the admiral's flag-ship in the Mediterranean, or on the caverns of the batteries of Gibraltar, or in the camp of Sir John Colborne in Canada, as of establishing it in Malta. A free press in Malta in the Italian language is an absurdity. Of the hundred thousand individuals who compose the population of Malta, three-fourths at least speak nothing but the Maltese dialect, and do not understand the Italian language. Of the one hundred thousand inhabitants of the island, at least three-fourths can neither read nor write. What advantages, then, can accrue to the people of Malta from the establishment of a free press? We do not want to teach our English sailors and soldiers to understand Italian. A free press will find no readers among them either. Who, then, is it for? These gentlemen say, that, unless the government support a free press in Malta, it cannot exist of itself, and they suggest an expense of £800 a year in its favour. They have done nothing more than this that I am aware of since their appointment, and it is plain, that the savings spoken of by the noble baron as having been effected by their recommendation are completely swallowed up by the project of a free press. My lords, I cannot help thinking that it is wholly unnecessary and greatly unbecoming of the government to form such an establishment, of such a description, in such a place as Malta; and the more particularly, as the object for which it is made, must be both of a dangerous tendency to this country, and fraught with evil to others. The free press which they propose, is to be conducted, not by foreign Italians, but by Maltese, subjects of her majesty, enjoying the same privileges as we do. Now, what does this mean? It means that the licence to do wrong is unlimited. If it were conducted by foreign Italians, you could have a check upon them if they acted in such a manner as would tend to compromise us with our neighbours—you could send them out of the island—you could prevent their doing injury in that manner by various ways. But here you have no such check—

you have no check at all—your free press in that respect is uncontrollable. If the free press chooses to preach up insurrection in Italy from its den in Malta, you have no power of preventing it. Were the conductors foreign Italians you could lay your hand on them at once, and dispose of them as aliens; but you cannot do that with the Maltese subjects, enjoying the same right and possessing the same freedom as ourselves. I did hope, that we should have been cured by this time of our experiments on exciting insurrection in the other countries of Europe—in the dominions of neighbouring princes—in the territories of our allies. I did think that we had received a sufficient lesson in these matters to last us a long time, even for ever, in the results which have taken place through such interference in Portugal, Spain, Italy—ay, and in Canada too—and that they had put an end to our dangerous mania for exciting insurrection in foreign countries. Such, my lords, I assert is the object of a free press in Malta—to excite insurrection in the dominions of our neighbour and ally, the King of the Two Sicilies, and in the dominions of the King of Sardinia—and I confess that I am ashamed of the government, considering the results that have taken place, from the doctrines promulgated by it, that they have not done everything in their power to suppress instead of encouraging and supporting it; and that they had not sent out their commissions with full power to do so, rather than instructed them to call for its establishment.

May 3, 1838.

State of Poverty in Ireland.

Of all the countries in Europe, Ireland is the one in which it has appeared to me to be least possible to establish anything in the nature of the English poor-laws. The opinion delivered by others has been, that there are no materials to be found in Ireland proper for forming, or if formed for administering with salutary effect, any system of poor-laws such as exists in this country; and I, my lords, believe that there is no doubt whatever of the justice and truth of that opinion, considering the English poor-laws, as they formerly existed, and as they were carried into execution up to the year 1834, when the noble lords opposite introduced the measure which amended them. While, however, I say this, I am bound at the same time to express my entire concurrence in the opinion declared by the noble viscount, that there never was a country in which poverty existed to such a degree as it exists in that part of the United Kingdom. My lords, I was in office in that country—I held a high situation in the administration of the government of Ireland thirty years ago—and I must say, that from that time to this there has scarcely elapsed a single year in which the government has not at certain periods of it entertained the most serious apprehensions of actual famine. My lords, I am firmly convinced that from the year 1806 down to the present time, a year has not passed in which the government have not been called on to give assistance to relieve the poverty and distress which prevailed in Ireland, and owing to circumstances over which no human power could have any control. One of the circumstances which has most frequently led to this lamentable state of things, has been the failure or delay of the potato crops, and there have been known times when two, three, and even as many as four months have intervened before these crops, which are used as a subsistence by the people, could be brought into the market; and such are the social relations in that country, that the people have no means of coming to market to purchase like the people of England. My lords, this is a fact that is undoubted, and one that I believe never existed in any country in the world except Ireland.

May 21, 1838.

The Numbers of a Meeting may render it Illegal.

The numbers of a meeting—that is to say, such an assembly of persons as would create terror in the minds of people living in the neighbourhood,—would justify the magistrate in taking measures to disperse it.

June 15, 1838.

Real cause of our interference in Spain.

The system of interference adopted by his late majesty's government, by means of the quadruple treaty, was with a view to the contest between extreme opinions—it was more with a view of aiding these extreme opinions, than to the arrangement of the mere differences between Don Carlos, upon the one side, and the queen, or her daughter, upon the other; to support certain opinions, and not to determine the succession, was the cause of interference. I regret interference upon that ground; I object to interference upon that ground; and I say, moreover, that we were not right in interfering upon that ground. I maintain that, more particularly on account of the extreme opinions that prevailed, we ought not to have interfered at all; but most especially we ought not, according to the common practice of this government, and in accordance with the declared political principles of the noble lords themselves, to have interfered in a question involving extreme political opinions. Now it has unfortunately happened that extreme political principles have been forced upon a great part of Europe by means of large armies and of great military forces, and it was consequently expected that the same thing would succeed in Spain. This, I believe, was the object of our interference with Spain, and not to determine the Spanish succession.

June 19, 1838.

We had no right to interfere against Don Carlos.

I say we had no business to interfere in the question of succession. There might have been some pretext for interference in the question of succession, if any of the powers of Europe had taken part with Don Carlos, but that was not the case. The noble baron (Lord Holland) cheers. I say, confidently, that not one of the powers in Europe had stirred a finger in support of the pretensions of Don Carlos. I say, then, that, according to all principles—the principles supported and acted upon by this country, in the case of the house of Braganza, and many other cases that I could mention—we ought to have avoided interference; and we ought to have avoided interference by armies more particularly, in the contests in Spain. I say, my lords, that not a sword had been moved in Europe in favour of Don Carlos. When Don Carlos went to Spain, in the summer of 1834, there were not three battalions in arms in that country in his favour. This I positively state as a fact. But, on the contrary, in the space of forty leagues there were forty fortified posts in possession of the queen's troops. Now, my lords, this is a positive fact; and I say that, in the year 1835, when the armistice was negotiated, when the exchange of prisoners was negotiated by Lord Eliot, Don Carlos had then acquired a superiority over the queen's forces, who were obliged to take up a position on the right of the Ebro. That is to say, between the interval of time I have mentioned,—and this is a positive fact upon which your lordships may rely, and to which I pledge my word,—between the summer of 1834 and the period at which the exchange of prisoners was agreed upon in 1835,—that is, in the course of a very few months,—the superiority had been gained by Don Carlos in that part of the country, so far that he had forced the enemy to take up a position on the other side of the Ebro, abandoning all their fortified posts, except Pampeluna and one other; and, I must add, they had very wisely abandoned them, because they found they could not march to their relief through the country. Now, my lords, this is literally and truly a fact; and it is a fact not to be forgotten, with respect to the present contest in Spain. I say, then, that it was the business of this government not to have interfered by force. We ought not to have done so, according to the noble marquis's principle—that there ought to be no interference between two hostile parties in a nation like Spain.

June 19, 1838.

The Legion a failure.

The noble viscount has told your lordships, certainly, that he sent out an expedition; and the noble marquis has informed us that it has always been the policy of this country to encourage such expeditions. Now, without meaning to assert that the result of that expedition was a dire catastrophe, I must be permitted to say that the legion has been, in my opinion and conviction, a complete failure. It has cost the Spanish government an enormous sum of money. Great expectations were raised respecting it, not one of which has been fulfilled. When the legion went to Spain, the Queen of Spain's army was in all the provinces, with the exception of Biscay and Navarre. Her government was established in all parts of Spain, excepting these places. Excepting them, all other places might be said to be in a state of tranquillity. But it appears the Queen of Spain could not carry on the war, unless she got ten thousand Isle of Dogsmen—a legion from England, and another from France. If the Spanish government had asked for officers, or for arms, or for money, or for artillery, I should not have been surprised, as I know well the manner in which the Spanish arsenals are supplied. But asking for 10,000 men from England to destroy Don Carlos, who was shut up in the mountains, was a matter really not to be seriously thought of. The object was not to bring 10,000, or 15,000, or 20,000 men into action, but to bring the red coats and the blue coats, the French and English troops, into the contest; that was the object, and the view was, to produce a moral effect. But the government ought to have known that that which gave them the influence on the one side, was fatal to that influence on the other. Thus was an end put to that moral influence which this country could, and ought to have exerted, but which can only be effectually exercised by strict adherence, throughout all her proceedings, to the plain principles of justice. If this country enter into a treaty, let her carry it honourably through; but let her not push her interference further than is necessary for exerting her influence over both parties, in order to settle existing differences. I have said that the legion was a failure. Of that there cannot be the slightest doubt. The war is now in the same state as it was in the year 1835, except that Don Carlos has more men.

June 19, 1838.

The Opposition should give aid to the Government when a war is inevitable.

The noble viscount tells us that we did not object to the appointment of the Earl of Durham as governor-general of Canada—that we did not object to the powers confided to him; that we—referring particularly to me—urged this government by all the means in their power to send out large forces, and take care to be strong in that part of the world; advice which, I admit, I did repeat over and over again, until I fatigued myself and the house by doing so. But why did I not object to those powers being given to the Earl of Durham? Because, seeing the government in difficulties—seeing the colony in a state of rebellion—and seeing that the government possessed confidence in another place—I thought it was not my duty to excite opposition to measures which they thought it might be proper to adopt; and therefore I took them all upon their recommendation. Very possibly I was wrong in so doing; indeed, it appears that I was wrong; but I took the course which I then considered it my duty to take. I declared that I would not follow the example of those who, being convinced of the certainty that the country would be involved in a war, yet thought proper to oppose all measures that were necessary for carrying on that war. Neither would I deny assistance to those who were absent, and who were carrying on the government to the best of their ability; but I would give the government a fair support, in order to pacify a country which might be in a state of war or rebellion. That was the course which I followed on the occasion alluded to by the noble viscount. With respect to the Earl of Durham, I am personally unacquainted with him; and I considered that the noble viscount and her majesty's government ought to have known best who was the person most qualified to act as governor of Canada.

August 9, 1838.

Lord Durham's Ordinance[20] a grossly illegal Act.

A grossly illegal act has been committed—not a mere technical error, or one having reference to small or nice points of law, but an illegal act of great magnitude, and relating to points of the most grave importance—an act so clearly illegal, that no man capable of understanding the first principles of justice can doubt of its impropriety. It is impossible that the people of this country can suffer any man to be driven into banishment without trial, or that they can allow him, afterwards, to be condemned to death, without having been convicted of any crime but that of returning to his own country.

[Footnote 20: The Earl of Durham, governor-general of the Canadas, had issued an ordinance, transporting to Bermuda Dr. Nelson and seven others, guilty by confession of high treason, and subjecting them to death if they returned to Canada. Lord Brougham, actuated, as was asserted by some, by personal feeling against Lord Durham, protested against this act in the face of the country. His speech on the occasion was one of the most powerful he ever delivered. It is scarcely necessary to add that Lord Durham immediately and precipitately resigned his governorship.]

August 9, 1838.

Inadequacy of our Navy.

There is nothing more certain than that, if you come to be entirely dependent for corn on the countries bordering on the Baltic, you would have the King of Prussia and the Emperor of Russia (as has been known before), levying a tax upon the exportation of that article of food to the Thames, and elsewhere in this country. * * I entirely agree with the noble and learned lord on the expediency of avoiding any interference with foreign powers on the subject of commercial matters; but I confess that I cannot view the state of our commercial relations, and of our position in the world generally, in connection with these commercial pursuits, with any degree of unmixed satisfaction. On the contrary, I do deplore the state in which we find ourselves placed in many parts of the world, particularly as it has been described in the course of the evening by my noble friend (Viscount Strangford). What I attribute that state of our commercial relations to, in a great degree, is, the extreme weakness and tottering condition of our naval establishments. I do not mean to complain of the distribution of our naval establishments; though, at the same time, I by no means intend to unsay what I have said in respect to the expeditions to Spain, which I cannot approve of; but I repeat my expression that I consider our naval establishments to be in too weak and tottering a condition to answer the purpose for which they were intended, which was to give protection to the commercial interests of the country in all parts of the world; for the commerce of England does extend to all parts of the world. There is not a port, not a river, which is not visited by the ships of her majesty's subjects; and her majesty's subjects have an undoubted right to protection in whatever part of the world they may think proper to visit in the pursuits of commerce. The circumstance of which I complain I do not at all attribute to neglect upon the part of the admiralty, neither do I include in my censure the noble earl who is at the head of the admiralty; but those I do blame are the individuals who have thought proper to reduce the establishments of the country to such a degree, that protection cannot possibly be given in all places where it is required.

I will remind your lordships that, since the peace, and particularly within the last twenty years, three great navies have sprung up in Europe, which are four times as strong as they were at any former period. Other navies, it is true, are put down; but we remain much the same. A great deal has been said, by way of comparison, between the strength of our navy in 1792, and in the years 1814 and 1815; but when we talk of strength in this case, we ought not to look at the subject without adverting to the naval establishments of other powers. Now, although our marine force should even be on the same footing as before, our commerce is not only tripled, but extended to a degree ten times greater than it ever was before; and there is not a part of the earth, from one pole to the other, in which the protection of our navy is not required for our commerce. I must say that, if we should at any time incur the misfortune of being involved in another war—which God forbid!—the only mode of keeping out of the difficulty would be to maintain such a navy as would give protection to her majesty's subjects in all parts of the globe.
August 14, 1838.

Neutrality of Belgium.
I hope that it never may be lost sight of in this country, that the original foundation of the independence of Belgium, as a separate kingdom, was this condition, namely, its perpetual neutrality. That condition I consider to have been the foundation of that transaction, and I hope that this will never be forgotten by this country, or by Europe.
February 5, 1839.

Aggressions on Canada from the United States.
I must say I should very much wish to see suitable measures adopted to carry into execution the intentions which her majesty declares in her speech, of

maintaining her rights of sovereignty over Canada. The system of levying private war which prevails on that continent is not wholly unknown in other parts of the world. I have read of it as existing in the deserts of Central Asia; I have heard of its being practised, as a system, by the Asiatics on the frontiers of the Russian monarchy, where a perpetual warfare is going on between those tribes and the troops sent to repress their inroads—a warfare that has been waged in those countries from century to century. We read also of circumstances of the same kind occurring in Africa—of wars carried on by barbarous tribes against the possessions of the British government in Africa, the contests of savages against a civilized people. But this is a war carried on by a nation supposed to be considerably advanced in the scale of civilization—by men governing themselves, electing their servants by ballot and general suffrage, and living under institutions of that description. Yet these are the very men who come in at night, and with fire and torch destroy the property of her majesty's subjects, for no reason whatever except that they obey her majesty's laws, and carry into effect her royal commands. Of such a system of warfare there are, I believe, no examples, except, as I have stated, among the most lawless of the barbarous tribes of the East and of Africa. It is quite out of the question that her majesty's loyal subjects, invited to their habitations, and fixed in them, by her majesty's authority and that of her predecessors, should not endeavour to retaliate the sufferings thus inflicted upon them, unless protected by the strong arm of government; but how can government protect them, except by taking strong measures, when these persons are found invading her majesty's dominions for the purpose of plundering and destroying the property of her majesty's subjects, to intercept them in their retreat, to take them prisoners, and punish them according to the laws of the country they have insulted?

There can be no doubt a civil government in any country is capable of preventing the collection of a body of troops, and the invasion of the territory of a neighbouring power. A body of "sympathisers" has been organised in the States to carry on the plan of invasion; and are we to sit down quietly and pass unnoticed this unwarrantable interference?
February 5, 1839.

Agitation by Authority.
I now come to the last paragraph of the speech, in which her majesty complains, that she has observed with pain the efforts which have been made, in some parts of the country, to excite her subjects to disobedience and resistance to the law, and to recommend dangerous and illegal acts. Now, I really think that this affecting paragraph cannot have raised very pleasant reflections in the breasts of many noble lords who are in the habit of supporting her majesty's ministers. It is but too true that various persons have endeavoured to excite her

majesty's subjects to resist the law; but I am afraid much of this spirit may be traced to what has taken place in this house on former occasions. I have heard persons, charged with the highest employments of government, insisting upon the rights of this people to assemble for the expression of their sentiments, declaiming against any restriction on that right, and preaching upon this doctrine without restricting it in the manner declared by law—namely, that these assemblies must not be in numbers sufficient to create alarm. It was but very lately that a great officer of state, travelling about the country, made a speech to the same purport at Liverpool, and stated those opinions in the most unreserved manner, at the very moment when men were assembling by torch-light meetings. We have heard for a number of years past of the extraordinary tranquillity of Ireland, and as often as I have listened to the phrase, I have protested against it; but there is a gentleman, high in the confidence of government, who goes about devising new modes of agitation every day. That gentleman ought to have a special copy of the speech sent to him! One time he talks of raising 2,000,000 of men—at another time of a fund of 20,000 l. sterling, which is deposited in his private bank, and ultimately to be deposited in his private pocket. In order to further his new schemes of agitation, that gentleman has declared his intention of raising 60,000 fighting men for her majesty, though he has never, that I am aware of, been employed as a recruiting officer. Sometimes these boasts do not turn out to be true; but if not 60,000 persons, there may be 6,000, or some force of that description, which would be a serious inconvenience to the government.

February 5, 1839.

Folly of carrying on war with a peace establishment.

This country is at war—at war in two quarters of the world—at war in America and at war in Asia; and what I say is this, that when a country is at war, I understand that the fleet of that country should be put upon a war establishment; whereas, these returns are made on a peace establishment—nay, I believe on one much lower,—on a reduced peace establishment; and yet we are pretending to carry on war in two countries of the world with such means! I warned your lordships a year and a half ago—indeed nearly two years ago, against any such attempt. I believe that we have been feeling the inconvenience of such an attempt from that period up to the present time, and I only hope and trust in God, that we shall not experience still further inconvenience and disasters from our perseverance in it. A peace establishment, and a reduced peace establishment, may be very fit and very proper for carrying on the service of the country in time of peace; but when we come to carry on war, our peace establishment is not found equal to the performance of the duties required from the establishment in time of peace, and still less to those extended duties which must be performed in time of war.

We are carrying on a war in North America, and a most expensive war in Asia; and both of them require all the force this country can employ in order to bring them to an early and an honourable termination. We are, however, engaging in both with a reduced peace establishment, and we are incurring all descriptions of risks, in every other part of the world, in order to do this. The noble earl (Minto) has been talking about a few masts and sails, when the whole force which the country can command ought to be engaged in the war now waging, in order to bring the contest to the honourable termination I speak of. I said this about a year and a half ago, and I now repeat it.

March 7, 1839.

The Corn Laws have improved Agriculture.
The system which it is the object of the existing law to establish, is one of encouragement to agriculture—a system which was established at the termination of the last century, and under which I will venture to assert, the agriculture of this country has made a progress, and has risen to a degree of superiority throughout these kingdoms, greater than exists in any other part of the world, not excepting even the Netherlands. Under this system of encouragement to agriculture, large sums of money have been laid out and invested in land, and property relating to land; and great sums are at this moment in the course of investment in the same way; and I call on your lordships not to agree to any resolution, or to any measure of the government (if they should think proper to propose any such measure), which will have the effect of withdrawing from agriculture this protection, and thus putting a stop to those great improvements which are at present in progress, and which, I say, have had such an influence on agriculture, that the amount of produce raised in this country is thereby greatly increased. I believe that the produce of the country has been immensely increased, and particularly in the valuable article of wheat, the annual production of which is now nearly equal to its greatest annual consumption. Such is the supply of wheat that the very lowest order of the people subsist mostly upon it; which is not, I believe, the practice in any other country. The practice is not known any where else; it is not known in France; it is not known in Germany; it is not known in the Netherlands; nor is it, in short, the case any where else. In fact, the lower orders live upon wheaten bread in no country of the world except England. I entreat your lordships to bear this in mind; I entreat you not to break down a system which has carried cultivation to such a pitch, that an amount of produce is raised in England, alone, which is found to be nearly equal to her greatest annual consumption. I think the annual amount of produce will increase. This is my firm belief; and I am confident that with the increase of produce there must come, and come naturally too, a corresponding decrease of price; and it is to that consequence that I look as being the solution of all the difficulties which at present attend this question. But, let your lordships recollect, it is absolutely necessary to keep up this

encouragement in order to arrive at the desired result of the reduction of price. Very lately, when wheat in this country was at 78s. the quarter, and the duty on importation was a merely nominal one of 1s. a quarter, was there any such quantity of foreign wheat introduced as was sufficient to lower the price? Not at all. The moment the ports were opened, the merchant importer stood on the same ground as the farmer, and he would not sell his corn for 1s. less than the price of the day. Did we ever hear of corn coming in from abroad, and being brought to market at a cheaper rate than it was selling for in this country? Never. But look to the operation of the law prevailing in the former part of the war; the prices varied from 70s. to 150s. the quarter. Did we ever hear of foreign corn being sold for 1s. less than what could be got for it in the general markets of this country? It must be sold by the merchant importer at the very same price as by the farmer. It is all very fine to say that the price would be exceedingly low, if these laws were abolished, and corn were allowed to be introduced without restriction. Why, if the price of corn raised in this country were low, the foreigner could not get more for his corn here, than the farmer; but if the price of home grown corn were necessarily high, the introduction of foreign corn would not reduce it.

March 14, 1839.

Repeal of the Corn Laws will raise the price of Corn.

It is very important to look at this question with reference to the interests of the commerce of the country, and also to consider the effect of the abolition of the corn laws on the price of provisions and on the price of manufactures. Now, if we discourage agriculture to such a degree that any large body of persons and a great amount of capital come to be withdrawn from it, the price of native produce must rise; there would be so much less produce raised than before, that its price—the price of the native produce I mean—must rise. Now, the price of the corn imported will be the price of the diminished quantity of the home-raised corn. Would the manufacturing labourer benefit by this? Would the manufacturer find any advantage in it, when the diminished value of their wages was forcing the labourers to raise the market upon him? Would the merchant exporter gain anything by the change? Would it not be found that, in proportion as the manufacturer must pay a larger amount of wages, the prices of his manufactures must be augmented; and therefore the disadvantages of competition with merchants abroad be augmented likewise?

March 14, 1839.

Foreign Governments would Tax the Export of their Corn.

There is another view of the question which I beseech your lordships to take—I mean the question of our dependence on foreign produce for a great part of our annual consumption, which would be caused by the abolition of the present law. On looking over the papers which have been produced on former discussions of this subject, I have seen proofs that in certain countries duties are paid upon the exportation of corn thence hither; and that statements are made by the sovereigns of those countries to this effect:—"As the corn is wanted by Great Britain, and her subjects can afford to pay the duty, therefore they shall pay it." This duty must come out of the pocket of her majesty's subjects, and be taken into account in the price of the goods of the manufacturers. Your lordships have heard a great deal upon the competition of foreign manufacturers with our own in foreign markets. I certainly am one who does not despise the consideration of these subjects; which, on the contrary, I think of very high importance; but this question is a large one, and it is necessary to consider it on rather broader grounds. This very consideration may be material with respect to some countries of which we have been the creditors; but I do not see how our relations with those which are not corn countries can be affected by any change in the corn laws. The power of taxation, which would be thrown into the hands of foreign powers, in the event of the repeal of the corn laws, constitutes, in my view, a most important feature of the case. Suppose we were involved in an arduous competition with Prussian or Russian manufacturers for the supply of a particular article: if we should make up our minds to rely solely on those countries for a supply of corn, as we are called upon to do by the opponents of the corn laws,—and if the success of our manufactures depends on the abundance and cheapness of corn among our population—must we not expect, according to the usual course of such affairs among mankind, that the corn exported from those countries would be taxed so as to render the food of our manufacturers as dear as it would be under any other circumstances? If that is likely to be the case, I would strongly advise you, my lords, to agree to no measure which may render this country dependent upon others for its supply of food. Let us persevere in those measures which have been successful in raising the agriculture of this country and increasing its produce; let us increase its produce to the utmost possible degree, and render all the articles of food as cheap as possible; and then let us see what can be done with reference to commerce and its interests; but let us, I entreat, begin by securing to her majesty's subjects a supply of the best food from the produce of her majesty's own dominions.

March 14, 1839.

As a public man, stands on public grounds.

The noble earl (Radnor) says that I am an advocate for a monopoly; and he talks about my not assisting the landlords, not assisting the farmers, and not assisting the labourers. My lords, I know nothing about landlords, farmers, or labourers, when I am advocating a legislative question of a public nature in this house. I have nothing to say to them any farther than as their interests are identified with those of the community at large. I beg the noble lord to understand, when I come into this house, I come here upon the public interest. I have no more to say to landlords, farmers, or labourers, than the noble earl himself; and I am thoroughly convinced there is not a noble friend near me who does not look at this question solely on public grounds, and those which he conceives it to be for the interest of the country to take.

March 14, 1839.

Objections to a free press in Malta.

I am one of those who have always thought, that if there existed any part of her majesty's dominions in which a free press was not necessary, Malta was that part. Our business there is to maintain a garrison and a great naval station. Malta contains a population of 100,000 persons, for whom I entertain the highest respect and regard, being convinced that her majesty has no better or more devoted subjects than they are. It is the duty of government, and the duty of this house, as far as it can, to superintend the good government of the people of Malta—a people who talk the Maltese language, and the Maltese language alone—a people, of whom not one in 500 can read a line. Surely, of all the institutions of this country which are the least necessary for men of this description, and I declare my belief that it is a true description of the people of Malta, I may venture to assert a free press is that one institution. I will not dispute that hereafter much good may arise from a free press, but education is much more necessary for the people of Malta. A free press cannot be rendered useful to them, much less advantageous, without that training which they require, and that education which ought to be given to them. There is a certain liberal set of gentlemen in this country who think a free press in Malta exceedingly desirable, not for the sake of any advantage to the inhabitants, but for the sake of the advantage to be produced on the neighbouring coast of France, and Spain, and Italy. This is the truth with respect to this free press. * * I believe that we have now had enough of private wars, and I believe that we now seek what advantage it would have been, if we had never undertaken those private wars, not only in other parts of the world, but also a little nearer home. I must say that the objects of them are inconsistent with the interests—aye, and inconsistent with the honour—of this country; inconsistent with the interests of the country, because, as I always have maintained, and always shall maintain, the interests of this country must depend, not only on the maintenance of peace for itself, but on its preventing, if possible, disturbances among other nations; and inconsistent with its honour, because I will say, that its honour does depend on not exciting rebellions and insurrections in other nations, at the same moment that the government here is ostensibly at peace with those nations. Now, that is the ground on which I have always objected to a free press in Malta. I object to it, because I contend that the intention entertained is to have a free press, not for Malta, but for the neighbouring regions of Italy, France, and Spain; and if

you must have a free press for the Maltese, in the name of God let it be in the Maltese language!
April 30, 1839.

Malta. Its riches and resources.
I have reason to know something of Malta; I know something of its resources; and, instead of its being misgoverned, I can only say that in the course of my intercourse with that island, I was astonished at the immensity of its resources of all descriptions, and at the readiness with which these resources were afforded to his majesty's troops and armies, in order to enable them to carry on war against an enemy. It is but an act of justice to those noble and honourable persons who have governed Malta, to say thus much; and I must add that, having known that island for a period of nearly twenty years, I really believe that, on the face of the globe there is not a place of the same extent and population which possesses one thousandth part of its riches and resources of all descriptions.
April 30, 1839.

Indifference to Reports.
I have served the sovereigns and the public of this country for fifty years, and throughout the whole of that period I have been exposed to evil report and to good report, and I have still continued to serve on through all report, both good and evil, and thus I confess myself to be completely indifferent to the nature of all reports.
May 14, 1839.

Personal Attendants of the Sovereign. Their Political Influence.
When the noble viscount announced in this house on Tuesday last that he had resigned his office, the probable consequences of that announcement occurred to my mind, and I turned my attention in consequence to the state of the government at the present moment—to the state of the royal authority—to the composition of the royal household—and to all those circumstances which were likely to come under my consideration, in case I were called upon to assist in advising the composition of another administration. I confess, that it appeared to me impossible that any set of men should take charge of her majesty's government without having the usual influence and control over the establishment of the royal household—that influence and control which their immediate predecessors in office had exercised before them. As the royal household was formed by their predecessors in office, the possession of that influence and that control over it appeared to me to be absolutely necessary, to

let the public see that the ministers who were about to enter upon office had and possessed the entire confidence of her majesty. I considered well the nature of the formation of the royal household under the civil list act passed at the commencement of her majesty's reign. I considered well the difference between the household of a queen-consort and the household of a queen-regnant. The queen-consort not being a political person in the same light as a queen-regnant, I considered the construction of her majesty's household—I considered who filled offices in it—I considered all the circumstances attendant on the influence of the household, and the degree of confidence which it might be necessary for the government to repose in the members of it. I was sensible of the serious and anxious nature of the charge which the minister in possession of that control and influence over her majesty's household would have laid upon him. I was sensible that in everything which he did, and in every step which he took as to the household, he ought to consult not only the honour of her majesty's crown, and her royal state and dignity, but also her social condition, her ease, her convenience, her comfort—in short, everything which tended to the solace and happiness of her life. I reflected on all these considerations as particularly incumbent on the ministers who should take charge of the affairs of this country; I reflected on the age, the sex, the situation, and the comparative inexperience, of the sovereign on the throne; and I must say that if I had been, or if I was to be, the first person to be consulted, with respect to the exercise of the influence and control in question, I would suffer any inconvenience whatever, rather than take any step as to the royal household which was not compatible with her majesty's comforts.

I cannot but think that the principles on which we proposed to act with respect to the ladies of the bed-chamber, in the case of a queen-regnant, were the correct principles. The public will not believe that the queen holds no political conversation with those ladies, and that political influence is not exercised by them, particularly considering who those persons are who hold such situations. I believe the history of this country affords a number of instances in which secret and improper influence has been exercised by means of such conversations. I have, my lords, a somewhat strong opinion on this subject. I have unworthily filled the office which the noble viscount now so worthily holds; and I must say I have felt the inconvenience of an anomalous influence, not exercised, perhaps, by ladies, but anomalous influence, undoubtedly, of this description, and exerted simply in conversations; and I will tell the noble viscount that the country is at this moment suffering some inconvenience from the exercise of that very secret influence.

May 14, 1839.

A war carried on by militia, volunteers, and troops of that description, will infallibly be carried on after the manner of civil wars.
May 30, 1839.

Reasons for passing the Poor Law.

I have been long enough in parliament to recollect that, before the present law passed, there were not less than half-a-dozen attempts made, by some of the greatest men this country ever produced, to amend the system of the poor laws. Among others, the late Mr. Pitt endeavoured to amend these laws, but failed, and for a reason which I believe occasioned the failure of every attempt to alter them until that which was successfully made within these five years, when the present poor law amendment act was passed, principally by the exertions of the noble and learned lord (Lord Brougham). The real truth of the matter was this— that in every parish in the country there existed some abuses, I will venture to say a hundred times greater than any of those with which the noble earl (Stanhope) entertains your lordships upon every vacant day that presents itself. In every parish, I repeat, there were abuses; and, in each, abuses founded upon a different principle from those existing in some neighbouring parish; so that no law could be devised to remedy them; for the measure which would apply to parish A, instead of removing the abuses existing in parish B, would only have tended to aggravate and render them intolerable. At length, there was a very general and searching inquiry into the whole state of the administration of the poor laws; the result of which was, that the present measure was arranged and produced to parliament. It passed both houses in a very short space of time, and, I believe, on the principle there was no division whatever, and hardly a difference of opinion, in this house; I believe there was none in the other house of parliament, and very little difference of opinion was expressed upon any part of the details. With respect to the administration of the law, I have observed it in different parts of the country, and I must say that its administration has been entirely satisfactory, and most particularly to those parties who are likely to become its more immediate objects. That part of the law of which the noble earl complains most, namely, the existence of the poor law commissioners, is, in my opinion, the most important part of it. The truth of the matter is, that the abuses in the administration of the poor laws were so numerous, so various, and, at the same time, so inveterate, that it was absolutely impossible to get the better of them, without the constitution of some central authority which should superintend the execution of the law; taking care that it was duly administered, and that those intrusted with its execution in the country did not infringe upon its provisions. Such, I believe, was the object of the institution of those boards of guardians and commissioners.

June 18, 1839.

The Ballot and Universal Suffrage dangerous. Open questions a symptom of weakness in a Government.

I fully concur with the noble viscount (Melbourne) in the propriety of opposing the further extension of the suffrage, and upon the very same ground, namely, that such extension would be inconsistent with the best interests of the country. I likewise concur in the sentiments which that noble viscount has expressed upon the subject of the ballot; that obnoxious, and, I must say, un-English measure; at the same time I deeply regret that the noble viscount did think proper to make it what is called an open question. I had the misfortune to be in office when there were such questions, and I must say, that I never could consider them as anything but a symptom of weakness on the part of those who were carrying on the service of their sovereign—a symptom that they were not acting together, that they did not agree amongst themselves, and that there was a division also amongst their supporters. Instead of its being a matter of satisfaction that an individual question like the ballot should be left an open question, I regard it as a circumstance most likely to prove disastrous to the government, and eventually so to the country.

June 25, 1839.

The Birmingham Riots in 1839. The town treated worse than if taken by storm.

I have been accused of "exaggeration."[21] That may be a parliamentary phrase; I will not presume to decide that it is an unparliamentary term; but I believe that it is a term not much used amongst gentlemen. It has been employed, however, in a privileged place, that must be nameless, and I shall advert to it no farther than to notice the conclusions which may be drawn from the use of such a term in reference to what I did say. I trust your lordships will excuse me for a few moments upon this subject, because I really think I have been most unjustifiably made the subject of a personal attack for what I stated in this, your lordships' house, with respect to the late riots in Birmingham. What I stated, my lords, was founded on the same species of information which, it appears, was in the possession of her majesty's government; for, neither the noble viscount, nor any of the other noble lords opposite, knew any more of the subject than I did; they knew nothing beyond what they had seen in the newspapers; and I stated, at the time, that I knew nothing beyond that, myself, with regard to the facts. But I compared the transactions at Birmingham with certain other transactions, of which, certainly, I have more knowledge than most noble lords in this house; matters on which I had a certain and positive knowledge; and I said (and I firmly believe that it was correct, and that, in making the comparison I did not, in the least degree, depart from the truth), that the peaceable inhabitants of the town of Birmingham were worse treated, upon that occasion, than the inhabitants of any town I had ever known or seen taken by assault. This is what I asserted; and, it is the fact, according to my opinion.

[Footnote 21: A member of the House of Commons had used this term as applied to the Duke's remarks on this subject, a few nights previously.] * * * * *

I cannot help thinking that it is extraordinary that, in the year 1839, after nine years of liberal government,—after nine years' enjoyment of the blessings of liberal government,—your lordships should be discussing whether or not the amount of destruction completed within a peaceful town within her majesty's dominions is equal to the mischief done to a town which is taken by storm. And yet this has been clearly demonstrated to be the case. It is clear, my lords, that in peaceful, happy England, which carried on a war for twenty-two years, and

which made the most extraordinary efforts to maintain that war, as she did, with circumstances of glory and success attending her arms in all parts of the world,—in order to avoid as it was hoped, these miseries, and so that no such disasters as these might ever approach her shores,—in this same happy and peaceful England, after nine years of liberal government, here is a town plundered, and its peace destroyed; and yet I am accused of exaggeration, because I say I never knew any town, taken by storm, to be so ill-used as this fine town has been. I confess I am not at all surprised, however, at the conduct of the noble lord who so liberally applied the term "exaggeration" to what I said, when I reflect who are the followers and supporters of that noble lord.
July 22, 1839.

Legal redress against Magistrates.

I apprehend that, according to the law of England, any individual is at liberty to complain of the conduct of a magistrate, and proceed against him in a court of law. No one has ever doubted that, in this country, every individual has a right so to complain of, and to proceed against, the magistrates, when the magistrates misconduct themselves. It is in accordance only with the *Code Napoléon*,—with the code of laws of that high priest of liberalism, the Emperor Napoleon,—that the consent of the council of state should be given, before a justice misconducting himself can be tried and punished. Hitherto, in this country, the practice and the law have been different on that head; and I hope we shall hear no more of such proceedings. But follow out the system laid down in the letter from the Home Office, and the result will be that no man—particularly if he have to complain of the conduct of a magistrate—will, without the consent of the home secretary, go into a court of justice to obtain redress. My lords, to such a course I trust I shall see some check put, before it is further established by precedents.
July 22,1839.

Reasons for Supporting the Penny Postage Bill.

In the preamble of this bill, it is stated to have for its object the establishment, in this country, of a low and uniform rate of postage. I admit the truth of the arguments stated by the noble viscount upon the expediency, and, indeed, the necessity, of establishing an uniform and low rate of postage in this country. These arguments have been urged more than once by my noble friend near me (Lord Ashburton), and by the noble duke who heretofore filled the office of postmaster general, but whom I do not see in his place this evening. If, however, the object be only to reduce the expense of postage, and to establish an uniform rate, I imagine that the power of the government is already sufficient for such a purpose, although the power was not granted for that immediate object; but the object with which the power was given was, for the purpose of enabling the government to adopt that particular plan which is called Mr. Rowland Hill's plan, and which, I am certainly disposed to admit, was, of all plans, if adopted exactly as Mr. Hill proposed it, the most likely to be successful. At the same time, I must say, I am afraid the present plan will not be entirely successful. I think, in the first place, that a great mistake is committed, in the assumption that the reduction in the rate of postage down to a penny, even to be paid on the delivery of the letter, would induce any very considerable increase of literary correspondence. I possessed, for many years, an extensive knowledge of the degree of advantage attendant upon such a system in the army; and I can safely assert to your lordships, that it is quite curious to remark how small an amount of correspondence is carried on by soldiers, notwithstanding they enjoy the utmost facility for doing so. One remarkable instance I will mention, just to show that it is not quite certain that a large increase of correspondence will take place in consequence of the rate of postage being reduced to a penny. In the case of a highland regiment, it was positively ascertained that, in the course of six or seven months, only sixty-three or sixty-four letters were written. Now this is a fact on which reliance can be placed; and it certainly demonstrates that the people of this country are not so ready to correspond, as some suppose, even when they can send letters at the rate of a penny for the postage. I would beg your lordships to observe just one point touching the application of this plan to the country parts of England. It is perfectly well known to you that the post-office is frequently six or seven miles, and sometimes ten or fifteen miles, from most of the houses and villages in the neighbourhood. Now, if a man have to take a letter to the post-office, he may lose half a day's work in going there; and it cannot be supposed that he would make such a sacrifice merely because he would only be charged a penny on the delivery of his letter. Then, again, let us look at the manner in which the plan will work in large towns. The plan will, no doubt, work beneficially in London. In London, there are a number of people employed for the purpose of delivering letters in all parts of the town several times in the course of the day. But let us take such towns as Manchester, or Leeds, or Liverpool; the people cannot resort to one post-office, and post-offices must therefore be established in different parts of the town for their accommodation; and the consequence will be, a vast increase in the establishment of the post-office,—of which increase, I do not think sufficient notice has been taken in the documents which I have perused. Upon the whole, then, I am very much afraid that this scheme for a low and uniform rate of postage wilt be found impracticable on account of the expense, and, also, from the small amount of profit which will accrue from the carriage of the letters.

At the time this subject was first mentioned in this house, and, indeed, in the other house of parliament, the noble viscount said that his main object would he to secure the revenue; and I certainly apprehended that the noble viscount would not adopt this plan, unless he could see some security for the revenue;

and this was the language held, also, in the other house of parliament, I understand. It seems now, however, that we have got no security for the revenue.

But my lords, notwithstanding I feel so little confidence in this measure, and notwithstanding that I must continue to lament that it should ever have been adopted, when all the circumstances of the present times are considered,—I, nevertheless, earnestly recommend you to pass it. It is a measure which has been most anxiously looked forward to by the country; at the same time that it is one as to which there has been much doubt: but your lordships should bear in mind, that there is not one clause of this bill upon which you can make an amendment, or in which you can give a vote, except in the negative or the affirmative, without committing a breach of those conventional rules which have been established for the conduct of the business between you and the House of Commons. On the other hand, my lords, suppose you were to reject this bill;—the government, supported by the other house, would have the power to destroy the whole revenue of the post-office; so that all the evil which this bill could do to the revenue, and which it is your object to save, might still be done;—and seeing that, at the same time, the measure of post-office administration, which it is the object of this bill to effect, and which it is desired should be carried into execution, must altogether lie over, unless you agree to some such measure as this;—I say, my lords, under these circumstances, I intend, though with pain and reluctance, to vote for the bill; and I earnestly recommend your lordships to adopt it.

August 5, 1839.

Danger of interfering with the Religion of the Hindoos.
My lords, I served in India for a considerable length of time; but I never saw—I never heard of—anything so revolting in the religious ceremonies of the natives as has been described by the noble duke and by the right reverend prelate. The whole army, while I was in India, except about 50,000 men, consisted of idolaters; but they were as good soldiers as could be found anywhere. They performed, in the best manner, any service that was required of them; and certainly, at that time, the object of the government, and of every man in the service of the government, was to avoid, not only interference, but even the semblance of any interference, in any manner, in the idolatrous rites and ceremonies of the country. I have not read one of the dispatches which have been alluded to; and I must say that I have seen too much, in my own experience, to encourage the practice of encouraging documents of this description. I beg your lordships to recollect, that with the exception of about 20,000 of her majesty's troops, and, with the exception of the civil servants of the government, and the few European residents in the country, there is not a

man in India who is not an idolater, to manage the affairs of that most extensive and important empire. I would entreat your lordships never to lose sight of that fact. I know, too, from experience, for I have seen the missionaries at work, the little progress which they make; and I know at the same time that their labours create a good deal of jealousy. I warn the government not to go too far in their measures against the idolatry of India; for the Indian empire is one of great importance, and they must not expect to convert 100,000,000 of idolaters to our holy religion by the small means at their disposal.
August 13, 1839.

Never said one thing and meant another.
I will not make any professions of my own anxiety to put down the slave trade. I have passed a long life, I trust with honour, in the service of her majesty's predecessors. I served her majesty's predecessors in diplomatic situations and in councils, as well as in the army, and I believe people cannot accuse me of saying one thing and meaning another.
August 19, 1839.

Impotent Colonial Administration of the Whigs.
We have sacrificed 20,000,000 l. of money to terminate slavery in the British colonies; and we are now calling upon other nations—upon the United States, upon Spain, upon the Brazils, and upon various powers which possess slaves—to imitate and to follow our example; but what have we done to secure the co-operation of those great countries in the great object that we have in view? We have offered no inducement to those nations to imitate our example, by the establishment of order and good government in our West Indian colonies; for nowhere have we properly or adequately availed ourselves of those advantages which we have, or of those advantages which we might procure, to give security to life and property in those islands, and to maintain peace and tranquillity among their inhabitants. The communities in the West Indies are all small societies; and there is not a man in any one of them, not in Jamaica, even, which is the largest of them, who is not within the reach of authority. The government of each of those islands is strong in the means of exercising authority—strong in garrisons, strong in troops, strong in a police force, and in everything necessary for the preservation of life and property, for carrying the laws into execution, and for affording security to every individual, even to the very lowest of the people;—but yet, I will venture to say, since the enactment of the law for the emancipation of the slaves, there have been and are no societies, in the whole world, in such a state of disorganization, disorder, and anarchy, as are those very West Indian islands of ours; but which, if they were well managed and governed by the noble lord, nominally at the head of the colonial department, instead of by the different factions that resort thither to interfere with the business of that

government, ought, and are calculated, to be of the greatest advantage to this nation. There are no societies in the world more capable of being well governed, than those islands are, if the noble lord opposite would only perform his duty in an independent manner, and keep all factions at a distance, instead of allowing every faction in this country to interfere, on all occasions, with the business of the government in relation to those colonies. But this is not all; let your lordships look round in all directions, and you will see the same lamentable state of things existing. Look at Lower Canada, look at Upper Canada, at Newfoundland—look where you will, you will see nothing but disorder and anarchy—and resulting from what? from nothing but the interference of factions in England; who, let your lordships recollect, have nothing to do with those colonies. These disorders result solely from the interference of those factions in the affairs of each of those colonies; and till the government shall put an end to such interference, and act altogether independently of it, it is impossible to hope for a restoration of tranquillity.

August 23, 1839.

The Melbourne Administration no Government.

I can assure the noble viscount, (Palmerston) that all I desire—and all I have desired for some years past—is this,—to see a "government" in the country. To see the country "governed." I wish that I could say that I had seen it "governed" for some years past; and I hope that the noble viscount will now turn over a new leaf, and "govern" the country a little better than he has done heretofore. I may tell the noble viscount, that I have had some little experience in these matters myself; and I humbly suggest to the noble viscount, that, before he announces measures to parliament through the speech from the throne, in future, he should first take care that those measures have already been properly considered; and that, before he inserts them in her majesty's speech, he should have them ready prepared, or in such a state of preparation as to be able to introduce them to parliament immediately after the speech from the throne. If he do thus, the measures in all probability, will be in such a state that they may be passed, or, at all events, they will not be scrambled for among partisans and factions in parliament: they will then, most likely, be considered by men who, I consider, from their official station, must be capable of deciding upon them; they will be their measures, and not the measures of factions and parties; or, at least, they will not be measures presented to parliament in such a state as that they ought not to pass. But I have desired to see a "government" in the country, for many other reasons besides those which are referable to the state and manner in which measures have been brought forward, after having been announced to parliament in the speech from the throne. I desire to have a "government" in this country, because I am anxious to see our colonies settled and governed—because I wish to see the interior of the country settled and governed as it ought to be governed—and because I wish to see all our establishments fixed and protected in that form and state in which they are to remain.

August 23, 1839.

Causes of the Weakness of the Melbourne Administration.

The noble viscount has been pleased to attribute the disturbances in the country, at the present moment, to the opposition which, he says, has been given by your lordships to the measures brought forward for the redress of grievances. Now I did not like to interrupt the noble viscount, when he was addressing your lordships; but I certainly felt much disposed to call upon the noble viscount to name what the measures were, to which he so alluded. I have been trying, ever since the noble viscount spoke, to recollect what those measures could be; and I declare that, with respect to England, particularly, I do not know of a single measure which has been discussed in this house, and rejected by your lordships, that would with any degree of propriety, be called a measure for the redress of the grievances of the people. If there be such measures, let the noble viscount bring them forward again next session, and I am sure they will receive from your lordships every attention. But, my lords, I have taken another view of the cause of the disturbances which now exist in the country. I think they have arisen from a very peculiar state of circumstances; and I will venture to submit them to the noble viscount, in answer to that part of his speech, in which he was kind enough to attribute those disturbances to the House of Lords. I believe that they have originated in the unnoticed and unpunished combinations which have been allowed by the government during so many years, to exist,—whether as political unions or as trade unions, or as other combinations,—clearly illegal combinations,—amongst workmen, to force others to abandon their work, by those who work at prices different from those at which they are content to be employed, and at which they have agreed to work for their employers. These combinations have gone so far in some parts of the country,—and more particularly in the north of England, and, indeed, throughout almost the whole of the northern part of the island,—as to threaten destruction to the trade and credit of the manufacturers; and at last they have arrived at that pitch, and have spread to that extent, that the country is brought to the situation in which we see it at the present moment. For, after all, what are these Chartists, that are found marching about the country, and engaged in the disturbances that prevail? I have inquired a great deal into the subject, and the result is, that I believe they are nothing more nor less than persons combined together for the purpose of driving other workmen—engaged, whether in manufactures, in the collieries, or agricultural pursuits, or in other districts—from their work; and for the purpose of destroying the machinery, and the buildings, and of interfering with the capital of the employers,—thus striking at the very root of employment, and at the chief means of the sustenance of the people,—striking at the foundation of the manufactures and the commerce of the country, and of all its prosperity. This is my sincere belief; and all this, I say, is owing to the want of early notice of the proceedings of those combinations by the government,—to their not having carried the laws into execution,—to their having left free from punishment those who have been submitted to trial,—and to their unfortunate selection of magistrates, and, above all, of the magistrates of the new reformed corporations of Birmingham, Manchester, Bolton, and other towns. The government may rely on it, that, until they adopt different measures, they will not induce parliament to look with favour on their proceedings. The government first reduced all the military establishments. Those military establishments are not, even now, nearly up to their proper footing; and I am firmly convinced that, in the disturbed districts, there is not one half the establishment equal to the ordinary establishment maintained in time of peace. This circumstance, and the want of a due execution of the law upon those who are tried, convicted, and sentenced to punishment,—and also the fact, that those who have been appointed to carry into execution the law are persons connected by habit, by association, and even by excitement, with those very Chartists who have violated the law,—suggest the true causes of these disturbances; and not the nameless grievances created by a nameless opposition in this house, to nameless measures, as alleged by the noble viscount.

August 23, 1839.
Speech on Her Majesty's Marriage.

There is no noble lord in this house who concurs more sincerely than I do in the expression of congratulation to her majesty upon her approaching marriage, which she has been pleased to announce a second time to the public from the throne this day. I sincerely wish, with the noble mover and seconder of the address, that this event may tend to the happiness and comfort of the Queen. Upon this occasion I should have been contented with the address, and should have offered not another word, if your lordships had not been called upon in the speech from the throne, to concur with the other house of parliament, in making a suitable provision for the prince, for whose future station in this country her majesty's speech has prepared us. But, my lords, it appears to me that when this house is called upon to express an opinion upon a detail of this description, the house ought to look into, and act upon, this subject—it ought not to be a mere congratulation. I conceive that the public have a right to know something beyond the mere name of the prince whom her majesty is about to espouse. My lords, I had the honour of being summoned to attend her majesty in privy council, when her majesty in council was graciously pleased to declare her intention of becoming the espoused of this prince. I observed, that the precedent of the reign of George III. was followed in all respects except one, and that was the declaration, that this prince was a protestant. [Loud cries of "Hear, hear!" from the opposition benches.] My lords, I, for one, entertain no doubt that the prince is a protestant. I believe he is a protestant. I know he is of a protestant family. I have the honour of being known to some members of that family, and I am sure that it is a protestant family. But, my lords, this is a protestant state, and it is absolutely necessary, by law, that the person who shall become the spouse of the queen be a protestant; and, if the precedent of George III. has been taken in part, it ought to have been followed throughout; and then the public would have had the satisfaction of knowing that the fact of the prince being a protestant, had been officially declared by her majesty's government. My lords, I know the noble lords opposite too well to suppose that they are not aware of the anxiety in the public mind on this subject; and I know, also, that they had it in their power to relieve that anxiety, and to gratify the public by making this declaration; nay, more, my lords, I am convinced that there exists the same anxiety in the royal mind, about the protestant character of the state as is felt by me or any of your lordships. And if so, my lords, I ask, why was the precedent of George III. departed from? Is there any doubt as to the religious sentiments of this prince? None at all; there can be no doubt that he is a protestant; he cannot be otherwise. Then, why is it not so stated? We have heard something of this marriage from another part of the country; we have seen some proceedings on this subject since the declaration in council, which show pretty clearly why the word "protestant" was omitted. My lords, I confess that I am one of those who read with great attention all that passes in Ireland;—all those speeches which come from that quarter;—and I do it for this reason: I have been accustomed to that kind of revolutionary discussions. It has been said by an eminent French writer, *en plein jour, on ne conspire pas*; but that is not so now. The object proposed is terror. These things are declared openly. This I can see from what appears in the public prints, as I read these public letters and missives in order to see what the real danger is, and that I may not be taken by surprise. Now, what I mean to say is this,—that I see in what has passed elsewhere, a very suspicious reason why the word "protestant" was not inserted in the communication made to the privy council, and why it has not been inserted in the speech from the throne. I say to the noble lords opposite, that I believe they are as much determined as I am, myself, to maintain the protestant ascendancy of the state. I think, then, if this be the case, that upon the first occasion, when this question comes before your lordships, and when the House of Lords shall be called upon to do any act, or to make any declaration upon the subject, beyond the mere congratulation of the queen, your lordships should take that course which may procure the country the satisfaction of knowing that Prince Albert is a protestant prince, and that this is still a protestant state.

January 16, 1840.
Approbation of the Conduct of the Affghanistan Expedition.

My lords, having been, for a great part of my life, selected to carry into execution, under superior authority, measures of this description, no man can be more capable of judging, from experience, of the merits of government in planning and carrying into operation such measures; and I should be the last man to doubt, at any time, the expediency of this or the other house expressing its approbation of the conduct of the political servants of the crown in planning and working out all arrangements preparatory to carrying into execution great military operations. My lords, it has happened to me, by accident, that I had some knowledge of the arrangements made for the execution of this great military enterprise; and, I must say, that I have never known an occasion on which the duty of a government was performed on a larger scale,—on which a more adequate provision was made for all contingencies that could occur, and for all the various events which could, and which did, in fact, occur during this campaign. My lords, it would be presumptuous in me to say more on this subject, having, I repeat, been made acquainted, only by accident, with the arrangements made preparatory to the campaign now brought under your lordships' attention. With respect to the military services performed, I can say nothing beyond, nor more deserving the officers and troops, than what has been stated by the governor-general in his dispatch. My lords, I am well acquainted with the officers who have directed and performed these services; and I must say that there are no men in the service who deserve a higher degree of approbation for the manner in which, on all occasions, they have discharged their duty; and that, in no instance that I have ever heard of, have such services been performed in a manner better calculated to deserve and secure the approbation of your lordships and of the country.

February 4, 1840.

Danger of Socialism.

It appears that this system (Socialism) has spread itself over a great part of the country; and, upon inquiry, I find that it has taken root rather extensively in the county in which I reside. I find that in Hampshire, or on the borders of the two counties, Wiltshire and Hampshire, there is a large institution for the propagation of Socialist principles, spreading over no less than five hundred acres of land, which this society have purchased for their purposes. In reference to that institution, I have this day presented a petition to your lordships, containing statements as to the doctrines of this society, regarding religion, the holy scriptures, God Almighty, and all the great points of our belief; which statements, in my estimation, demand the most serious inquiry. When I read that petition, which I did the moment it was placed in my hands, I felt it to be my duty, as the lord lieutenant of the county, to call the attention of the magistracy to the facts which it set forth. That I considered to be my duty; and I say, also, that the House of Lords, now that the facts have been brought before them, have a duty to perform to the country, on this question. These doctrines of Socialism are rapidly gaining strength—are spreading themselves throughout the country. They have now got beyond that point at which your lordships might say, "We will take no steps in the matter; the system is absurd, and will fall to pieces of itself." I say, my lords, we have got beyond that point; and the people should be made to understand that the legislature and the government look on those institutions only with disfavour, and are determined to discountenance them. And they should also be made to know, that wherever, in the promulgation of the doctrines of this society, there shall be a breach of the law committed, it will be treated as such, and punished as such. I say, then, that it is incumbent on your lordships to take such steps as will satisfy the country that your attention has been directed to the subject, with the view to remove the evil and ensure tranquillity. If the government will allow the motion to pass, and take the subject into their own hands, and inquire into it, through the magistracy, or by any other means, I, for one, am willing to leave the matter with them on that condition, merely adding that I shall be happy to afford them any assistance in my power in carrying out their inquiry, and in enabling them to annihilate this mischievous and demoralising system.

February 4, 1840.

Compliment to the Navy.

I know a great deal of the gentlemen of that profession; and, for my own part, I have always had, and still have, the greatest and the highest respect for them, and the very utmost confidence in them. I have always endeavoured to emulate their services in the service in which I have myself been engaged; and I am sure that in nothing have I endeavoured to emulate them in a greater degree than in that confidence which they feel, not only in themselves, and in the officers of their own rank, but in all officers and troops under their command.

February 6, 1840.

Eulogium on Lord Seaton.

I had the honour of being connected with the noble and gallant lord in service at an early period of his life; and I must declare that, at all times, and under all circumstances, he gave that promise of prudence, zeal, devotion, and ability, which he has so nobly fulfilled in his services to his sovereign and his country, during the recent proceedings in Canada. I entirely agree with the noble viscount in all that he has said, respecting the conduct of my noble and gallant friend, in remaining, under all circumstances, at his post, and in taking the command of the troops, although it was not thought expedient by the government to place him again in the government of the provinces. I agree with the noble viscount in wishing that such examples as that which has been shewn may be always followed in her majesty's service; for I must say that there never was a brighter example of fortitude and discretion than that which has been manifested by the noble and gallant lord.

March 27, 1840.

Opinion on the Printed Papers' Question.

I wish—as, indeed, everybody wishes—that the House of Commons should have the power of printing and publishing its papers. But what I want to do is this—to provide that, when it proceeds to the sale of them, the law should take its course. As to the printing and publishing of papers, I have no objection, until it comes to the point of sale. The sale ought not, in my opinion, to be made by the authority of the house; it ought to be made by individuals, and they should be responsible for what they sell, as they were previously to the passing of the resolution in 1835; and, up to that time, it must be admitted that the House of Commons and the House of Lords had the advantage of all their privileges quite as much as they have had ever since. My lords, I must confess that I look a little further into this question than the mere matter of libelling individuals. I consider all this as it affects the public generally; and, I say, the public is mainly interested in its being understood that the House of Commons and the House of Lords are not to be the privileged sellers of libels against individuals.

April 6, 1840.

Libels on foreign Sovereigns ought not to be permitted.

I remember reading with great satisfaction, the history of a great case, which was pleaded and argued at considerable length, some years ago, in this country— I mean the case of the "King v. Peltier," in the court of King's Bench. That was the case of an action brought against an obscure individual, for a libel which he had published upon the sovereign of a neighbouring country, with whom we were then in a state of peace and amity. Now, I ask your lordships whether, supposing, in the course of the late Polish revolution, the libels, some of which we have seen printed in this country, and others which we have heard spoken of in the other, and, I believe, in this house of parliament, reviling, in the strongest terms, the sovereign of Russia, had been stated in the petitions, or in the proceedings of the House of Commons, and had been printed, published, and sold by its authority; I ask your lordships whether such a proceeding would not have been calculated to disturb the peace of this country, and of the world at large? In short, I ask your lordships whether it is desirable that there should be an opportunity of publishing and selling, on the part of the two houses of parliament, libels against the sovereigns of all the foreign powers in Europe? My lords, I am one of those who consider that the greatest political interest of this country is, to remain at peace and amity with all the nations of the world. I am for avoiding even the cause of war, and of giving offence to any one, and of seeking a quarrel, either by abuse, or by that description of language which is found in these libels. I am against insulting the feelings of any sovereign, at whom individuals may have taken offence, and against whom they may seek to publish libels under the sanction of parliament. Let them state what they please in their private capacity, and let them be answerable for it individually, as Peltier was. What I want is, that parliament should not, by the combined privilege of publication and sale, run the risk of involving the country in the consequences of a discussion of such subjects, and in all the mischiefs and inconveniences which might arise from it.

April 6, 1840.

Reasons why the Chinese stopped the Opium Trade.

It is perfectly true, as is stated by the noble earl, that the trade in opium has been carried on contrary to the laws of China. But then, my lords, it has been so carried on with the knowledge of the local authorities on the spot, who received large payments, in the shape of bribes, or in the way of duties, possibly both, for allowing the import of this opium,—its admission into the ports of China. It appears that, although the trade was forbidden by the law of China, it was known to the authorities of China, to the emperor himself, and to all the servants of the government, that it had existed for many years, and that the discussion had continued for many months, upon the question, whether the trade should be allowed, and continued, under a duty, or whether it should be discontinued altogether. Allow me to ask the noble earl, who has contended so very strongly for the Emperor of China, whether that morality was so very great while he allowed that trade to be continued? and whether his morality can be improved in any respect by opium being introduced upon the payment of a large duty, instead of its being introduced by means of smuggling, and under bribes paid to the officers of his government; and even, as it has been shown, from the exterior waters into the interior of the country, in the Mandarin boats, that is, in boats, either in the service of the country, or, at all events, under the charge of officers of the government? I really cannot see the force of the noble earl's argument with respect to the illegality of the trade, when it is as clear as possible that its existence was well known to the government of China, and that no step had ever been taken to put it down; but, on the contrary, the means of continuing it, and of raising a larger duty upon it, were under consideration; and, in fact, the trade was finally put down, and discontinued only because it was supposed that it occasioned the export of a larger quantity of native or Sycee silver.

May 12, 1840.

The Opium not the cause of the war with China. Defence of Captain Elliot.

The noble earl says that this war is to be attributed to the opium! Why? there was no British opium in China at the very time these other outrages were committed, and when this very language was held; and, as far as I am able to judge, there was then no opium in the possession of the British merchants there. An order had been issued to deliver it up, and this gentleman had gone down the river for the purpose of surrendering the whole. The war, then, has grown out of another state of circumstances. First of all, there was a claim for the surrender of an Englishman to be put to death, because a Chinese had lost his life in an affray. Captain Elliot, as became an English officer, instituted an inquiry to discover whether a certain number of persons, stated to have been in an affray, had been guilty of the murder or not, and the result of the inquiry was, that he could not bring the charge home to any one; that he had no reason to suspect any one. The Chinese government still insisted that these six men should be given up. Captain Elliot refused, and that, I take it, is one of the causes of the war.

Another of the causes of the war is this—that a provision had been made that matters should be restored to their former state, in proportion as the opium should be delivered up; that the British inhabitants should have the use of the native servants; that they should have the common comforts of life, provisions, and all that was necessary for subsistence; and, finally, that the trade should be re-opened, and matters allowed to resume their usual course. After having given that promise, it is discovered that this Chinese lost his life in an affray in which American seamen were engaged as well as the English; and then a fourth proposition was advanced, which was this, that every master of a vessel, proceeding up the Canton river, should sign a bond, submitting himself, and all on board his ship, to be dealt with according to the laws of China. The noble lord has found fault with Captain Elliot upon this, as well as upon another matter. Now, this objection is most extraordinary, and it rather tends to prove that the noble earl, though he has paid great attention to this particular blue book, is not very well acquainted with former transactions in that country, or he would have found that former traders with China had invariably refused to subscribe to such proposals, and that they had broken off the trade with the Chinese, rather than do it; rather than give up British subjects to be dealt with according to the laws of China. I think they acted most properly; and that Captain Elliot, very much to his credit, refused to do it; at the same time, he did no more than his duty. He did what others would I trust have done under the same circumstances; and he is entitled to great praise for his firmness in resisting that demand. Then there is another circumstance in which Captain Elliot acted as became him. I allude particularly to his refusal to give up Mr. Dent. It was declared that the opium trade was not to be continued; that it was an illegal trade; and that dealing in opium should not be suffered. It was supposed that Mr. Dent had been a person very much concerned in that trade, and had made a large fortune, as I believe many others have done, by that illicit trade. And Captain Elliot was blamed, when it was sought to have Mr. Dent given up, because he, her majesty's representative and the chief superintendent of trade in that country, stepped forward and said, "I won't allow this gentleman to be given over to the Chinese government, and to be tried as the Chinese government may direct." I should, my lords, be ashamed of the name of Englishman, if there could be found one in her majesty's service capable of acting otherwise than this gentleman did, under such circumstances. The noble earl has stated that a great deal of difficulty would have been got rid of, if Captain Elliot had complied with the request of the Chinese; and that the Americans gave up a seaman to be dealt with according to the Chinese laws. I am sorry for it. I must say, it was not their duty to do so. They would have done better to have taken a leaf out of our book, and to have followed the example of the East India Company, to put an end to the trade rather than risk the life of one of her majesty's subjects, or give him up to be tried by the Chinese government.

May 12, 1840.

If we cannot sustain our power in the Canadas, we must necessarily lose all our dominions in North America.
June 30, 1840.

Colonial responsible government, and the sovereignty of Great Britain, are completely incompatible.
June 30, 1840.

Importance of Colonies to the Mother Country.

I have observed in this country, for some length of time, a growing desire to get rid of our North American dominions—a desire that they should become republics. This desire prevails amongst a very large party in this country. I am aware that there are also others—not, however, acting from the same motive—who desire that the separation should take place; tranquilly, if possible, but that at all events it should take place. In my opinion, these gentlemen are mistaken. It is my decided opinion, that, considering the resources and the power of these colonies, this country would sustain a heavy loss, indeed, if these colonies were to be separated from it.
June 30, 1840.

Religious Education must be provided out of the Funds of the Church.

It appears to me that there is no difference of opinion amongst us on these points—namely, that means must be found of preaching the word of God to the people of England; and I go further—for this point is also not disputed—and I say that those means must proceed, in the first instance, from the church, and that they must be exhausted before the public is called on for other means; in providing those means, you will not only be performing a duty incumbent upon you, but you will also be following the example of every other nation in the world. It has been my lot to live among idolaters—among persons of all creeds, and of all religions; but I never knew yet of a single instance in which public means were not provided sufficient to teach the people the religion of their country. They might be false religions; I know but of one true one; but yet means were never wanting to teach those false religions; and I hope that we shall not have done with this subject until we have found sufficient means for teaching the people of England their duty to their Maker, and their duty to one another, founded on their duty to that Maker.
July 30, 1840.

Necessity of administering Oaths.

I entreat your lordships to pause, and recollect that the foundation of all justice is truth; and that the mode of discovering truth has always been to administer an oath, in order that the witness may give his deposition under a high sanction. I hope your lordships will not adopt another of those bills which have been before your lordships only a few days, and which suggest, in truth, nothing more than a way of enabling a witness, who thinks proper to say he has conscientious scruples, to escape the solemnity of an oath. I admit that the inconvenience of the present state of the law falls on the community rather than on the individuals; but, at the same time, I think that, by every one of those relaxations, we shake the foundations of justice.

August 4, 1840.

Church-rate Martyrs—true state of the Case.

In my opinion, this case is a very simple one, and one on which there can be no doubt as to the course which should be taken. Here is a man who has been sued for a sum of money, which, it is understood, was lawfully due by him. The law renders him liable to pay that sum of money, and the law supports the proceedings against him for the recovery of it. This person could have easily avoided these proceedings, by simply paying the sum of 5s. 6d., which was demanded of him; or he could have gone into court and had the question fairly tried, whether he was lawfully bound to pay it or not, according to the laws of the country in which he resides; for, of course, he must be bound by the laws of his country, as well as all other British subjects. But he has not chosen to take either course. He has said, "I will not pay that money;" and, in consequence of his own conduct, a large amount has been incurred in the way of costs. These costs are not matters of speculation or amusement, they are realities; they are sums of money paid for the labour of certain individuals, for certain services performed in the execution of their duties, under the legal authority of the ecclesiastical courts, and in this suit. Now, those costs must be paid. Were we to let the man off from paying the 5s. 6d. for the rate, that remission would not get rid of his liability for the costs; these latter must be paid, either by himself or his friends, or else they must be paid by the other party, by the lawful suitors, by the lawful plaintiffs, who had a right originally to recover the money. They are the persons who would have to pay the costs, unless your lordships consent to insert the clause proposed by my noble friend. Somebody must pay the costs after all. But it is said that the defendant is not to pay the costs, and that he is to be let out of prison. Well, you may let him out, if you please; but, surely, you would not call upon the plaintiffs to pay the costs incurred by *his* conduct? That would not be justice. That would not be fair between man and man. Not a soul in this house could be of that opinion. It is not consistent either with law or justice to throw these expenses upon those on whom the law of the country has laid the necessity of incurring them. Not they, but he who, by his own conduct, rendered the proceedings imperative, ought to be made to pay the costs.

August 7, 1840.

The Duke of Wellington not a War Minister.

No noble lord nor any other man that I know has done half so much for the preservation of peace, and above all, for the pacification and the maintenance of the honour of France and for the settlement of all questions in which the interests of France were involved, as the individual who is addressing your lordships. From the period of the year 1814, down to the last month of my remaining in the service of the king, I did everything in my power for the strengthening and preservation of the peace of Europe, and more particularly for the maintaining and keeping up the best understanding between England and France. I repeat, that I have done more than any one else to place France in the situation in which she ought to be in the councils of Europe, from a firm conviction,—which I feel now as strongly as I ever did,—that if France is not, then there is no necessity for the preservation of the peace of Europe, or for a sound decision on any subject of general policy. I am sure that the noble viscount would find, if he would take the trouble to search the archives of the government, papers written by me shortly before I went out of office in 1830, that would fully justify the assertion which I have just made. I am sure that those who were in office with me were as anxious for the preservation of the peace of Europe as any politicians, be they liberals or otherwise. They were as anxious for the preservation of a good understanding between France and this country, and that France should be on a perfectly good understanding with all the powers of Europe, and that she should take the station which becomes her in the rank of nations, and which her power, her wealth, and her resources entitle her to.

January 26, 1841.

The Capture of Acre, the greatest deed of modern times.

I have had a little experience in services of this nature, and I think it my duty to warn your lordships on this occasion, that you must not always expect that ships, however well commanded, or however gallant their seamen may be, are capable of commonly engaging successfully with stone walls. I have no recollection, in all my experience, except the recent instance on the coast of Syria, of any fort being taken by the ships, excepting two or three years ago, when the fort of St. Jean d'Alloa was captured by the French fleet. That is, I think, the single instance that I recollect; though I believe that something of the sort occurred at the siege of Havannah, in 1763. The present achievement I consider one of the greatest deeds of modern times. That is my opinion, and I give the highest credit to those who performed such a service. It was altogether a most skillful proceeding. I was greatly surprised at the small number of men that were lost on board the fleet; and, on inquiring how it happened, I discovered that it was because the vessels were moored within one-third of the ordinary distance. The guns of the fortress were intended to strike objects at a greater distance, and the consequence was, that the shot went over the ships that were anchored at one-third of the usual distance. By that means they sustained not more than one-tenth of the loss which they would otherwise have experienced. Not less than 500 pieces of ordnance were directed against the walls; and the precision with which the fire was kept up, the position of the vessels, and lastly the blowing up of the large magazine, all aided in achieving this great victory in so short a time. I thought it right to say this much, because I wished to warn your lordships against your supposing such deeds as this could be effected every day. I repeat, that this is a singular instance, in the achievement of which great skill was undoubtedly manifested, but which is also connected with peculiar circumstances which you could not hope always to occur. It must not, therefore, be expected as a matter of course, that all such attempts in future must necessarily succeed.

February 4, 1841.

A blow at the Reformation.

There is no doubt that that body (the Roman Catholic seminary of St. Sulpice) was made a corporation by means of that ordinance, yet until that property had been legally vested in them by the ordinance, they had no legal right whatever to it. * * * I was very much struck, I must confess, when first I read the petition and the ordinance relating to this subject; I was very much struck by the total departure it evinced from the principle of the reformation; a principle untouched up to this present moment. And I entreat your lordships, whatever you may think on the subject of this ordinance or other questions—I entreat the attention of your lordships and of the British public to this, that this ordinance was the first blow openly struck by authority at the principles of the reformation; principles hitherto upheld, particularly throughout Canada, from the period of the conquest down to the present moment. I felt strongly on this point the moment I saw the petition and the ordinance, and I still continue to feel strongly on the subject, since I have heard the right reverend prelate state that it was the governor-general, not a member of the legislative council, but the governor-general of the province who brought forward this measure, acting on the part of the queen, whose rights, interests, and prerogative it was his duty to protect, and which he should have protected in the legislative council.

March 5, 1841.

Australia.

It would be much the best plan to put an end to all the Australian commissioners, to whom allusion is made in the bill before your lordships, altogether. A worse system was never adopted for the management of a colony. We ought to place that colony in the same position as the other colonies under the government of her majesty, and rule it in the usual way by the Colonial Office. I disapprove of these commissions altogether.

April 30, 1841.

Evils of Reduced Establishments.

It was stated that the British were expelled from Canton on the 5th of May. I, however, infer from what took place, that the British were obliged to retire at the end of March. Looking to the events of the present year, they appear to me to be exceedingly unsatisfactory. And to what, I would ask, is this owing? It appears to me that this state of things is to be attributed to improper advice. The interests of the country in various parts of the world, have not been properly protected. If there is not a general war, we are placed in a situation that tends to it; and this arises from our having reduced our establishments far below what they ought to be, even in a time of peace. This was the true cause of the present state of things in China, and of delay and consequent misfortune elsewhere; and I much fear that circumstances will occur to cause still further regret at the course that has been adopted with respect to our establishments. I told ministers so at the time they were making those reductions in 1837. I stated to them then that they were not taking such care of our establishments as would enable them, in the event of war, to contend with success against our enemies. The reduction of our establishments has been pursued in different parts of the world, where we are engaged at present, and now we see the consequence.

April 29, 1841.

Poor Law Commissioners must be made to do their duty.

I voted for the Irish poor law bill, and proposed amendments, which, I believe, induced your lordships to pass the bill. I am sure that those amendments had the effect of inducing others to approve of that bill, who would not have done so if those amendments had not been introduced. I did all this on the faith and assurance, not only of the house and the government, but of those gentlemen themselves, that it would be carried into execution in Ireland, with the same strictness and fairness as it was in this country. In this expectation I have been altogether disappointed, and for this reason I am determined, when I get the other papers, to read every line of them, and probe the matter to the bottom, in order to see where the mischief lies. But recollect there is not only this case, but several other cases before your lordships, in every one of which there is corruption. We cannot stop here with the resolutions of my noble friend. The Clonmel case is a very gross case. The noble lord opposite has told us that the office can be but of little importance, as the salary is only 10l. to 30l. a-year; but see what power the office gives. In this very case let your lordships see what happened next day, when the brother-in-law of this individual was appointed valuator, a situation which puts the property of every man, in some degree, in his power. We must go deeper into this question, if we wish to do justice to Ireland, and to the gentlemen who hold property in that country. We must take care that their property shall not be left at the disposal of such miscreants, and we must make the poor law commissioners do their duty. I cannot think of asking him any question on the subject, for it was sufficient for him to know that he was the nephew of a person called the archbishop, to be satisfied of his fitness.

It would be mere stuff to stop here; the persons on whom the house must call are the poor law commissioners themselves. Let them be taught to feel it their duty to keep a correct record of their proceedings, which they shall be ready to produce at any time that the house or the government may call for them. Let them be taught to feel that the house will not permit such conduct as this, and we shall soon see an end to such abuses as those out of which the resolution of my noble friend arises.
May 3, 1841.

Why Corn Laws were imposed.
These laws (corn laws) were not invented, nor have they been maintained, for the purpose of keeping high rents in the pockets of noble lords, but they were invented and have been supported for the purpose of maintaining and supporting agriculture, and of maintaining this country independent of all other countries and parts of the world; and it is also perfectly true, as stated by my noble friend behind me, that such has been the policy of England for centuries, sometimes by one mode, and sometimes by another; sometimes by imposing protective duties when corn rose above certain prices, and sometimes by giving bounties, and occasionally very large bounties, on the exportation of corn. But whatever has been the means, the object has always been to support the agriculture of the country, in order to render this country, in respect of its subsistence, independent of other nations. This was the object of the improved system introduced in the year 1828; this was the object of those principles which have been maintained ever since; at least it was the principle on which I gave those laws my support, and on which I more than once asked your lordships to render this country dependent only on itself for subsistence. This was the object of the corn laws, and not that dirty object which has been imputed to your lordships—and which, I must say, it is too bad to impute to your lordships—of obtaining large rents from your land. It is also perfectly true, as has been stated by my noble friend behind me, that there is not a country of Europe in which corn laws do not at this moment exist; but, nevertheless, I suppose if it were proposed to repeal these laws, and adopt the measures recommended by the petitioners, your lordships would be told of the quantities of corn that might be had from Russia and from Prussia, and other parts of the world. But are there no corn laws in those countries? Has the noble earl heard of no laws prohibiting all exportation of corn to other countries? That fact alters the whole state of the question of corn laws in this country. The effect of such a state of things would be most serious if there came a bad season here and there, too. Then, again, has

the noble lord not heard of the high duties imposed on the exportation of corn from those countries during the late wars? Have not your lordships got evidence before some of the committees—have you not got letters from some merchants at Dantzic to one of those governments on the subject of the prices of corn in England, and on the rate of duties imposed at that port? and was it not stated that the increased price obtained from England might be expected to enable those merchants to pay the duties imposed by their government on exportation? Let it be observed, that I do not blame the sovereign to whom I allude for imposing those duties—I should not have blamed him if it had been an act of war, whereas it was a mere measure of finance. I do not say, that I agree with him in his notions of protection; but I say, that when I consider it a question of protection, that sovereign is not to be blamed, and that his object was like that of your lordships, to secure the subsistence of his subjects, and not to cause a rise of rents.

May 7, 1841.

The Corn Laws.

The first man who brought forward those opinions (Adam Smith) which I have read as well as noble lords opposite, made an exception upon this very subject. He excepted corn from the doctrines he laid down as to all the other articles of trade. In relation to the subsistence of the people he says, that we must always take care to ensure that subsistence within the country itself—and accordingly he excepts corn from the several doctrines which he lays down. I confess I have heard nothing during these discussions to alter my opinion, that the corn laws which were adopted almost unanimously in 1828, have perfectly answered the purposes for which they were intended, and have kept the prices as steady as the nature of the commodity will allow. Yes, my lords, in this country, when we have produced corn for our own subsistence, and it is our object invariably to produce it, prices have been more steady than in any other country of Europe. It it my opinion, on all these grounds, that these laws have operated as successfully as any laws could have done.

May 11, 1841.

Agriculture and Manufactures.

I cordially concur in the feeling that the prosperity of the agriculturist must depend on the general prosperity of the manufacturer, and of commercial interests in general. There can be no doubt about that, and then corn laws are supported, not with a view to the advantage of any particular interest or class of men, but with a view to render the whole country independent of foreign countries in respect of its supply of food. I believe that all parts of the country, and every individual resident in it, are interested in this subject.

May 17, 1841.

Cotton and Corn.

Allusion has been made to the increase in imports in cotton. It has been said but small profits were made upon the manufacture of this immense quantity of produce, but that appears to me to have no connection with the question of the corn laws. The fact is, the improvements in the machinery, and the introduction of steam, have enabled the manufacturers to manufacture with very little cost. They do not make the profit now they did fifty years ago; but they still make profits, although diminished by competition—not by competition with the foreigner, but by competition at home. Other manufacturers who were aware that profits were to be made, although not so large as formerly, entered the field, built new manufactories, established machinery, and thus introduced fresh competition.

May 25, 1841.

Grounds of Complaint against the Whigs in 1841.

These grounds are neglect and mismanagement of the finances of this country by her majesty's government, the future consequence of which, as has been stated, it is impossible to foresee, and the improper, impolitic and unconstitutional means which they took to recover themselves. These things were proved by reference to the actual state of the finances, when it was found necessary to review them in the last parliament; and it was shewn that, in point of fact, after a period of about five years, a debt had not alone been accumulated of five millions, but there had also been a vast deficiency in the public revenue. This debt and deficiency are to be attributed to the practice adopted by her majesty's government of carrying on extensive operations, of which nobody approves, mind you, more than I do when done as they should be, and at the same time not making due provision for the increased expenditure, occasioned by their carrying on war in several places with a peace establishment, being the most crying of these evils, and neglecting to employ the proper means for meeting the increased charge, and putting an end to the impending danger. The next allegation against them, my lords, is for not making financial provision in the way of ways and means for the expense and charge incurred by the country from the exertions made to put an end to the danger which menaced it. A noble lord has stated that, though a large amount of army and ordnance was kept on foot after 1831, no provision had been made for the additional expenditure in the usual way of an application to parliament, but that irregular and unconstitutional modes were adopted by her majesty's government for finding means of defraying those expenses. In this, my lords, my noble friend spoke but the simple truth. In one case the whole charge of a war had been thrown on the East India Company, and then converted into a debt on this country; in another the funds of the savings' banks had been tampered with; in another the Exchequer bills had been funded; and, in short, several most irregular modes has been adopted. Then, my lords, what happened? Besides these expenses; besides the failure of the government to make due provision by the mode of ways and means to defray the charges incurred by their naval and military operations; besides these, my lords, her majesty's government thought proper to repeal a large amount of taxes, by which means they reduced the revenue of the country to such a degree as materially and inevitably left a most serious deficiency.

August 24, 1841.

Hasty adoption of Free Trade by the Whigs.

My lords, it is not more than fourteen months ago since I heard the noble viscount (Melbourne) say,—making use of the strongest language I ever heard in opposition to a motion merely for taking the corn laws into consideration,—the noble viscount on that occasion declared before God, with reference to the abolition of the corn laws, that he believed the man must be mad who dreamed of such a thing. Now, my lords, I do not pretend to say that the noble viscount has not a perfect right to change his opinions. I believe he thought that he had good grounds for doing so, and I think I have myself read the report which induced him to change them. But this I do say, that, before your lordships and the country were placed in this situation in regard to the queen, the noble viscount was bound to give parliament and the country an opportunity of obtaining that knowledge and information as to the true merits of the question, which he imagines himself to have obtained.

It is by such inquiries as these, my lords, calmly and patiently conducted, that men are enabled to judge respecting the consequences of great changes of this nature, and of the bearings and tendencies of each particular part of what is intended to be done. But, instead of such a course being pursued, what has been done in the present instance? Nothing. * * I further think, that the committee and report were *ex parte* ones, upon which no legislative measures ought to have been founded. But what I chiefly complain of is this, that before the noble viscount put this speech into the mouth of her majesty, he did not give us full and fair information to guide us as to what we ought to do. I believe, my lords, that conduct like this is sufficient to induce you to say that the noble lords opposite do not deserve your confidence.

August 24, 1841.

Lord Melbourne's services to the Queen.

I am willing to admit that the noble viscount has rendered the greatest possible service to her majesty. I happen to know that it is her majesty's opinion that the noble viscount has rendered her majesty the greatest possible service, in

making her acquainted with the mode and policy of the government of this country, initiating her into the laws and spirit of the constitution, independently of the performance of his duty, as the servant of her majesty's crown; teaching her, in short, to preside over the destinies of this great country.
August 24, 1841.

England the best country for the Poor.
With respect to the corn law question, my opinions are already well known. I shall not argue the propriety of these laws, but I shall be ready to discuss them when a discussion is brought forward by a government having the confidence of her majesty's parliament. But, my lords, I earnestly recommend you, for the sake of the people of this country, for the sake of the humblest orders of the people, not to lend yourselves to the destruction of our native cultivation. Its encouragement is of the utmost and deepest importance to all classes. My lords, I have passed my life in foreign countries, in different regions of the earth, and I have been in only one country in which the poor man, if sober, prudent, and industrious, is quite certain of acquiring a competence. That country is this. We have instances every day; we have seen, only within the last week, proofs that persons in the lowest ranks can acquire, not only competence, but immense riches. I have never heard of such a thing in any other country. I earnestly beg of you not to lose sight of this fact, and not to consent to any measure which would injure the cultivation of our own soil. I have seen in other lands the misery consequent on the destruction of cultivation, and never was misery equal to it; and, my lords, I once more conjure you not to consent to any measure tending to injure the home cultivation of this country.
August 24, 1841.

Opinions on Abstract Questions of Policy inexpedient.
My lords, the noble viscount states, and he states truly, that it is not a habit in this house to call on your lordships to give an opinion on abstract questions of policy. That, my lords, is perfectly true, and I have myself endeavoured to bring the house to that view on more than one occasion, that is, to prevent the expression of any opinion on abstract questions of policy, in the shape of an address or otherwise, until it should be brought before your lordships in the shape of a distinct legislative measure. More than once I have succeeded in persuading your lordships to withhold such opinion, and on some occasions, even, I have supported the government (whig) against them, however much I may have disapproved of their policy with regard to them.
August 24, 1841.

It is at all times desirable that the sovereign should not be pledged in the speech from the throne.
August 24, 1841.

Abolition of Oaths.

The foundation of all justice is truth, and the question is, how truth is to be ascertained. Before I can receive any application of this description, and before I can vote for the bill lately laid on your lordships' table, I would like to hear the opinion of some of those learned men who are at this moment engaged in the administration of the law, and who must have made up their minds as to the best means of ascertaining the truth. Hitherto it has been understood in this country that the best means was by administering oaths. I am aware that the legislature has made certain exceptions. It may be very well to make these exceptions—and let further exceptions be made if they are expedient—but I do say, that we ought to have some solemn examination of the question, and some certainty that the new mode proposed is as good as the old one for ascertaining the truth, which, as is said, is the foundation of all justice.
March 18, 1842.

The Income Tax only justified by Necessity.

I can answer for myself, and I believe I can also answer for my colleagues, that nothing but necessity could have induced us to propose such a tax. We are perfectly aware of all the inconveniences that must result from it. We are perfectly aware of the provisions of the act of parliament upon your lordships' table. We are perfectly aware of the odious powers with which these commissioners and others must be trusted—and we can reconcile it to ourselves only by the necessity of the case. Your lordships must feel it. We have been now for several years engaged in operations involving great expense in all parts of the world. I will not say, my lords, that we have been at war, but, I believe, we have been at something as like war, if it be not war, as anything could well be. We are exactly in the situation of persons who have incurred a great debt, and who are called upon to pay the bill. I say again, my lords, that nothing but a strong sense of the necessity of the case, and that there was no other course which we could take to produce such a revenue as would enable us to meet the difficulties of the country, or to do what is necessary for its prosperity, would have induced us to propose such a measure; and it will not last one moment longer than it shall be absolutely necessary.
June 17, 1842.

The Poor Law has worked well.

I was one of those who supported the poor law as it was introduced some years ago by my noble and learned friend, and I did so on ascertaining the inconveniences and evils which attended the system of working under the old poor law up to that period; and being sensible that the only remedy which could be found for those evils and inconveniences, was in the measure proposed by my noble and learned friend. My lords, I have since had the satisfaction of contemplating the working of the measure, which then became the law of the land, and I must say that I have been satisfied with its results. It has, undoubtedly, improved the condition of the working classes, and it certainly does place on a better footing the relations between the working classes and their employers. It has enabled those who had the care of them to provide better for the aged and destitute than has been hitherto the case; and it has, in general, given satisfaction throughout the country. My lords, I don't mean to say that I approve of every act that has been done in carrying this bill into operation. I think that, in many cases, those who had charge of the working of the bill have gone too far, and that there was no occasion whatever for constructing buildings, such as have acquired throughout the country the denomination of bastiles, and that it would have been perfectly easy to have established very efficient workhouses without shutting out all view of what was passing exterior to the walls. I say, then, that in some respects, the system has been carried farther than it ought to have been, and, I shall also say that its features have assumed a harsher character in some parts of the country than was necessary; but this has been owing, I must admit, in a great degree, to the adoption of another law by parliament, I mean what is called the dissenters' marriage act, the regulations depending on which were connected with the execution of the poor law act, and rendered necessary the establishment of unions in many parts of the country which were not yet ripe for the formation of those unions. But, notwithstanding the circumstances to which I have just now alluded, I must, in general, state my approbation of the working of this act. I have paid great attention to the subject. Wherever I have resided, I have attended the meetings of guardians of unions in my neighbourhood; I have visited several workhouses in different parts of England, and I must say that I never visited one in which the management was not as good as could be expected in such districts of the country, and which did not give universal satisfaction.

July 26, 1842.

The government of Lord Melbourne carried on war all over the world with a peace establishment. That is exactly what we (Sir Robert Peel's government) do not.

February 2, 1843.

Real cause of the Chinese War.

I was almost the only individual who stated that the real ground of complaint against the Chinese government was its conduct towards the person employed in the service of her majesty, and representing her majesty in China. I was the only person in this house who defended her majesty's servants. I said that the war was a just and necessary war. I will go further, and say, if it had been otherwise—if it had been a war solely on account of the robbery of the opium—if her majesty's government were engaged in that war, and if their interests and honour were involved in it, I should have considered it my duty to make every effort for carrying it on with success, and have asked parliament for the assistance which would have enabled her majesty's servants to bring it to an early and successful termination.

Eulogium on the Indian Army.

My lords, I know something of that (Indian) army; I have served in its ranks, and I know pretty well what its feelings are; and though there are different castes and religions composing it, the discipline of that army, and the military spirit by which it is actuated, totally do away with all such distinctions. You will never hear in India of any difference of caste or religion in that army, any more than you would in the ranks of the British army. All do their duty,—all are animated by the true feelings of soldiers.

March 9, 1843.

Evils of the Press in India.

The state of things in that country is one of much greater difficulty now than when I was there, because there is now established in India what is called a free press, but which I should make free to call a most licentious press; and by referring to these papers your lordships will see that the mischievous influence of that press is repeatedly complained of. For my own part, I must own, I do not see how the operations of war can be carried on in a satisfactory manner in India, with such a press constantly exercising its influence, and connected through its correspondents with every cantonment of the army.

March 9, 1843.

The Union must be maintained inviolate.

There can be no doubt of the intention of her majesty's government to maintain the union inviolate; and it is the duty of every government, and I will say it is the determination of her majesty's present government, to maintain that union inviolate, and to come down to parliament and call upon parliament to give her majesty's government its support in carrying into execution any

measures which may he considered necessary to maintain the union inviolate, and to preserve from turbulence the peace of her majesty's dominions.
May 9, 1843.

The House of Lords should disregard popular Clamour.

As to the remarks which are made on your lordships elsewhere, I am one of those animadverted upon, and I am glad to find myself upon this occasion in such extremely good company. For myself, I can only say that I have been for a great number of years in the habit of treating such criticisms and such assaults with the smallest possible attention; and I shall continue to do my duty to the best of my ability, in the service of my sovereign, or elsewhere, and continue to treat the language referred to with as little attention as heretofore; and I recommend noble lords on both sides of the house to follow my example in this respect.
May 15, 1843.

Sees of St. Asaph and Bangor.

There can have been no object in the measure (the bill for the union of the sees of St. Asaph and Bangor), but to make all the arrangements in the manner most convenient to the country generally. There could have been no desire to injure the dioceses of St. Asaph and Bangor, or any other district in the kingdom; but the object was to make a better distribution of the revenues of the church, and to satisfy the public of a sincere desire to effect such a reformation as would be a real one, and such as would give satisfaction, not only to those who were attached to the church, as my noble friend and myself, but also to others who looked upon it with indifference.
May 23, 1843.

The Duke of Sussex.

My lords, his late royal highness was well known to all your lordships. His royal highness frequently took part in the discussion of those subjects which came under your lordships' consideration; and although it was impossible for every person endowed with such acquirements, and possessed of such an understanding, as belonged to his late royal highness, not to have felt strongly on the various events and questions which from time to time were brought under the consideration of this house, yet his late royal highness always treated those subjects, however exciting they might have been, with much moderation, and with great forbearance towards others with whom he might have a difference of opinion. I must do his late royal highness the justice to say, that though I had the unhappiness to differ from him in opinion on several subjects which came under discussion in this house, yet, notwithstanding that difference of opinion, his late royal highness ever treated me with unvarying kindness, and with the utmost condescension. My lords, his late royal highness having received the benefit of an excellent education, and having in his youth passed a considerable portion of his time in foreign countries, was a most accomplished man; and he continued his studies, in all branches of literature and science, until almost the latest period of his existence. His late royal highness was, during his whole life, the protector of literature, of the sciences, and of the arts, and of the professors and representives of all branches of knowledge. For a number of years his late royal highness was elected president of the Royal Society, and he received the learned members of that body in his house with the greatest amenity and kindness. Having himself sedulously cultivated all subjects of literature, science, and art, his late royal highness was, I may say, the patron, protector, and friend, of all those who pursued such studies, on every occasion when that protection was necessary. But other praise belongs to his late royal highness. His royal highness was not backward—on the contrary, he was equally forward with all the princes of his family—as a patron and upholder, as a supporter and protector, of the various charitable institutions of this metropolis; and, my lords, up to the last moment of his life, he was the friend of the indigent and the unfortunate wherever they might be found.

April 27, 1843.

Reasons for the Dismissal of the Irish Magistrates.

These gentlemen having been some of the persons to instigate and encourage the assembly of those large meetings in Ireland, on which the first law authority had pronounced in writing the opinion that they had a "tendency to outrage;" that "they were not in the spirit of the constitution, and may become dangerous to the State;" the lord-lieutenant of the government could not put any confidence in the performance of their duties by these magistrates and deputy-lieutenants, who had thus excited these meetings, or who presided at them. Your lordships are perfectly aware that on one occasion it was proved that these meetings had a tendency to outrage—indeed, outrage was actually committed. I told your lordships on a former occasion that there was a great difference in Ireland on the subject of the repeal of the union. Now, suppose that two assemblies representing such opinions assemble on the same occasion and in the same neighbourhood, why it is obvious that outrage and bloodshed may occur, and it must be likewise obvious that those magistrates and deputy-lieutenants are not officers on whom the Lord-lieutenant can rely for carrying into execution measures for the repression and suppression of outrage which he may think proper to take on such an occasion. My lords I have besides to observe to your lordships, that for a very considerable period of time it has been a matter of notoriety in Ireland that the members of her Majesty's council, her majesty's servants in this and the other house of arliament, declared it to be the fixed and positive determination of the government to maintain inviolate the legislative union between the two countries. Some of the most distinguished members of both houses of parliament declared, in their places, that they had the same intention; and this declaration of opinion has been communicated to the public more than once; and in no one instance, as I believe, has there been an intention avowed to promote the object of this repeal of the union. Well, then, what must be inferred from the notoriety of that fact? What but that the repeal of the union, so far as a vote of parliament is concerned, is hopeless? It is to be carried then by intimidation, by force, and violence; and, of course, as the government, whose duty it is to resist and repress such acts of intimidation, force, and violence, whenever they should be attempted, by all the means at their disposal, cannot use such instruments as those who excite the people to appear at their head, the lord-lieutenant and lord chancellor have taken measures to remove them from the commission of the peace, and deputy-lieutenancies of their several counties. This is the principle, my lords, on which I conceive the government has acted.

June 9, 1843.

After what passed in both houses of parliament it became a matter of notoriety that the opinion of parliament was, that the legislative union should not be repealed, and that every effort on the part of the government should be made to resist the attempt to occasion that repeal. Then, my lords, under these circumstances, the lord chancellor finds Lord French and other magistrates calling meetings to repeal the union, assisting at the meetings, presiding at them, and urging all the proceedings. At this time the opinion of parliament was notorious, yet meetings consisting of 10,000, 20,000, 100,000, no matter as to the number of thousands, continued. My lords, I wish to know with what object they were continued? Was it with a view to address parliament to repeal the union? No, my lords, they were continued to obtain the desired repeal of the union,—by terror, if possible,—if not, by force and violence. And the persons calling these meetings, I beg your lordships to observe, were the magistrates, the very men who must have been employed by government to take measures to resist this violence, to prevent breaches of the peace, to arrest those who should be guilty of such breaches, and to bring them to justice; and then the noble lord says, that the government ought not to have removed those magistrates from their situations, and that they ought not to draw a distinction as to the time when it became notorious to the whole world what were the views entertained by parliament and the government on this important question. My lords, in this and the other house of parliament, no one would have any idea of repealing the union except in regular course, like another act of parliament; but with these meetings of 50,000 and 60,000 men, was there any question of discussion? No, my lords, the question was terror, force, and violence. That was the ground on which the lord chancellor told these magistrates after the views of the government had become notorious, you must be dismissed if you attend, or excite others to attend, such meetings. I am as much concerned that this state of affairs should exist as the noble lord can be; but of this I am quite certain, that the way to be prepared is not to have in the service of the government—not to have government dependant upon the exertions of—a number of magistrates who have excited and encouraged these proceedings, assisting at and presiding over these very meetings. That could not have been desirable, and I say that the lord chancellor and situation as that of governor-general of India, an officer who was so for little more than two years—an officer who has given satisfaction in so high a situation to those by whom he was intrusted and employed—whose acts have been concurred in and sanctioned in every instance; to recall that officer suddenly, making no provision for the performance of the great duties which are to be performed, and which must be performed in that country—to recall an officer in whom the government fully confided, without the concurrence of that government—is, my lords, an act, to say the least of it, that cannot be called a discreet exercise of the power which is conferred on those who have so used it. My lords, I will say nothing— I will advert to nothing that is not notorious— that is not strictly in reference to the act of parliament. I beg your lordships to observe, that the body which did this act—which I must call an act of indiscretion, at least—that body, as a body, has no knowledge whatever of the instructions sent out to the governor-general, and under which he acted. They stated reasons for withdrawing the governor-general from India; but, as a body (except the secret committee appointed under the act of parliament), they had no knowledge whatever of the instructions under which the governor-general acted, or of the events which had taken place in that country, except that which is within the general knowledge of this and the other house of parliament, and the whole public of this country. And yet, my lords, they take this responsibility upon themselves—having no knowledge of the instructions which it was deemed at Waterloo. Very possibly not, my lords. Bear in mind what he said in respect to the augmentation of his numbers, and the means of assembling those persons. He said on one occasion, that by the post of one night, he could collect the whole of this force in different parts of the country; and it is perfectly true,—I have not a doubt of the fact.

July 14, 1843.

Remedial Measures of no avail whilst Agitation continues in Ireland.
My lords, I must say, that grieved as I am that there should be so much truth in the representations made by the noble lord of the existing state of the country, and of its prospects, threatened as they are by the continuance of agitation, I must say, that no measure that could be proposed, no new measure which could be adopted, would have the smallest effect in removing any of these evils or inconveniences. My lords, the only mode, the only course to be adopted on the part of the government, is to oppose a strong resistance to everything like

a breach of the peace or public order, and to be prepared, as I hope they are prepared, to enforce measures for preserving quiet, and protecting property, in Ireland. My lords, I know of no remedy but that for the state of affairs which exists at present; particularly as it appears that whether the peace of the country shall be disturbed or not, depends on the will of one man, and his influence over the wills and actions of some thousands, who possess influence in various parishes of the country.
July 14, 1843.

Agitation no Relief for the Poverty of Ireland.
My lords, it certainly is true that there is in Ireland a vast number of poor. I have been sorry to see that it is stated in some returns on the table, that there are as many as 2,000,000 of poor in Ireland. My lords, it happens unfortunately, that in all parts of the empire there are poor; but I will beg to observe, that it is not in the power of this government, nor of any government, nor of any parliament, in the course of a few weeks, or a few months, or, I may say, a few years, to relieve the poverty of a great country like that, extending as it does to such a portion of the population. But, my lords, I beg to know whether poverty can be relieved by this description of agitation for the repeal of the union? Is poverty relieved by marches of twenty-five and thirty Irish miles a-day, during the period of spring and summer, to hear seditious speeches? Is poverty relieved by subscriptions of thousands of pounds to the repeal rent, and the O'Connell rent, and other funds of that description? No, my lords, that poverty must be relieved by a perseverance in industry and sobriety; not taken up by fits and starts for the sake of a more orderly appearance at seditious meetings, where the people are marshalled by bands of music and flying colours. The evils, whence that poverty proceeds, are not to be cured in a day. The remedies must be some time in operation; and all I can say is, that the government are sincerely desirous to avail themselves of every opportunity that may tend to benefit the people of Ireland, and to relieve that poverty of which the noble lord so eloquently complains.
July 14, 1843.

Assistance of Foreigners to the Repeal Agitation.—Their Anti-English Motives.
My lords, I do not dispute the extent of the conspiracy—I do not dispute the dangers resulting from organization in Ireland—I have stated it publicly on more than one occasion—I do not deny it—it is notorious, it is avowed, it is published in every paper all over the world. I do not deny the assistance received from foreigners, not from foreign governments,—I have no right to say so,—but from foreigners of nearly all nations; for there are disturbed and disturbing spirits everywhere, who are anxious to have an opportunity of injuring and deteriorating the great prosperity of this country.
August 8, 1843.

The Military in readiness to preserve the Peace in Ireland.

I, whose duty it is to superintend one of those offices on which the execution of the measures of the government depends, feel confident that everything that can be done has been done, in order to enable the government to preserve the peace of the country, and to meet all misfortunes and consequences which may result from the violence of the passions of those men who unfortunately guide the multitude in Ireland.

August 8, 1843.

Mr. O'Connell's Proceedings.

To plunder the public in Ireland of money for the purpose of O'Connell rent, or repeal contribution, or the lord lieutenant would not have done their duty if they had not removed those persons from her majesty's service.

July 14, 1845.

The "Monster" Meetings in Ireland.

The noble lord (the Marquis of Clanricarde) has stated that these meetings were not illegal. I certainly do not consider myself competent to decide whether they were or were not illegal. This I know, that they consist of very large numbers—whether of 10,000 or 100,000 I am sure I cannot tell, and I do not believe any man can tell to a certainty. They are assembled in very large numbers, regularly organised, marching under the lead of persons on horseback, with bands and banners, in regular military array. After having attended these meetings, those present are dispersed by word of command, without trouble, violence, or breach of the peace, and march back, perhaps twenty or thirty miles. * * * My lords, I have had some experience, in the course of a long life, which I have passed in the service of the sovereigns of this country, of revolutions. A distinguished author has written of the French revolution. "*On ne conspire pas sur la place.*" There is no secret in these transactions, and the reason why there is no secret is this, that the great means of operation are deception of their followers, and terror in respect of their adversaries. Accordingly, we hear a learned gentleman exclaiming to his audience, "Napoleon had not in Russia such an army as this is; the Duke of Wellington had not such a one repeal of those laws upon which the reformation in this country has been founded. My lords, I have already taken opportunities of warning your lordships against the assertion of such doctrines in this house, and I must again express a hope that you will observe and beware how they are introduced into it, because you may rely upon it, that there is not an individual in this country, be his religious opinions what they may, be his position what it may, who is not interested in the maintenance of the reformation. Not only our whole system of religion, but our whole system

of religious toleration, in which so many people in this country are interested, depends upon the laws upon which the reformation was founded; and I therefore entreat your lordships to give no encouragement to doctrines that might induce a belief that there exists in this house any indifference upon the subject of those laws.
March 18, 1844.

The Compact entered into for the Maintenance of the Protestant Church in Ireland should be held sacred.
The Protestant church in Ireland has existed in that country for a period of nearly three hundred years, and was maintained in that country during a century of contests, rebellions, and massacres; and during a contest for the possession of the crown, the Protestants of that country encountered that contest, and kept possession of their church; and during another century it was maintained through much opposition, and under difficulties of all descriptions. At the period of the union, the parliament—who had the power to consent to the union, or to refuse their consent—stipulated that the Protestant church in Ireland should be maintained, and maintained on the same footing as the Protestant church of England in this country. The parliament had, under the auspices of the king of this country, the power of either making or not making that compact. Your lordships entered into that compact with the parliament of Ireland, and I entreat you never to lose sight of the fact. I entreat you not to suffer yourselves to be prevailed upon to make any alteration in, or to depart in the slightest degree from, the terms of that compact, so long as you intend to maintain the union between this country and Ireland. It is the foundation upon which the union rests,—it is a compact which you have entered into with the parliament of Ireland, and from which you cannot depart without being guilty of a breach of faith, worse than those which have been referred to in other countries,—worse than those pecuniary breaches of faith which have been alluded to in the course of the discussion which took place in your lordships' house this evening upon another subject. I entreat you to listen to none of those petitions or speeches which tend to the injury or the destruction of the church in Ireland. Do what may be necessary,—do what it may be proper to do, in order to render that church more beneficial to the people of that country; but I entreat you to adhere strictly, in spirit and according to the letter, to the compact you have made, and not permit it to be supposed in any quarter whatever that you entertain the most distant intention of departing, in the slightest degree, from that arrangement.
March 18, 1844.

The recall of the Governor-General of India, by the Court of Directors, an act of gross indiscretion.

My lords, I conceive that this right (of recalling the governor-general of India) is one which the court of directors are bound to exercise with due discretion; as all bodies and all individuals ought to do, when they possess extraordinary powers under the provisions of the law. In such cases, my lords, they are bound to exercise that power with the utmost discretion. Now, my lords, I will venture to submit to your lordships, as the opinion of an individual who has had some experience in these matters, that the exercise of the power belonging to the court of directors is not, in this instance, to say the least of it, a discreet exercise of that power. My lords, the court of directors has this power. It has also the power of nominating a successor in the room of the person recalled. But, my lords, it has no other power whatever, as your lordships will find in looking into the law on the subject—it has no other power whatever, my lords, except under the direction and control of the board of commissioners for the affairs of India, and for the acts of that board of commissioners her majesty's government is responsible. Under these circumstances, my lords, I venture again to say, what I before said, that it is not a discreet act of authority to recall from power—to recall from such an important what not, is one thing; to excite the common people of the country to approach as near as possible to the commission of crime, and to do all the mischief that is possible to be done to the country, without exposing one's own person, is another thing; but to corrupt the army is quite a different thing, which, I hope and trust, I may promise your lordships will not be fulfilled.

August 11, 1843.

Eulogium on Major-General Sir Charles Napier.

My lords, I must say, that, after giving the fullest consideration to these operations (in Scinde), I have never known an instance of an officer who has shown in a higher degree that he possesses all the qualities and qualifications to enable him to conduct great operations. He has maintained the utmost discretion and prudence in the formation of his plans, the utmost activity in all the preparations to ensure his success, and, finally, the utmost zeal, gallantry, and science, in carrying them into execution.

February 12, 1844.

Persons of every Religious Denomination interested in the maintenance of the Reformation.

The noble lord (Earl Fitzwilliam) has propounded to your lordships a something, neither the nature of which, nor the period at which it is to be carried into execution, is he himself exactly certain of. Something or other must be done; to that something this country must make up its mind; the noble lord does not state what it is to be; but it is, at all events, to involve the necessary to send out to that part of the globe—and the act of parliament will shew they are bound to have none—having no share in giving those instructions—in short, having no knowledge on which to found a judgment on so important a subject as the recall of a governor-general, they took upon themselves to pronounce their judgment on the conduct of this officer, and to disapprove of it. Now, my lords, I must say, that having no knowledge which could enable them fairly to pronounce their judgment on his conduct, or that could justify them in depriving the government and the country of the best instrument—I say it again, the best instrument to carry on and perform the various duties of that great office, making no provision whatever for the performance of those duties which are now to be provided for by her majesty's government, is an indiscreet exercise of the powers they possess. My lords, as I have said so much on this subject, I will, in order to illustrate the indiscretion of this act (that is the best word I can find for it), go yet a little further. My lords, though I believe this is the first time in the history of the government of India that this extreme measure has been resorted to by the court of directors, it has more than once been in contemplation; but upon the advice and remonstrance of the ministers of the day, the resolution of the court of directors has been always withdrawn. And it is the fact, that it has been in contemplation by these very gentlemen, with reference to this same governor general, in the course of the last twelve months; but they were at that time prevailed upon to withdraw that resolution, and not to persist in the recall of my noble friend. This was previous to the late great military operations in Gwalior, of which we have all heard with so much satisfaction,—operations which I am sure your lordships will have perceived from the perusal of the reports which have been laid upon your table, must have been founded upon the most just and discriminate measures, for the equipment and maintenance of the armies placed in the field, under the direction and superintendence of the governor general—not the equipment only of these armies—but the support of the troops in the field, the maintenance of military communication, and the moans of advance and retreat—in short, all that could tend to insure their success—were amply provided for. Then, my lords, suppose the case to have occurred of the court of directors thinking proper to recall the noble lord six or eight months ago, whilst the measures to which I have just alluded were in contemplation, what would have become of the great operations at Gwalior—operations carried on under the superintendence and direction of my noble friend the governor general. Why, the gentleman who was senior in the council must have succeeded my noble friend—a respectable man no doubt he is, but without the experience of my noble friend; and without the knowledge of the manner of equipping armies, and making proper arrangements for their being called into action, it is needless to add, that such great and successful operations as those to which I have alluded could not be carried on, and I leave your lordships to judge what the situation of India would have been if that expedition had failed, and if such an army as the one which we have seen described in one of the blue books upon this table had continued in existence, threatened, as we were, at the same moment, by a similar body in the Punjaub, on the north-west frontier, and with the province of Scinde still in an unsettled state. Why, my lords, the danger would have been imminent, and this would have been the consequence of the recall of my noble friend six or eight months ago, a measure which was in contemplation, and was only prevented by our representations to those who have now committed this gross indiscretion of recalling the noble lord—it was prevented only by the representations made to those gentlemen of the danger which would ensue to the public interest from the measures which they were about to adopt, the dangers resulting from the impossibility that they would be able to provide for events which most probably would occur if they recalled their officer without the consent of her majesty's government, who would thus be deprived of the instrument in their hands best fitted for carrying their instructions into execution, while the directors, in this country, must be unable to direct the means in existence for securing the safety of their troops, for guarding their frontier, for upholding the honour of Her majesty's arms, and the security of our vast dominions in that part of the world. I say again, as I have said before, and I say the least of it, when I pronounce it to be the most indiscreet exercise of power that I have known carried into execution by any body possessed of power since I have had a knowledge of public affairs, which I am sorry to say is upwards of half a century.

April 29, 1844.

His Support of the New Poor Law (Ireland.)

I will take the liberty of reminding your lordships that the New Poor Law was originated by noble lords opposite, while they were in the service of her majesty, and that I gave the measure my support from a sense of duty, because I thought it was calculated to benefit Ireland. I have throughout supported the measure; I proposed some amendments which I thought likely to promote its beneficial action; I have given it my support ever since; and I am prepared to do all in my power to ensure its successful operation.

May 17, 1844.

The Echo Library
www.echo-library.com

Please visit our website to download a complete catalogue of our books. We specialise in out-of-copyright reprints in all subjects. We publish a range of Large Print Editions of classic titles.

Books for re-printing

Suggestions for re-printing can be sent to titles@echo-library.com. Titles must be out-of-copyright or you must own the copyright. They can be in digital or published form.

If we do not wish to add the title to our catalogue then we can reprint for you. Costs depend on the format of the manuscript or book and its size.

Feedback

Because we have no direct contact with our customers we would welcome constructive comments to feedback@echo-library.com

Complaints

If there is a serious error in the text or layout please advise us by sending details to complaints@echo-library.com and we will supply a corrected copy, usually within 15 working days (it may take longer outside the UK and USA).

If there is a printing fault or the book is damaged please refer to your supplier.

Printed in the United Kingdom
by Lightning Source UK Ltd.
122043UK00002B/111/A